Structural Change, Welfare Systems, and Labour Reallocation

Structural Change, Welfare Systems, and Labour Reallocation

Lessons from the Transition of Formerly Planned Economies

TITO BOERI

OXFORD

UNIVERSITY PRESS

OXFORD
UNIVERSITY PRESS

Great Clarendon Street, Oxford OX2 6DP

Oxford University Press is a department of the University of Oxford.
It furthers the University's objective of excellence in research, scholarship,
and education by publishing worldwide in

Oxford New York

Athens Auckland Bangkok Bogotá Buenos Aires Calcutta
Cape Town Chennai Dar es Salaam Delhi Florence Hong Kong Istanbul
Karachi Kuala Lumpur Madrid Melbourne Mexico City Mumbai
Nairobi Paris São Paulo Shanghai Singapore Taipei Tokyo Toronto Warsaw

with associated companies in Berlin Ibadan

Oxford is a registered trade mark of Oxford University Press
in the UK and in certain other countries

Published in the United States
by Oxford University Press Inc., New York

British Library Cataloguing in Publication Data
Data available

Library of Congress Cataloging in Publication Data
Data available
ISBN 0–19–829365–8

1 3 5 7 9 10 8 6 4 2

Typeset by HK Typesetting Ltd.
Printed in Great Britain
on acid-free paper by
T.J. International Ltd., Padstow, Cornwall

Contents

Acknowledgements

Writing a book is an endless task—something as tiring as cycling over the Alpe d'Huez. If I were a publisher, before offering contracts I would submit potential authors to a physical-fitness test. I am very grateful to Oxford University Press for not having asked me for a medical certificate.

Actually, the test should also be performed by the author's family. I am very much indebted to my wife, Silvia Milesi, and my children, Bianca and Carlo, for having been so patient with me during my literary efforts.

The analogy with the *Tour de France* is inspired by the crucial role played by France in the drafting of this book. I decided to embark upon this task while still in Paris, at the end of a very enriching experience at the OECD. I am very grateful to this organization for having given me the opportunity to follow the transition process from its very start and from a privileged vantage point, halfway between policy making and research. It would take too long to list the names of the colleagues who interacted with me during this period and hence influenced my way of thinking about transition.

Without the initial support and constant encouragement of Olivier Blanchard, and his insightful comments on the structure of this book and its main conclusions, I would have never reached this stage. Another French native speaker, Micael Castanheira, spent time reading through the book and prevented me from making mistakes and omissions. I ruined Randall Filer's visit to Italy in the Spring of 1999 by giving him the manuscript to read. I believe that by now he hates me, but I was rewarded with very acute and detailed observations.

Many other people have contributed directly or indirectly to this book with informal discussions, data and institutional information. Among these I would like to recall Michael Burda, Fabrizio Coricelli, Irina Denisova, Michael Forster, Janos Köllö, Jop Konings, Hartmut Lehmann, Mattia Makovec, Branko Milanovic, Daniel Munich, Gerard Roland, Mark Schaffer and Vit Sorm.

I will never forget the skilful assistance that Lapo Anzilotti provided to my work on transitional economies during my fellowship at the European University Institute in Fiesole. In addition to being a very promising young economist, Lapo was one of those rare people who could keep smiling while doing for you the most boring data manipulations. Patricia Arden prevented my English from being unreadable. Randolph Bruno has been a very skilful and hard-working research assistant.

I am also grateful to my students at Bocconi University in Milan for having provided an excellent sounding board for my book. I am likewise indebted to seminar participants in Berlin, Bonn, London, Montreal, Moscow, Prague, Stockholm, and Vilnius for their comments, which greatly improved this book.

Finally, the analogy with the *Tour de France* forces me to thank two persons who indirectly contributed to this book by supporting my efforts to cycle around the Italian countryside no sooner than I was back from my long French *séjour*. I owe much to Carlo Favero and Luca Paolazzi for having taught me that you can suffer while going uphill and still be happy, even if your opponents—not to speak of your team-mates—are several hundreds of metres ahead of you.

List of Abbreviations

ALMPs	Active Labour Market Policies.
CEECs	Central and Eastern European countries (Bulgaria, Czech Republic, Hungary, Poland, Romania, Slovak Republic and Slovenia).
CIS	Community of Independent States, including as Member states or as associates all former Soviet Republics, with the exception of the Baltic countries.
CMEA	Council for Economic Mutual Assistance, composed of USSR, Bulgaria, Hungary, Poland, Romania and the former Czech and Slovak Federal Republic (CSFR).
LFS	Labour Force Survey.
OECD countries	Australia, Austria, Belgium, Canada, the Czech Republic*, Denmark, Finland, France, Germany, Greece, Hungary*, Iceland, Ireland, Italy, Japan, Luxembourg, Mexico*, the Netherlands, New Zealand, Norway, Poland*, Portugal, South Korea*, Spain, Sweden, Switzerland, Turkey, the United Kingdom, and the United States. (Those countries with an asterisk have joined since 1994.)
OST	Optimal Speed of Transition.
PES	Public Employment Service.
POS	gross job creation (sum of *net* employment variations in expanding units).
NEG	gross job destruction (sum of *net* employment variations in declining units).
NET	net employment growth (the difference between POS and NEG).

SA   social assistance.

UB   unemployment benefits.

Visegrad group   Czech Republic, Hungary, Poland and Slovak Republic, all countries that signed an economic cooperation agreement in Visegrad in February, 1991.

Introduction

The economics of transition is no longer *the* topic. The transformation of formerly planned economies into market economies is a much less fashionable area of operation for 'research commuters' than it was just a few years ago. Some of the 'gods' (an expression used at the Ukrainian Ministry of Finance the day before a famous Western economist landed in Kiev), flying in daily to dispense policy advice to the new governments of Central and Eastern Europe and the former Soviet republics, have since long abandoned the region. There are far fewer articles in the newspapers devoted to the issue, and fewer large conferences organized around the world with big names on the agendas. This is, no doubt, an ideal scenario to carry out serious research on transition.

There are at least three reasons why the economics of transition can be highly rewarding for researchers.

The first reason is that transition involves, almost by definition, rapid structural change that we still understand very little about. The pace of change occurring in the last decade of the twentieth century has no historical precedents. Although changes have been radical everywhere, some formerly planned economies have been faster than others in their systemic transformation. There are also significant differences in transition trajectories across the various countries of the region. By studying the different timings of reforms and analysing in depth the wide variation of outcomes amongst the nations affected, it is possible to further our knowledge of the interactions between structural change and reallocation. These interactions are, on the one hand, still largely unexplored and, on the other, bound to become increasingly important in the years to come—not only for formerly planned economies but also for Asia, Latin America and an eastwards enlarged European Union. Formerly planned economies are being transformed while having a significant welfare state in place. Hence, some of the lessons that can be drawn from their experience can also be valuable for developed market economies struggling, in this era of globalization, to achieve greater flexibility of structure through the adjustment of quantities rather than prices, while having in place a large welfare state. From this experience we can better understand the role of insitutions in structural change and the effects that structural changes have on institutions themselves.

The second reason is that transitional economies, notably those of Central and Eastern Europe, offer a wealth of data, because one of the few advantages of their previous system was to have *de facto* censuses at much higher frequencies than Western countries. Some of the datasets one can find for the period before the transition track all eligible individuals for years across different jobs, labour market states and dwellings. Moreover, very competent statisticians were (and are still) operating in these countries and they, unlike many of their Western counterparts, also know where to draw the line, in the treatment of data about individuals, between the protection of privacy and the interests of the research community. Hence anonymous microeconomic data is available to researchers and it is possible, unlike in quite a few countries in the OECD (the Organization for Economic Cooperation and Development), to carry out policy evaluation studies exploiting the many 'natural experiments' of the transitional experience.

The two reasons provided so far are sufficient to justify an investment of intellectual effort on something that is, by definition, transitory. They suggest that research on transition does not finish with the completion of transition.

The third reason is less cynical than the other two. It does not look on the arena of transitional economies as a research topic or as a 'natural experiment', but as an ongoing event involving a little less than 30 per cent of the human population, about 6 per cent of the world's gross domestic product (GDP), and roughly 8 per cent of world trade. This third reason is, in my view, the most important and one of the main inspirations of this book. Transition has generated diverging trajectories, yielding a few success stories, many failures, and the risk of further economic derailments. Interpreting these divergent dynamics and, if possible, providing sound policy advice is one of the most challenging and intriguing tasks that an economist can be faced with at the present time.

According to Vaclas Klaus, transition was already over by the mid-1990s. In his opening speech at the X Congress of the European Economic Association in Prague in August 1995, the former Prime Minister of the Czech Republic bluntly stated that his country had already crossed the dividing line. He did not spare complaints to the scientific community, which had underestimated the Czech miracle story. Since that glorious day, the Czech Republic has gone through a major currency crisis, experienced a drop in GDP—while all the neighbouring countries were rapidly growing—and seen a threefold increase in its unemployment rate, increasing political instability, several austerity packages (repetitions in this case being a clear sign of a lack of credibility), and a series of bank failures inducing the government in the end to put the largest private banks under compulsory administration.

At first sight, Klaus was right. His country, as well as many of the former Central European members of the Council for Mutual Economic Agreement (CMEA), could display impressive figures: from being virtually nil at the start of transition, the share of the private sector in value added had risen to about 70 per cent, and a massive reallocation of resources had occurred from industry and agriculture to the service sector, which was undersized in the centrally planned era. In 1995 the Czech Republic, unlike the other Visegrad countries (Hungary, Poland and the Slovak Republic), also enjoyed low unemployment rates, and hardship related to reallocation in the labour market was much less pronounced than in other countries of the region.

Other prime ministers in the regions are perhaps not marketing themselves in the same way as Klaus did; but some of them at least can display impressive records in terms of privatization, price liberalization, an opening-up to trade, substantial progress in closing down enterprises that were not viable (if not producing negative value added!), and structural change in their GDP.

The Inner Fragility of Transitional Economies

However, there was, and still is, a specificity and 'inner' fragility of transitional economies that Klaus overlooked, which holds also for those countries of Central Europe, that are so far displaying the most promising transitional records. Small open economies, as most of these countries are, coming out of a deep 'transitional recession' and growing faster than their trading partners are bound, sooner or later, to hit a balance of payment constraint unless they succeed in selling more and more products abroad. The growth of exports are, however, continuing to be constrained by the narrow and ill-founded product specialization inherited from the previous system; and imports are booming, not least because of a repressed demand for product variety.

Under the previous system, consumers were constrained in their choice of different specifications of the same product. There was generally just one type of good—a standard, poor-quality, homogenized version. In other words, consumers could at best choose *how much* to buy but not *what* to buy. This repressed love for variety is an important factor behind the collapse of CMEA trade and the strong growth of imports from Western countries, experienced by all countries in the region from the very start of transition. Trade balances of the countries in the region are likely to improve over time as a critical mass of firms, a *mittlestand* of small producers, takes root. Not only will this change reduce import penetration, but it will also make exports less sensitive to prices and hence to exchange-rate dynamics. In a world where consumers like variety, and where they prefer to get some of many different products rather than a lot of just one of them, new varieties create their own demand. When global demand is stagnant, export volumes can increase even without lowering prices, so long as the number of varieties being produced domestically increases.

Unfortunately, it takes time to develop an export base sufficiently diversified to be less vulnerable to global demand shocks hitting particular products, and even more time to increase the enterprise density (the average number of personnel in manufacturing plants under the previous regime was about 1,000, compared with 20–30 in the United States or Japan) and the number of varieties being produced domestically. All this requires the development of new entrepreneurship—something very much lacking in countries coming out of central planning—and a real-location not only of labour but above all of capital for small businesses. Although the risk of failure may be lower where there are many market niches to be filled compared with where markets are more crowded, the underdeveloped capital markets of the transitional economies have trouble in channelling resources to small private initiatives. Available evidence suggests that startup costs are high and liquidity constraints significant for new businesses.

Capital inflows can soften the external constraint while badly needed structural change gains momentum and small businesses gradually develop. Capital inflows did indeed significantly pick up in some countries in the region, at least before the Russian August 1998 crisis. However, capital inflows generate (often short-term) claims that will sooner or later have to be honoured, and globalization makes them more and more volatile because they can easily leave the country at any moment in response to events occurring elsewhere in the world or to a sudden loss of credibility. Capital markets lacking depth, liquidity and effective supervision, and banking sectors still to a large extent unreformed and unregulated, magnify the information problems faced by investors, leading to overreactions to changes in perceptions of a country's risk. Hence, external financing of trade deficits increasingly needs to be sustainable in terms of the economy's overall ability to pay, not only in the medium to long run but also in the very short run.

Another way to deal with the external constraint is to let the currency depreciate repeatedly or to abandon a fixed exchange-rate regime altogether. This option is not at zero cost, for repeated devaluations reduce purchasing power over imports and hence living standards; they also make progress more difficult on the inflation front, which is still significantly higher in Eastern Europe than in the West. Yet deteriorating trade balances signal, after all, that a country's exports are overvalued, and pegging the currency to a foreign anchor when domestic inflation continues to be significantly higher than in the major trading partners implies experiencing a real appreciation of the exchange rate. Thus, letting the currency depreciate may be sensible.

However, many countries have already accumulated a large foreign debt, which is often denominated in foreign currencies and is to a large extent short-term. Many large firms in the area have also issued equity in Western stock exchanges because the domestic markets lack depth and liquidity. Devaluing the currency under these circumstances implies increasing the burden associated with the servicing of the debt, and, in some cases, may pave the way for insolvency crises. Nor are a rescheduling of the external debt, improvement in its term structure, or the issue of government bonds in domestic currencies often feasible options, as spreads imposed by foreign investors on issues not hedged against exchange-rate risk can be extremely high. Moreover, the adoption of a flexible exchange-rate regime, when accompanied by tight monetary policies in order to keep imported inflation under control, may stimulate short-term speculative investment. Many developing countries, after abandoning a fixed exchange-rate regime, have experienced strong appreciations of their exchange rate, making it more difficult to absorb the trade deficit that originally caused the crisis. The experience of the Czech Republic is indicative also in this respect: a few months after being forced to let the currency depreciate and float in May 1997, the real exchange rate returned to its level before the speculative attacks.

The other side of the coin of the external constraint is the public deficit. The cost of servicing the foreign debt, if not the foreign debt itself, is strongly associated with public dissaving. Almost all transitional economies are experiencing government deficits. Although the imbalances may not be too large (to the extent that some of the Central and East European countries could actually satisfy the Maastricht criteria on these grounds), public deficits have a marked structural component; in particular, they tend to persist even in years of strong economic growth. Moreover, the experience of Russia in August 1998 suggests that the loss of confidence of investors in a country's ability to pay, even from a relatively small public debt, can set in motion a sequence of events leading to an insolvency crisis. Thus, there is a risk constantly hanging over these economies. In order to deal with the external constraint, they need to convince foreign investors that their public finances are in order; that they can close the budget deficit.

Needless to say, economies undergoing a systemic transformation are, by definition, heavily investing in the future. These are the typical conditions where deficit financing would be justified. However, governments in the region often face a static, rather than an intertemporal, budget constraint. The instability of global financial markets makes foreign investors' decisions increasingly driven by short-term considerations, and often also by perceptions based on non-economic factors—on 'animal spirits'.

How else can the asymmetries in the propagation of the Russian crisis between countries such as Poland and Hungary be explained? The two countries in August 1998 manifested broadly similar macroeconomic indicators: a rate of inflation close to 15 per cent, a budget deficit running at about 3 per cent of GDP, and output growth of the order of 5 per cent. Hungary had succeeded in significantly reducing its external debt position, bringing down the external debt-to-exports ratio to roughly 100 per cent (more or less the same level as Poland) from 250 per cent in 1995; and the current account deficit was larger in Poland (4.5 per cent of GDP) than in Hungary (3 per cent). Both countries had been included in the first round of Eastern Enlargement of the EU and had covered quite a lot of ground in structural change. And trade exposure to Russia was low in both countries, hardly attaining 5 per cent of exports. Yet spreads on Eurobonds increased in August 1998 much more sharply in Hungary than in Poland: while in Hungary spreads were of the order of 350 base points at their peak, in Poland they never exceeded 150 base points.

One may argue that these instability problems are common to many developing countries around the world in an era of globalization. However, there are important differences in degree. Moreover, the legacies of central planning offer a combination of systemic risks and of opportunities, which is almost unique in the arena of middle-income countries. Ten years after the start of transition, some of the inherited features of the Communist regime have disappeared; privatization and the development of services have been relatively fast, so that state-sector shares in GDP exceeding 50 per cent survive only in a few former Soviet republics and there are no longer signs of overindustrialization. Other legacies of the past are, however, still there—for instance, the striking contrast between a persistent excess of regulations in some areas and an institutional vacuum in others. These economies are overregulated and underregulated at the same time. The overregulation results in large, inefficient and often corrupt bureaucracies. Employment in the state administration, which was sizeable to start with, compared with other middle-income countries, has actually increased over time in most countries, just at a time when overall employment rates were falling by 10 to 15 percentage points per annum. The underregulation of crucial aspects of economic life, notably the financial markets, does not help in gaining the confidence of investors, and discourages long-term commitments by those able to assist with badly needed foreign direct investment. Regulatory reforms represent the only way that CEECs can succeed in transforming into a dynamic form the static budget constraint they are facing. Only by gaining the confidence of investors will governments of CEECs be able to issue debt in the manner they should in order to transform their economies at reasonable interest costs.

Thus, in order to deal with the external constraint, countries in transition not only have to be virtuous on the fiscal side but also need to deal with their 'regulatory mismatch'. Institutional reform is at least as important as macroeconomic stability for transitional economies, and institutional *reform* is longer to achieve than institution *building*. It is not a matter of starting from scratch.

Social policies are at the core of the problem. Fiscal pressures and failures in institutional reforms typically arise in this field. In the Central and Eastern European countries, social policy expenditures increased significantly over the 1990s, reaching between one-quarter and one-third of GDP and on average absorbing far more than 50 per cent of government expenditure. There is a complex mixture of provisions and cash transfers in place in urgent need of reform, many of them overlapping and some of them subject to mutually inconsistent regulations, which feed a large social security administration.

There was a window of opportunity at the outset of transition to phase out some of the multitude of cash transfers inherited from Communism, to reform pensions without necessarily grandfathering existing entitlements and, within the framework of a broader social policy reform, to introduce unemployment benefit systems. In times of economic upheaval, it is possible for governments to renege on commitments made under previous regimes, to streamline regulations, and to build social welfare systems adequate for market conditions. This opportunity has been lost. New schemes were introduced into the transition economies on the top of those previously existing; pension reforms were postponed; supplemental measures were the norm; comprehensive reforms were the exception. The outcome was to create an excessive number of benefits and beneficiaries of low, sometimes negligible, amounts. Even though it is still possible to reform social welfare systems, it is much more difficult to achieve.

Cuts to social spending are particularly hard to make, given that employment rates have sharply declined since the start of transition. Even supposing that cuts to social spending are politically and socially feasible, they may not be appropriate. The literature on growth accounting keeps on finding that social policy expenditure matters. In some cases it is found to negatively affect growth; in others, it is found to support it. These conflicting results confirm—if there was any need for it—that the composition of social spending is important for long-term growth. Transitional economies are, almost by definition, economies undergoing structural change. Thus, the link between social policy and growth is in these countries even stronger than elsewhere. The different social policy models adopted in Central and Eastern Europe and in Russia led to significantly different results in terms of speed and scope of labour reallocation, and those spending in social transfers were often the least successful. Changing the composition of social spending may be even more difficult than cutting cash transfers altogether. Weak governments can let inflation erode the real value of all cash transfers, but they can rarely reduce transfers to the pensioners and the inactive and give more support to jobseekers.

Reallocation Through Transfers

*Re*allocation is the word for the transitional economies. We are not dealing with countries starting from scratch, without an industrial base and with a large surplus of labour, but with countries having for the most part (the exception being China) exploited their extensive margins for growth. Full employment along a product specialization (and division of labour within the CMEA), which had been imposed by the planner rather than by market forces, implies that new jobs can only be created by redeploying labour.

The inherited social-transfer system was inadequate for transition in so far as it penalized mobility and conditioned the access to benefits (often provided in kind) to the holding of a job in a specific firm. Thus, at the outset of transition, cash transfers were detached from jobs: unemployment benefits were introduced in order to relieve employers from their social responsibilities with respect to their workers and to provide income support to those experiencing unemployment, a condition that was legally banned in most countries under the previous (Communist) regime. Pensions were also improperly used to reduce the social costs of redundancies.

The design of these 'non-employment benefits' differed significantly from country to country in the region. By comparing the various national experiences, one can make inferences as to the interactions between cash transfers to individuals in working age and labour reallocation.

The countries of Central Europe started the transition with rather generous non-employment benefits. It was frequent to find transfers having unlimited duration, either because of gross mistakes in the design of unemployment benefits (as in Poland) or deliberate choices to put workers leaving state enterprises into bridging schemes towards retirement. This version of non-employment benefits induced not only a large decline of employment rates—something that was after all foreseen by most scholars of transition and that was often advocated as a necessary by-product of the privatization of large segments of these economies—but also a strikingly long duration of unemployment spells. A vicious circle of entitlements and declines in effective labour supply was set in motion, which soon brought the social security burden on the active population to unbearable proportions. These cash-transfer systems had to be cut and were indeed significantly tightened a few years (in some cases even only a few months) after being started from scratch. When such cuts were made, they often resulted in a mere transfer of the burden from one social expenditure item to another, for instance from unemployment insurance to social assistance. Moreover, cuts to non-employment benefits were not successful in bringing people back to work—which is ultimately the only way to cut transfers across the board—except in the countries intervening before a high level of unemployment had built up.

At the other end of the spectrum, there is the experience of the former Soviet republics. Being geographically and politically more distant from Western Europe, and hence not subject to the influence or 'fatal attraction' of its welfare states, these countries entered transition without introducing significant cash transfers to non-employed individuals of working age. Problems in revenue collection and, in some republics, a lack of foreign capital inflows also played some role in the social policy model that was adopted by these countries. The transfer systems that had been put in place before the start of transition and the collapse of the Soviet Union (for example the unemployment benefits introduced under Soviet employment law) were only partly indexed or not indexed at all, leaving to inflation the task of silently eroding the real value of these transfers. Employment in these countries declined less as a result, and unemployment did not rise as steeply as in Central Europe. But countries taking the foregoing approach proved less successful in reallocating labour across industries, occupations and jobs than countries with a meaningful unemployment benefits system in place. There were no floors to wage setting and no insurance was provided against job loss; hence, employment in the new sector was unappealing for most workers of former state enterprises where a compressed wage structure still prevailed. Private firms, where unions are weak if not totally absent, were found often to pay unskilled workers less than the state enterprises and, on the top of that, to offer less job security. The outcome was less labour reallocation and more downward wage adjustment than in other transitional economies.

These two extreme experiences suggest that there should be an optimal design of benefits that would allow the fostering of mobility of workers without putting a large fraction of the population of working age at the margin of the world of work. Identifying these optimal design features is a dauntingly difficult task. Nor do Western countries offer blueprints in this respect, because they themselves are struggling to improve incentives related to benefits provision, so as to make work pay in spite of significant transfers to non-working able-bodied individuals. Further complications arise from the fact that these optimal features are not time-invariant, because they depend among other things on the level of unemployment, and on the extent of reallocation that has already occurred. There is a timing issue, which should not be overlooked.

Once these optimal features have been identified, it still remains to progress from one position to the other, by transforming the cash-transfer systems already in place, building an effective policy-delivery mechanism, and forming an administration capable of actually enforcing restrictions to eligibility—for example a work test and means testing when required. This is an even more difficult task. There are always strong pressures to do a bad job in reforming welfare systems, and while tight external and fiscal constraints put pressures on governments to intervene, they also do not help the shift from one system to another. Politically feasible reforms of key social-policy programmes may involve transient increases of public spending because it is necessary to win the cooperation of the losers—and, in some cases, also of the bureaucracies that are called upon to implement the reforms.

The political economy of reforms may appear less intricate in formerly planned economies than in Western Europe. There was, and there partly still is, a window of opportunity to reform the cash-transfer systems of transitional economies. In the West there is often strong agreement among economists about the need for cuts in social spending, but these are rarely implemented as they face strong political opposition. Significantly, social-policy expenditure as a percentage of GDP has hardly changed in the OECD countries in the course of the last fifteen years, in spite of mounting criticism about the excessive size of the European social welfare budget. In transitional countries, political resistance to social expenditure cuts is much weaker than in Western Europe. After all, significant cuts have already been made—in Russia, for instance, large arrears were accumulated in pension payments, which is certainly quite a radical way to cut transfers—and such cuts have not met the strong political opposition one would encounter in the West. Moreover, unions were, and still are, rather weak throughout the countries in transition, and certainly much less powerful than has been depicted in the early literature on work councils and self-managed firms.

Governments in the Eastern European region did not efficiently use the degrees of freedom at their disposal in reforming social policies. As mentioned above, pensions were not addressed at the outset of economic transformation, when it was possible to renege on commitments made under a different regime. Later on, when fiscal consolidation forced governments to cut social expenditure, savings were only pursued in the field of unemployment benefits, leaving the rest of the welfare system untouched. The case of the former Soviet republics is revealing in this respect: their shrinking social budget has been increasingly concentrated on pensioners, while the unemployment benefit system introduced under Soviet law was in effect dismantled. Furthermore, in Central Europe the first programmes to be cut under the fiscal crises of the early 1990s were, needless to say, unemployment benefits. As these after all represent new transfers, there was not much need to grandfather existing entitlements in. Unemployment is deemed to be a condition that can be altered at will by individuals, and a social stigma is often placed on the unemployed; if you do not work, it is your fault. An Interfax–AIF survey carried out in Moscow in December 1997 is quite revealing in this respect: among the main causes of poverty listed by the respondents, a prominent position is taken by 'laziness and drinking' (included in 77 per cent of the answers) and 'lack of effort' (44 per cent).

Then why were Central European countries more generous than Russia towards their unemployed? Jobseekers in the Visegrad countries were not more represented in the bargaining over the allocation of social transfers than in Russia. Yet, transition was for the countries of Visegrad like a 'return to Europe' and they inevitably felt the attraction of the Western European welfare systems. Although this choice involved very steep declines in employment rates (overshooting the employment to working-age population ratios of countries at comparable GDP per capita levels), it ultimately turned out to be good for labour reallocation. Whether the 'fatal attraction' of the EU will continue to play a positive role in the future is open to debate. Pressures to comply with the *Acquis communautaire* made on countries seeking accession are mainly in the direction of increasing the degree of protection of those who already have a job. This would make Central Europe's welfare systems look more and more like those of Southern Europe—countries where strong employment protection goes hand in hand with long-duration unemployment and where the unemployed count very little in all respects.

Another feature that these countries have in common with Southern Europe is the presence of a large underground economy escaping payroll and income taxation. A vicious circle has been set in motion whereby a declining tax base forces governments to increase statutory contribution rates for social policies and this, in turn, induces more firms and workers not to pay contributions. The problem of revenue collection is compounded by weak tax administrations and, more broadly, an ineffective and highly corrupted policy-enforcement mechanisms. Insisting on strengthened controls over tax compliance and a repression of illegal behaviour, as the EU countries are doing *vis-à-vis* candidates for accession, without improving incentives to declare employment may just make things worse and increase the dualism of these economies. Enforcement is not simply a matter of labour inspectorates and tax administration. Excessive emphasis on controls (for instance, assigning inspectorate functions to labour offices that register jobseekers) may actually be counterproductive and end up inflating the informal sector. It is better to rely on incentives and improve the social welfare system in this respect. Even a more costly, but better-designed, unemployment insurance may contribute to reduce the informal sector by inducing workers to declare their jobs and make sure that their wages are not underreported by employers when paying social security contributions.

Summarizing, we can note that countries in transition on the one hand face the same external pressures as developing nations and have to move along the same narrow pathway, and on the other they face the reality that they are not starting from scratch. They have to reallocate, not allocate; they have to reform, not build something new. This means more opportunities, but it also brings a high risk of stumbling off the path, because there are strong pressures to make wrong decisions. The increasing asymmetry in the performance of formerly planned economies is a clear indication of these opportunities and the risks of doing things that should not be done.

Comprehensive reforms of social welfare systems rather than selective cuts are needed to address the ultimate causes of the inner fragility of transitional economies. In the countries included in the first round of EU accessions, a more effective way to redistribute has been found— one that involves transfers to individuals and no longer forces them to hold unproductive jobs, but also one that creates strong disincentives to work. Cutting social transfers, notably those to able-bodied individuals, makes workers stay in their unproductive jobs and occupations. It is a strategy that reduces employment decline in the early stages of transition but does not generate employment later on; these economies may have less job destruction at the outset, but they certainly have less job creation later on.

This Book

This book is on the subject of labour reallocation and the reform of welfare systems, particularly the so-called non-employment benefits (namely the transfers provided to fit individuals of working age) throughout transition. The focus is on transition rather than on the legacies of the past, because there are many books that have already carefully described the characteristics of formerly planned economies. The institutional features inherited from the Communist regime will only be recalled when they are instrumental to understanding developments since the beginning of the 1990s.

The existing literature on labour market and social policy adjustment in transitional economies is fairly extensive. Ten years after the start of the transition process, it is possible to do something more ambitious than simply report evidence and draw conclusions relevant from both a heuristic and a policy standpoint. There is, in contrast, little, if any, work on the interactions between labour and social policies and on the relation between ongoing reforms of the education systems and labour market flows, because the existing literature tends to treat each of these issues separately. This book attempts to address the issues of transition within a framework encompassing the relationship between labour (including human capital development) and welfare.

Surprisingly enough, labour supply is absent from the models developed by the scholars of transition. The labour force is generally assumed to be fixed; all the action takes place on the demand side. However, the transitional countries entered the 1990s with participation rates—notably the participation rates for women—significantly higher than those of countries at comparable stages of development and are now displaying employment rates in some cases lower than those of nations with similar GDP per capita levels. Thus the labour supply has played a major role so far in transition and is bound to play an even more important role in the years to come. Low employment rates are the main factor behind the high, sometimes unbearable, social security burden placed on the active population in these countries.

There is also no literature on institution-building and policy-enforcement mechanisms in countries in transition. This book aims to fill this gap by drawing on information that the author collected while he was coordinating the activities carried out by the OECD in transitional economies in the domain of labour-market, social and education policies. These activities included cross-country analytical work as well as policy reviews and technical assistance projects. In this context, a network of contacts was developed and maintained with senior policy makers, government officials and researchers in the various countries. A wealth of data on labour-market flows, labour-market and social-policy expenditure, and beneficiaries was gathered, with detailed information on national regulations and institutional details.

The interpretations offered in this book for the 'puzzles of transition' (see Chapter 1) are mainly related to the interaction between structural change, cash transfers offered to non-employed individuals of working age, and labour reallocation. Clearly, there are many other factors that play an important role in affecting the speed and scope of transition. These factors are mentioned in later chapters but are not necessary for explaining the basic puzzles; they simply strengthen the storyline running throughout the book, embodied in the three elements mentioned in its title: structural change, welfare systems, and labour reallocation.

How can this storyline be summarized in a few words? There are two features of structural change that play a crucial role in making transition successful. The first is the *speed* of transition, in other words the time required to create more efficient units of production and dismantle the old ones. The second feature, which has so far been neglected by the literature, is the *scope* of transition, meaning the number of individuals actually in transit from an old to a new sector. Speed and scope interact closely and in a way that changes over time. Transition can gain in speed when job destruction in an old sector is achieved by inducing many workers to leave the labour force altogether. However, there are significant locking-in effects—related to informational asymmetries as to the ability of workers in the new occupations, which are particularly acute in economies undergoing radical structural transformations, urban–rural migration, and other changes—whereby economies get trapped in low-participation equilibria.

Hence, too speedy a transition, one that quickly downsizes the old sector, and is likely to lack scope. The opposite does not necessarily hold true: that is to say, a slow transition may not succeed in achieving greater scope. Rather, to the extent that a slow transformation holds resources within the old sector, the new sector never takes off and hence non-employment slowly builds up. This case is clearly less desirable, according to any normative criterion proposed, than the case of fast structural change with little scope. There we have at least a buoyant sector of the economy, albeit involving perhaps too few people, capable of leading the economy out of the transitional recession, in contrast to a small new sector with limited scope.

By a modelling of reallocation and participation decisions along these lines, it is possible to account for the wide international variation of transition trajectories, and for the differences in unemployment and non-employment created throughout the process. In particular, it is possible to explain why Russia has experienced low unemployment in the midst of dramatic output losses, but has not gone very far in transforming its economy. It is also possible to unfold the secrets behind the 'Czech low-unemployment miracle' of the mid-1990s in a region dominated by high and long-duration unemployment, and better understand the wide and persistent regional imbalances in Central and Eastern Europe.

From a policy standpoint, the interpretation of the puzzles of transition offered in this book sheds some light on the optimal design of income-support schemes for those transiting from the old to the new sector. It also suggests that there is an issue of right timing of reforms. Put another way, it is not only a matter of properly fine-tuning non-employment benefits but also of intervening before it is too late.

The plan of the book is as follows. Chapter 1 discusses what was expected to occur in these countries and what actually happened. It offers a critical review of the literature relating to the optimal speed of transition, and it points out a number of puzzles—facts that are at odds with that train of thought and also with commonly perceived wisdom on transition. Chapter 2 addresses some of the puzzles, namely those relating to the stagnancy of transitional unemployment and the presence of locking-in effects preventing the pickup of outflows from unemployment when non-employment benefits are reduced. Chapter 2 also draws on a model that combines the reallocation processes framed by the literature on the optimal speed of transition with matching frictions. Variants of this basic model are used in the remaining chapters of the book.

Chapter 3 discusses the interactions between non-employment benefits, income distribution and job reallocation. This makes it possible to characterize and understand the asymmetries in labour-market adjustments between Central and Eastern Europe on the one hand and the former Soviet republics on the other. Chapter 4 draws policy implications from the previous analysis and tries to understand why different policies were implemented in different countries and why policy mistakes were made. The objective of Chapter 4 is to provide policy prescriptions that take into account factors of political economy as well as the state of the policy-enforcement mechanism in these countries.

In the first and last chapters, theory comes before facts. In the second and third, it is the other way round as facts are essential in order to understand where existing models should be revised. The book is written in a style that targets economists working close to policy making, officials from international organizations, policy makers from transitional countries, and students involved in the large number of courses being taught around the world on the economics of transition. The book targets a non-specialized audience, and so the most technical parts are relegated to annexes to the various chapters.

1
The Puzzles of Transition

1.1 Introduction

When transition of the Eastern European economies began, there was no historical precedent to draw upon while making inferences on the future course of events. Educated guesses were allowed and were made, quite many of which turned out subsequently to be wrong. It is easy to be wise after the event, but knowledge evolves by comparing actual with expected outcomes and learning from these deviations. Thus, I will be pitiless in pointing out departures from the predictions made at the outset. Actually, I will do more than that: I will try to understand why wrong predictions were made. This is my primary goal. From the common wisdom prevailing at the beginning of the 1990s we need, in any event, to start.

There were three common predictions made at the outset:

- The removal of state subsidies and associated hardening of budget constraints would force many state enterprises to close down, inducing large-scale labour shedding. In order to restructure these enterprises, rather than simply closing them down, it was essential to win the strong resistance of workers to change, that is to 'buy them off'.
- As a result of this shake-out, striking at the core of 'socialist employment', large inflows into unemployment of redundant workers would have to be expected. As the size of these inflows was related to the pace of closure of state enterprises, it was also argued that unemployment could be considered as an indicator of the determination of government to push through reforms and impose tough budget constraints on enterprises.
- Unemployment would gradually be absorbed by the growth of the

emerging sectors, namely private firms (mainly clustered in retail trade), the service sector, and industries producing light consumption goods where such industries had previously been artificially compressed under central planning because of its emphasis on primary accumulation.

In a nutshell, labour reallocation was deemed to occur mainly through unemployment, the single most important indicator of the speed of transition trajectories.

From a normative point of view, a careful timing of reforms was called for. Most of the models used to speculate on the future course of events yielded a multiplicity of equilibria and a non-trivial relation between the speed and final outcomes of transition. On the one hand, reforms had to be enforced in such a way as to avoid creating too much unemployment before a critical size of the private sector had been reached; otherwise, social unrest relating to increasing unemployment, the associated political backlashes of reformers, or the fiscal burden induced by unemployment benefit payments or other 'feedback' mechanisms (e.g. income effects of dis-employment) would block reforms. On the other hand, reforms could not be too slow as resources had to be freed for the growth of the private sector, unemployment had to start exerting its moderating effects on wage claims (and employers were deemed not sufficiently organized to resist such claims), and increased productivity had to stimulate investment. This was the essence of the trade-offs entailed by the models of the optimal speed of transition (OST) developed at early stages of the process and widely used in policy advice throughout the region.

In this chapter we will start by reviewing the extensive OST literature. Next, we will assess the empirical relevance and predictive accuracy of these models based on information on aggregate stocks and flows. The final section of this chapter will list the various pieces of evidence left unexplained by this rich (and still flourishing) literature and will argue that solving these puzzles is important in the light of the challenges facing the transitional countries in the years to come. Thus, we will start with theory and go on to facts. The reader knowing the OST literature can skip section 1.2 and go directly to the evidence presented in section 1.3.

1.2 What Did We Expect to Occur?

When I first visited Warsaw at the beginning of January 1990, the policy makers I met were largely underestimating the growth of unemployment. I distinctly remember that their estimates for Poland ranged from 50,000 (according to the most optimistic views, shared *inter alia* by the first Labour Minister of the new Poland) to 200,000 unemployed. Needless to say, at the end of that month, there were already 56,000 people registered unemployed in the Polish labour offices and the 'pessimistic' 200,000 threshold was attained after just two months. One year later there were 1.2 million individuals registered unemployed. One-and-a-half years later the 2 million threshold had been crossed. Four years later about 3 million Polish citizens were registered as unemployed at labour offices.

The climate in the international organizations and within the scientific community was very different. The comparative view across nations that organizations such as the IMF, the OECD and the World Bank could draw upon, and perhaps also the 'distance' from which they could observe developments in the transition world, dictated much less optimistic views as to the likely rise and magnitude of transitional unemployment. The experience of Eastern Germany on unification was, after all, emblematic. Even if Eastern German unemployment had been to a large extent a by-product of the political decision to fix a 1-to-1 parity of the ostmark to the deutschmark (and of the extension to the East of the Western system of industrial relations),[1] these large cohorts of jobseekers were coming from enterprises often generating negative value added, and this evidence was even more striking as coming from the technological leader of the former CMEA bloc. Thus, there were many Cassandras around.

Not only was unemployment considered inevitable, but it was also deemed to be an indicator of the speed of transition.[2] To a common way of thinking, there was a simple mechanics of transition: on the one hand, the removal of subsidies to state enterprises and their exposure to market discipline would force the managers of these firms to shed labour; on the other hand, a flourishing private sector would generate employment opportunities in the numerous market areas (e.g. the retail trade) and niches (because central planning did not allow for product differentiation

---

[1] According to von Hagen (1997), the fact of exporting Western-type collective bargaining institutions to Eastern Germany reduced the competitivity of new Länders even more seriously than the exchange rate established at the time of unification.

[2] Cf. McAuley (1991).

satisfying consumers' preferences for variety) that had been artificially compressed under the old system. Thus, inflows into unemployment coming from the downscaling of state enterprises and outflows from unemployment associated with the emergence of the private sector were expected, with the former exceeding the latter during early stages of transition because of the small scale of the private sector at the start of the process. Hence, unemployment would increase even if employment growth in the private sector was faster than job destruction in the state sector.

As an illustration of this scale effects, assume that a proportion 's' of employment in state enterprises E_s is shed per period whilst in the meantime employment in the private sector E_p generates 'g' new posts for any job type existing at the beginning of the period. Then we have that unemployment U evolves according to the following law:

$$\Delta U = I - O = sE_s - gE_p \qquad (1.1)$$

where I represents unemployment inflows and O represents unemployment outflows. From (1.1) it follows that unemployment inflows can exceed unemployment outflows, and hence unemployment can grow (ΔU positive) even if g is greater than s, provided that E_p is small compared with E_s.

Put another way, unemployment should have been unavoidable at early stages of transition because even a buoyant private sector could not compensate employment losses in the overmanned state enterprises inherited from the previous system.[3] However, further down the transition path, i.e. for large E_p and small E_s, unemployment would have to decline because the scale effects would begin to work the other way round. Overall, a bell shaped curve representing the dynamics of unemployment was expected, with unemployment initially increasing and then declining.

---

[3] Several estimates were provided at the beginning of transition of the amount of 'labour hoarding' (e.g., see OECD, 1993a), that is employment kept in excess of what needed to attain the targeted output level. Most of these estimates were just guesses as there were no time series of employment under different cyclical conditions or ad-hoc surveys to draw upon. The estimates pointed to overmanning accounting for between 30 and 60 per cent of state-sector employment at the beginning of the 1990s. Interestingly, the reduction in labour hoarding was considered by many Eastern European economists as the single most important sign of 'marketization' as if (1) restructuring had involved only cost-minimization, (2) firms also in the West, particularly in downturns, were not keeping workers in excess to the extent needed to reach a given level of output, and (3) reducing overmanning could be always crucial, even in countries and time periods when real wages were falling dramatically, for example.

Unemployment was also deemed to be an indicator of the speed of reforms: inflows into unemployment were determined solely by the parameter s, capturing the pace of labour shedding in state enterprises and hence the timing of removal of state subsidies and, more broadly, the tightening of the budget constraints of state enterprises.

Although unemployment was unavoidable, governments could at least prevent too large an initial rise in the number of jobless. They could do this by fine-tuning employment reductions in state enterprises with the absorption capacity of the emerging private sector. However, the slowing down of restructuring in state enterprises could negatively affect the development of the private sector by preventing excess labour from exerting downward pressure on wages, and possibly via fiscal displacement effects related to the financing of subsidies to state enterprises.

1.2.1 Fine-tuning the Speed of Transition

The interactions between 's' and 'g, and policy trade-offs between the tightening of the budget constraints of state enterprises, unemployment and the development of the private sector are at the core of the theoretical literature on the optimal speed of transition, which offers a valuable framework for researchers and relevant background material for policy advice throughout the region. As the building blocks and main implications of the various models are reviewed in the annex to this chapter (Annex 1.), I can confine myself herein to summarizing the key findings of this literature and the basic assumptions it relies upon.

Transition is modelled as a process involving the reallocation of labour from state to private enterprises. A common feature of these models is the assumption that labour supply is fixed, so that persons are either employed or unemployed; in other words, labour market adjustment does not involve flows to and from the out-of-the-labour force (OLF) status. Another key simplifying assumption is that flows of labour from the public sector to the private sector are necessarily mediated by intervening unemployment spells, so that there is no direct shift of workers from state to private enterprises. The kind of flows allowed and 'banned' under this literature are summarized in Fig. 1.1.

This literature also considers the speed of closure of state sector jobs as a control variable. Governments can affect labour shedding in state enterprises in various ways—for instance by granting them subsidies, and by imposing strict employment protection legislation (e.g.

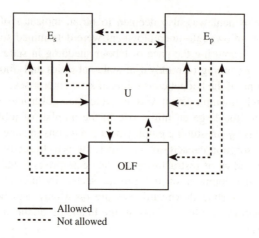

———— Allowed
------ Not allowed

Figure 1.1. Labour market flows in the optimal speed of transition literature
Notes: E_s = employment in state firms; E_p = employment in private firms; U= unemployment; OLF = out-of-the labour force.

non-negligible severance and advance notification requirements on firms implementing layoffs). The other key policy variable is the generosity of unemployment benefits (summarized by the ratio of benefits to the ongoing wage, or 'replacement rate') provided to those displaced in the transition. Unemployment benefits cannot, however, exceed the amount raised by (specific) taxes on employment in the public *and* private sectors.[4] The government budget constraint is generally assumed to be static, that is, no deficit financing is allowed. Only the model by Coricelli (1996) allows for intertemporal budget constraints.

All the models aim at capturing institutional features of transitional economies, such as the important role played by workers in decision making in state enterprises, and they typically generate unemployment even at the steady-state equilibrium. Although the micro-foundations of these models are not spelled out, reference is occasionally made to two sources of involuntary unemployment, namely the presence of moral hazard (associated with imperfect monitoring of workers' effort) or adverse selection (because of poor signals to workers' actual productivity,

[4] In this model, subsidies to state enterprises are treated as falling from the heavens. They are simply a policy instrument that governments can freely adjust—that is, without taking resources away from other public expenditure items—in order to affect the speed of transition.

for instance), both of these sources leading employers in the private sector to set wages above the market-clearing level (efficiency wages). Frictions in the labour market making it more costly and time-consuming to reallocate workers from the state sector to the private sector are also framed, notably in the models by Burda (1993) and Gavin (1993).

Thus, the literature departs from the standard assumptions and the basic setup of neoclassical growth theory. The price of this greater realism is that models are very rich in structural assumptions and it is more difficult to disentangle the role played by each market imperfection and to identify what drives labour-market dynamics. The OST literature also follows, more or less consistently,[5] a partial equilibrium approach, the main exception being in this case the general equilibrium model by Castanheira and Roland (1998), which is also an attempt to bridge the gap between these models and standard growth theory.

The policy trade-offs involved in the transition process are embedded in these models in a number of feedback mechanisms: unemployment growth is, on the one hand, influenced by the speed of the removal of state subsidies; but, on the other hand, high unemployment may strike back on speed because of fiscal effects related to the funding of unemployment benefits, political economy factors eroding the consensus gathered around the reform effort, or other mechanisms.

In the seminal model by Aghion and Blanchard (1994), the basic feedback mechanism is one coming from the fiscal side: high unemployment means large outlays to fund unemployment benefits (because subsidizing overmanning in state enterprises is supposedly costless, while paying people who are out of work is not), and hence there is higher payroll taxation. This in turn reduces job creation in the private sector. This 'fiscal externality' is at work also in the models by Burda (1993) and by Chadha and Coricelli (1994). The last two authors, unlike Aghion and Blanchard, allow for differential taxation of state and private enterprises. In particular, effective tax rates are assumed to be higher in the state than in the private sector, owing to problems in revenue collection faced when dealing with private (and small) businesses. Hence, in Chadha and Coricelli's model, the fiscal balance deteriorates in the transition process even when unemployment is stable, because an increasing proportion of the total wage bill of the economy is being paid by private employers.[6]

---

[5] Even if ad hoc assumptions allow some authors to claim that these are general equilibrium models, their setup is a partial equilibrium one.

[6] The model by Castanheira and Roland (1998) does not have such a feedback

Another class of models identifies potential feedback mechanisms in political economy factors.[7] This is the case of the frameworks proposed, *inter alia*, by Przeworski (1993); Rodrik (1995) and Dewatripont and Roland (1992, 1996). Rodrik's model shows that the window of opportunity existing at the outset of transition rapidly erodes as workers in state enterprises find it more and more difficult to shift to the emerging private sector and hence vote against further cuts to subsidies to state enterprises (which are, contrary to reality, supposed to be entirely financed via the taxation of private enterprises).[8] In Dewatripont and Roland (1992), a big-bang reform strategy is bound to be stopped under majority rule. The only way to enact reforms is to introduce them gradually using divide-and-rule tactics whereby only the workers hurt by each reform will oppose it.[9] Divide-and-rule tactics are also essential to start restructuring firms whose workers exert substantial control over managerial decisions. Under these circumstances, a sharp initial rise of unemployment may block reforms. If unemployment increases too much at the outset of transition, workers will oppose restructuring as they face low re-employment probabilities in the case of job loss (Blanchard, 1997). Intuitively, the job-finding probability is given by outflows from

mechanism. However, too fast a process of sectoral reallocation of workers can still end up perversely slowing down the transition process and can generate mass unemployment because the (negative) income effects associated with plant closures dominate the (positive) substitution effects of wage declines induced by increasing unemployment.

[7] To be fair, political economy considerations are present also in the model by Aghion and Blanchard (1994). As spelled out in a subsequent work by Blanchard (1997), the generosity of unemployment benefits plays a key role in allowing worker-controlled state enterprises to begin (strategic) restructuring. However, the political economy of reforms—notably industrial relations within the enterprise—matters in these models only in so far as it hastens or postpones the restructuring of state enterprises. In other words, political economy factors do not play the role of a feedback mechanism potentially reversing the process once this has started.

[8] This window of opportunity is present also in the case of strategic voting when state enterprises are highly inefficient at the outset of transition. Even by initially voting against the reforms, state sector workers are not able to prevent the median voter (whose preferences ultimately drive policy decisions) from getting out of the state sector. Moreover, if state sector workers succeed in shifting to the private sector, they will have to bear the burden of the subsidy they initially voted for. As long as private sector workers and the unemployed always vote against the subsidy, strategic voting rules out the possibility of policy reversals.

[9] This applies also when workers are forward-looking, provided that the 'old' sectors (e.g. state enterprises and cooperatives) are bound to disappear at some finite date. This is not the case in some OST models. For instance, in Rodrik's 1995 model, the state sector is supposed to survive even at the steady-state equilibrium in spite of persistent productivity (and wage) differentials *vis-à-vis* the private sector.

unemployment over the unemployment stock, and high unemployment means a large 'denominator' for any given absorption capacity of the private sector, that is for any given numerator.

The presence of such feedback mechanisms opens up the possibility of a multiplicity of equilibria. This may be a desirable property of these models in so far as they aim also at explaining international differences in the levels at which unemployment is stabilizing throughout Central and Eastern Europe and the former Soviet republics. For instance, in Aghion and Blanchard (1994) model, depending on the expectations of private sector employers, the economy may end up at a low-unemployment equilibrium or the transition may fail, leading the economy to be trapped in a high-unemployment equilibrium. Expectations matter because private employers decide on hirings on the basis of their assessment of their lifetime tax liabilities. Expectations are self-fulfilling as pessimistic private employers end up paying more taxes: they absorb workers shed by state enterprises too slowly and hence have to pay more for unemployment benefits. A credible commitment by governments to reduce unemployment benefits (or to slow down restructuring in state enterprises) when unemployment is too high can prevent the occurrence of the high-unemployment equilibrium.[10]

1.2.2 Policy Implications of the OST Literature

Multiple equilibria and non-linearities in the adjustment paths point to the role of economic policies in ruling out 'bad' equilibria,[11] easing transition and reducing the risk of derailments. Thus, the OST literature has relevant policy implications as to (1) the magnitude and timing of reduction of subsidies to state enterprises, (2) the generosity of unemployment benefits, (3) the form and speed of privatization, and (4) the scope for deficit financing of social policies in the course of transition.

Although all models imply that subsidies to state enterprises will sooner or later have to be lifted, the OST literature suggests that there is a need for careful timing to be followed in the tightening of the budget con-

[10] The announcement that benefits will be reduced if unemployment becomes too high may not be credible *ex ante*. However, as discussed in Chapter 2, governments in the region have proved capable of significantly tightening up unemployment benefits when unemployment was at its transitional peaks.

[11] High and low unemployment need not necessarily be synonymous in these models with 'good' and 'bad' equilibria, respectively. For example, in the model by Chadha *et al.* (1993), the economy may get trapped in a low-unemployment equilibrium dominated by state firms, where no accumulation of physical and human capital takes place.

straints of state enterprises: too quick a reduction of subsidies means too large an initial rise of unemployment and associated fiscal burden (and/or income effects), hindering the growth of the private sector. Hence, subsidies have some role to play at the outset of transition. In other words, the OST literature makes a case for gradualism in spite of the fact that two key factors that generally move the balance in favour of gradualism rather than big-bang[12]—the presence of a political learning process, and the possibility of early reversals—are not taken into account.

Unemployment benefits play a twofold role in these models. On the one hand, inasmuch as they increase the value of the outside option of state sector workers, they ease the restructuring of state enterprises by reducing the opposition of insiders to employment reductions and to privatization.[13] On the other hand, the financing of unemployment benefits puts a brake on the creation of private-sector employment and hence reduces its capacity to absorb labour shed from state enterprises. Owing to this trade-off between the effects of benefits on restructuring and on private job creation, unemployment benefits should be rather generous at the start of transition and, if necessary, be reduced later on. Actually, in order to rule out bad equilibria, governments should from the beginning commit themselves to reduce benefits if unemployment reaches a certain threshold.

As shown by Blanchard (1997), when unemployment is large, the 'fiscal externality' tends to dominate. At that stage, a case for high benefits can only be made on equity grounds. This holds even when unemployment benefits are also meant to promote better matches between jobseekers and vacancies. In that individuals are not very risk-adverse (and hence the provision of insurance does not significantly affect voluntary decisions to undertake risky job search) and have a large demand for precautionary savings, unemployment benefits aimed at promoting better matches ultimately slow down restructuring (Atkeson and Kehoe, 1997).

The choice among different privatization rules is framed in these models as a change in the proportion of post-privatization profits going

---

[12] The literature on gradualism versus big-bang is reviewed in Roland (1994).

[13] However, higher unemployment benefits negatively affect job-finding probabilities of the unemployed by putting a higher floor to wage bargaining in the private sector, which means lower job creation. If individuals place a relatively high value on future consumption (if they have a rather low discount rate), the negative effect of higher benefits on unemployment outflows may offset the positive effect on the instantaneous value of being unemployed. See Annex 1. for a characterization of these two mutually offsetting effects.

to insiders (Aghion and Blanchard, 1996), which is zero in the case of pure outsider privatization. More generous privatization rules (reflected in an insider share close to one unit) reduce the opposition of insiders to restructuring by increasing the benefits they can get if they do not lose their job in the process. Unlike unemployment benefits, insider privatization rules do not involve fiscal externalities (they do not increase taxes paid by private enterprises) and hence they do not exert negative feedback effects on the reallocation process. More importantly still, insider privatization tends to reduce wage claims in the private sector because workers involved in privatization will be due to receive a share of their firms' profits, and may also stimulate job creation.[14] Hence, these models generally argue in favour of insider privatization, a case against this method being made mainly on distributional grounds (as insider privatization makes everybody worse off except those who happen to be employed in privatized firms).

Finally, debt financing of social insurance is generally advocated by these models because it allows offsetting of the feedback effects associated with the initial rise of unemployment. Excessively strict borrowing constraints—established in the context of macroeconomic stabilization packages, for example—may therefore have a negative effect on the pace of job reallocation and even jeopardize the success of economic transformation (Chadha and Coricelli, 1994). Yet the kind of foreign borrowing allowed in these models is a foreign transfer not involving future repayment obligations; more than foreign borrowing, it is a gift offsetting the fiscal-externality effects associated with the rise of unemployment.

Summarizing, we should note that the OST literature assumes that labour supply is fixed: one can be either employed or seeking a job, but inactivity is banned. In the light of this assumption, the many variants of the basic Harris–Todaro model that have been developed in recent literature all consider the rate of decline of state sector jobs as a parameter (s) that can be altered at will by governments. The control over s is both direct—in so far as governments decide upon the amount of subsidies to be granted to state enterprises—and indirect—because workers controlling state enterprises can be induced to accept restructuring plans by more generous unemployment benefits. Unemployment benefits them-

[14] These models underplay (if they consider them at all) the effects of different privatization rules on enterprise behaviour via changes in corporate governance and managerial incentives. Hence, they neglect a possible feedback effect of insider privatization at the time of restructuring.

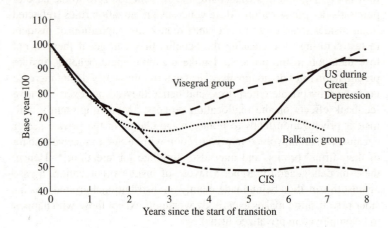

Figure 1.2a. Comparative evolution of GDP since the start of transition

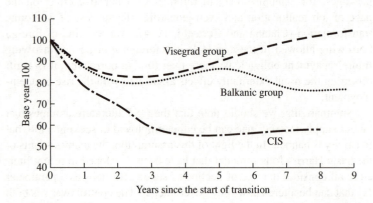

Figure 1.2b. Comparative evolution of industrial production since the start of transition

Notes: Visegrad group includes the Czech Republic, Hungary, Poland and the Slovak Republic. Balkanic group includes Bulgaria and Romania. CIS = Commonwealth of Independent States. United States during Great Depression refers to the 1929–37 period.

Source: OECD, 'Short-Term Economic Indicators and EBRD', *1998 Transition Report*.

selves should be relatively generous at the start of transition, in order to set in motion the reallocation process, but governments should be committed to reduce the generosity of benefits when unemployment is above a certain threshold. Because of the heavy fiscal burden imposed by the financing of these benefits on private job creation, employers need to be convinced that the transition will not eventually fail.

1.3 What Happened?

1.3.1 The Output Collapse

All transition countries experienced after the beginning of the systemic transformation in the early 1990s one of the deepest economic recessions ever observed in modern history. In the first two years of transition, GDP declined on average between 15 and 20 per cent (Fig. 1.2a). Output declines affected all sectors, but were particularly marked in the manu-facturing industries. Gross industrial production fell everywhere more sharply than output, and in Bulgaria and Romania (the Balkanic group) industrial output halved between 1990 and 1992. The 'transitional reces-sion' was no less dramatic than the Great Depression. Actually, output declines were sharper and, at least in Russia, more protracted than in the United States in the 1930s (Fig. 1.2b).

The transitional recession is often characterized as a U-shaped evo-lution of output. However, this is true only for the Central European countries, and yet some of them at the end of 1999 were still lagging behind the GDP levels of the previous decade. The Balkanic countries, after a short recovery around the mid-1990s, experienced a new marked decline of GDP six to eight years down the road of transition. In Russia, the recession had not reached an end eight years after the beginning of the systemic transformation. With an acknowledgement of measurement errors in largely demonetized economies such as those of the Common-wealth of Independent States (CIS), recorded GDP levels in this region were in 1999 at about 50 per cent of the pre-transition levels and the shape that could best describe the evolution of output is a letter L rather than a U.

The OST literature did not predict such a marked decline of output. As acknowledged by Kornai (1994), the transitional recession came as a surprise: only a mild slowdown had been predicted (by a few economists) at the outset. And, after all, there was no reason to believe, *a priori*, that the transition from a less efficient to a more efficient production system should have involved dramatic falls in output. Also, from an empirical standpoint, labour- and capital-reallocation costs involved by structural change could not have been expected to generate sizeable output losses. The empirical relation between structural change and output observed in OECD countries—the so-called Lilien's hypothesis[15]—cannot yield comparable falls in output, and the losses were in any event initially uniform across the board rather than concentrated in specific sectors.

Although a number of statistical issues (some overreporting of output under the previous regime; changes in the composition of output and in the availability of goods to consumers as well as quality improvements not captured by official statistics, which consequently overstated inflation;[16] a large hidden economy; etc.) could contribute to explain some of the GDP decline, the size of output losses could by no means reflect mere measurement problems. Industrial output statistics are generally more accurate than GDP figures and—albeit gross output statistics may overstate declines in value added in so far as before the transition some firms were operating at low, or even negative, value added—point to sharp declines in economic activity. Moreover, data on electricity consumption (EBRD, 1995; Kaufmann and Kaliberda, 1995; Lacko, 1999) are in line with reported GDP declines in the Central and Eastern European Countries (CEECs). All this suggests that the transitional recession was not simply a statistical artefact.

Some explanations for the output losses were only provided *ex post*—externally with respect to the OST literature[17]—and were, for the most part not entirely convincing. The most ingenious interpretation is that provided Blanchard and Kremer (1997). They point to the disorganization in the production network, notably in the provision of materials and intermediate inputs, associated with the removal of central planning, the unbundling of the vertically integrated conglomerates inherited from the previous regime, and rent-seeking behaviour on the

[15] Cf. Lilien (1982).

[16] Filer and Hanousek (1999) estimate that the upward bias in inflation statistics for the Czech Republic could have been as high as 20 per cent. This means that the GDP decline would have been shorter (two years rather than three) and resembling much more a cyclical downturn than a so-called 'transitional recession'.

[17] The only explanation for the output fall provided within the OST literature is associated with the work of Atkeson and Kehoe (1997), who point to labour-market frictions associated with sectoral shifts. Yet output fall was experienced uniformly across the board and preceded sectoral shifts in employment. For earlier explanations of the output fall, see Gomulka (1991) and Kornai (1994).

part of input providers as soon as the coercive power of central planning (in enforcing the production and delivery of intermediate goods) ceased to exist. Under asymmetric information as to the reservation price of input providers or incomplete contracts, bargaining over input provision is inefficient and may lead to a collapse of production in the state sector. At any stage along the chain of production, the input provider may indeed find it more advantageous to break the chain.

These problems arising from the interlocking of firms along the vertical links of production are bound to become less and less important as transition proceeds, because rents induce the multiplication of suppliers and hence the firm standing uphill in the production chain can always change input provider. Thus, this explanation can only hold for the initial stages of transition. Based on measures of the 'complexity of production' (capturing the number of intermediate inputs required by final goods in any given sector) obtained from input–output tables and business surveys reporting shortages of materials and intermediate inputs, Blanchard and Kremer found some support for the theory in the Balkanic group and the CIS,[18] but in all of these countries output falls were much more protracted than implied by a transient disorganizational shock. Moreover Blanchard and Kremer's model is based on two key assumptions: the presence of Leontief-type technologies (where such technologies do not allow the replacement of inputs that are temporarily underprovided), and a marked specificity of the inputs required by the firms inherited from the previous regime. The latter assumption may sound particularly unrealistic for firms that were frequently subject, under the previous system, to input shortages and were producing homogeneous goods using intermediate inputs that were much less specific or specialized than in market economies. Surveys of enterprises carried out in these countries suggest that it is the *new* firms producing the *new* products that find it difficult to secure domestically an adequate provision of intermediate goods and often have to use imported inputs. [19]

The explanation for the output fall provided by Roland and Verdier (1997) differs only slightly from that of Blanchard and Kremer (1997). Unlike the latter, Roland and Verdier emphasize the existence of frictions in the search of new partners down the chain of production and relation-specific investment: firms do not invest until a long-term partner has

---

[18] Based on data from enterprise surveys in the Ukraine and Russia, Konings and Walsh (1999) found little support to the role played by disorganization in the output fall in these two groups of countries.

[19] See Konings and Walsh (1999).

been found. Thus, output fall in their model arises not only because of the disruption of previous production links but also because of a fall in investment and the depreciation of capital associated with the absence of replacement investment. Many of the points made concerning the empirical relevance of Blanchard and Kremer's model apply also to this explanation of the output fall.

1.3.2 Behind the Stocks

For quite some time, labour-market developments in the transitional nations seemed closely to conform to *a priori* expectations and to the predictions of the models summarized in section 1.2. Employment in state enterprises was plummeting, unemployment was skyrocketing, and private employment was growing rapidly. Projecting over time the monthly growth rates of public and private employment experienced in 1989–91 by Poland—the first country to embark on a comprehensive structural transformation-cum-stabilization process—and imposing, as is customary in the OST literature, a constant labour force, one obtains the pattern of unemployment displayed in Fig. 1.3, which bears a close resemblance to the evolutions implied by the models reviewed in the previous section. Unemployment is initially rising, reaches double-digit levels, and then vanishes as quickly as it appeared: we have the predicted (and quite reassuring) broadly bell-shaped evolution of unemployment. Everything seemed to be working in line with expectations.

However, a closer scrutiny of labour-market dynamics and access to flow data soon revealed (Boeri, 1994) that the adjustment of labour markets in the CEECs was very different from what was predicted by these models and anticipated in most policy forums and academic discussions. While employment reductions were expected to be driven by layoffs, data on separations from state enterprises indicated that a significant component of outflows from state-sector jobs was associated with voluntary quits. Available evidence from Labour Force Survey (LFS) data (reported in the top panel of Table 1.1), points to rather large ratios of job *leavers* (persons currently non-employed because they had quit their previous job) to total employment in comparison with non-CEEC countries, whereas proportions of job *losers* (persons currently non-employed because they were laid off from their previous job) are roughly comparable to those observed in the European Union. Quite strikingly, in Poland and the Czech Republic the ratio of job losers to total employment was even lower than in Italy, a country located at

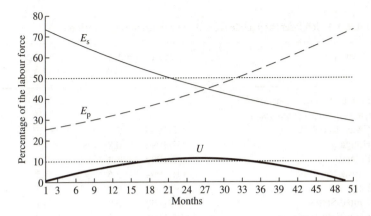

Figure 1.3. The mechanics of transition (simulations of the mechanic model based on Poland's 1989–91 experience)

Notes: The simulations are based on the following initial conditions and values of the parameters: $E_s(0) = 0.75$; $E_p(0) = 0.25$; $U(0)$; $s = 0.019$ and $g = 0.021$, where E_s = employment in state sector, E_p = employment in private sector, U = unemployment.

the top of rankings of employment protection against dismissals[20] and experiencing among the lowest layoff rates in Western Europe. It should be stressed that the LFS questionnaire asked only those at the time non-employed about the nature of the separation, and many quits are likely to end up in the take-up of another job rather than in non-employment. Hence the data reported in Table 1.1 are likely to significantly underestimate the proportion of quits in the total number of separations. The large number of quits occurring at the outset of transition is even more striking when account is taken of the transitional recession: voluntary separations are in OECD countries strongly procyclical and tend to fall significantly during downswings.

Disentangling quits from layoffs on the basis of administrative data is notoriously difficult because separations classified as 'mutual' agreements may often hide actual layoffs. That fact notwithstanding, data from the unemployment registers (reported in the bottom panel of Table 1.1), which also have the advantage of covering the very beginning of the transition process, suggest that the bulk of flows from employment to unemployment in 1991–2 was indeed represented by quits. Rela-

[20] See OECD (1999).

Table 1.1. Job losers and job leavers at the early stages of transition

Country	Dates	Job leavers (%)	Job losers (%)
Labour Force Survey data [a]			
(percentage of employment)			
Czech Republic	Q2/1993	2.1	1.5
Hungary	Q2/1992	0.8	4.5
Poland	Q2/1992	1.4	2.0
Slovak Republic	Q1/1994	2.6	4.3
Italy	1993–94	0.4	2.3
United States	1991–92	0.9	3.1
EU weighted average	1991–95	1.2	3.2
Data from the unemployment registers [b]			
(percentage of total separations)			
Czech Republic	1991–92	72.1	27.4
Poland	1991–92	65.7	34.3
Slovak Republic	1991–92	79.2	20.9

[a]Non-employed for less than six months with previous work experience by reason of termination of their previous contract, as a percentage of LFS employment.

[b]Registered unemployed for less than 12 months with previous work experience by reason of termination of their previous contract, as a percentage of total inflows from employment into registered unemployment.

Source: For the CEECs, estimates are based on individual LFS and unemployment register data; OECD, *Employment Outlook, 1997*, for data on Italy, the United States and the European Union.

tively many voluntary separations were also observed in countries that embarked later upon a structural transformation process, such as Russia. Based on an enterprise survey carried out by the World Bank, (Commander *et al.*, 1995) report that only about 25 per cent of separations from state enterprises in Russia were associated with individual or collective layoffs.

Information from the registers of jobseekers pointed to monthly inflow rates into unemployment (unemployment inflows as a proportion of the working-age population) of half a percentage point in most transitional countries (OECD, 1994b), compared with more than 1 per cent in Western Europe and 2–3 per cent in North America. Thus, unemployment was rising not because of the predicted large cohorts of workers being laid off from state enterprises, but as a result of remarkably low outflow rates. Outflows from unemployment to jobs, in particular, were marginal. With the notable exception of the Czech Republic, only up to 5 out of every 100 jobseekers were leaving unemployment every month because they had found a job.

When using administrative records (data from the unemployment register), outflows to jobs generally offer a better measure of actual exits from unemployment than total outflows. This is because exits from the unemployment registers not associated with the take-up of a job are often merely a by-product of the exhaustion of the maximum duration of benefits.[21] Thus, outflow to job rates of the order of 5 per cent implied that, had unemployment stabilized at these levels, the average duration of unemployment would have been of the order of 20 months!

Hence, while *stocks* seem to have behaved as anticipated, for labour market *flows* it was a different story—and quite a different one. The differences between actual labour-market flows and their characterization under the OST literature can be highlighted by matched records across household surveys. By tracking the same individual over different LFS waves, it is possible to map transitions from one state in the labour market to another.[22] LFS data are based on a similar methodology and on harmonized questionnaires across Europe, hence offering a better basis than data from the unemployment registers for cross-country comparisons. Unfortunately, transitional countries started carrying out such surveys only three to six years down the road of transition,[23] which means that available data does not reflect the early stages of transition.

With the above caveats in mind, Fig. 1.4 characterizes yearly transition probabilities (gross flows over the base-year stock of origin) estimated on the basis of the LFS carried out in Poland, the first country in the region to have introduced such a survey, in 1992–3. Similar patterns emerge by matching records across LFS waves in other Central European

[21] This comes out very clearly when inspecting data from the Hungarian labour offices. There is almost a one-to-one correspondence between unemployment benefit receipt and registration at a labour office for those who cannot claim social assistance—i.e. for those who do not pass a means test (Boeri and Pulay, 1998).

[22] A statistical problem involved by using matched records across different LFS waves is that sample attrition, non-response and errors in the classification of the labour-market states of individuals at different points in time tend to bias results in a direction that is not predictable *a priori*.

[23] See OECD (1993a) and Chernyshev (1997) for a discussion of the reform of labour-market statistics in formerly planned economies.

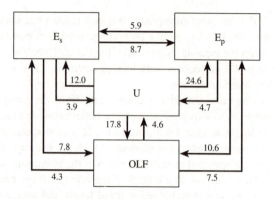

Figure 1.4. Yearly labour market flows in Poland 1992–1993 (LFS)

Notes: Numbers in the chart denote estimated flows as a percentage of the population of origin.

Source: Matched records across quarterly LFS waves.

countries, such as the Czech and Slovak republics and Hungary (Boeri and Bruno, 1997).

Three facts are striking. First, outflows from employment to inactivity are twice as large as flows from employment to unemployment. Second, large direct (and genuine [24]) shifts from state-sector employment to private-sector employment occur that are not mediated by intervening unemployment spells: in Poland such job-to-job shifts were in 1992–3 more than twice as large as flows from public-sector employment to unemployment (almost 9 per cent of state-sector employment moved directly to the private sector compared with a modest 4 per cent becoming unemployed). Third, a very significant component of outflows from unemployment (about 35 per cent!) involved withdrawals from labour-force participation rather than flows to private-sector employment.

Thus matched LFS records suggest that the stagnancy of unemployment pools in these countries was a by-product both of the fact that (1) employment reductions were accommodated mainly via flows into inactivity, and (2) significant direct shifts of workers from the state to

---

[24] Workers in privatized enterprises by definition shift from the public to the private sector without experiencing unemployment spells. We removed these spurious flows by combining matched records with the retrospective information contained in the survey. In particular, we counted as yearly flows from public to private employment only workers who had tenures in the private sector shorter than 12 months.

the private sector were occurring.[25] Needless to say, both channels of labour-market adjustment are banned under the OST literature, which assumes a constant labour force and focuses solely on flows between public and private employment mediated by intervening unemployment spells. Indeed, Fig. 1.4 looks quite different from the standard flowchart of the OST literature (see Fig. 1.1). The OST models can account for slightly more than 10 per cent of the actual gross flows summarized in Fig. 1.4.

1.3.3 Major Structural Change with Low Worker Flows

Labour markets where shifts of workers from declining (e.g. state-owned) enterprises to expanding (private) units occur without intervening unemployment spells typically generate relatively small worker flows. This is because there is just one shift rather than two. Workers go directly to the new sector, rather than moving from employment to unemployment and vice versa. Moreover, mobility is low when the two non-employment states (not only inactivity, but also unemployment) tend to become 'absorbing states' of the sort where, once in, it is very difficult to get out. In spite of the radical and historically unprecedented transformation occurring in these economies, transition countries have indeed displayed remarkably low mobility of workers across labour-market states, occupations and sectors.

Table 1.2 reports worker mobility indexes and measures of structural change for all transitional economies for which LFS data were available, for the remaining OECD countries, and for Italy, the Western European country typically indicated as being endowed with the most sclerotic labour market, and traditionally very low mobility of its workforce. In particular, the first four columns display summary measures of structural change, namely the standard deviation of employment growth across nine sectors (STD), two summary measures of job reallocation, respectively across sectors (SR) and firms of different ownership (PR),[26] as well as the average yearly change in the share of private employment in total employment (ΔPS). The next two columns display scalar mobil-

---

[25] The relevance of direct job-to-job shifts from public to private firms at early stages of transition is confirmed by evidence from the Hungarian Household Panel (Köllö, 1993), Czech and Slovak household surveys (Vecernik, 1993), and data on Bulgaria (Beleva *et al.*, 1995).

[26] The two indexes SR and PR are increasing in the pace of job reallocation across sectors and between the public and private sectors respectively. In particular, the two

ity measures for yearly transition matrices:[27] where such measures are bounded between 1 (maximum mobility) and zero (no mobility, i.e. each individual is in the same state as one year before).

Quite strikingly, all transitional economies display lower worker mobility than a sclerotic country like Italy during a cyclical downturn (when, typically, worker' flows are lower). Moreover, such a low mobility stands in sharp contrast to the pace of structural change in these countries: indicators of structural change across sectors and occupations are indeed consistently larger than those computed for the whole group of OECD countries. Taken together, the evidence presented in Table 1.2 suggests that dramatic changes in the distribution of employment across sectors and by ownership type of firms have occurred in these countries with relatively low worker flows.

The presence of large job-to-job shifts and, more broadly, relatively low churning rates (namely the rates of hirings and separations simultaneously occurring within the same firm) provide a statistical explanation for the coexistence of fast structural change and low workers' mobility in transitional economies.[28] However, the economics behind these sizeable shifts without intervening non-employment spells is somewhat puzzling.

indexes are given by:

$$SR = 1 - \frac{|\Delta E|}{\Delta E^+ + |\Delta E^-|} \quad \text{and} \quad PR = 1 - \frac{|\Delta E|}{|\Delta E^{\text{PUB}}| + |\Delta E^{\text{PRIV}}|},$$

where ΔE^+ denotes the sum of sectoral employment variations over expanding sectors and ΔE^- is the sum of employment variations across declining industries, while the superscripts PUB and PRIV stand, respectively, for public sector and private sector employment. Both indexes are bounded between 0 and 1, and increasing in the extent of job reallocation from declining to expanding industries and from public to private jobs. Unlike the standard deviation measure, which can take high values even when all sectors and firms of different ownership are experiencing employment declines, these two indexes isolate the extent of the job reallocation *from declining to expanding units* involved in the transition process.

[27] In particular, the scalar measure is given by the index: $\frac{(n-tr(M))}{(n-1)}$ where n denotes the number of states (the number of rows of the transition matrix, M). As shown by Shorrock (1978), when matrices have a maximal diagonal—that is, when stayer coefficients are larger than any mover coefficient—this index is bounded between 0 and 1, is monotonically increasing in mobility, and attaches value zero only to identity matrices and value unity to matrices with identical rows (hence probabilities of moving independently of the state originally occupied). All the computed matrices had a maximum diagonal; hence in our case the index satisfies the four properties just listed.

[28] These are significantly larger than those that can be estimated for a country such as Italy. Using retrospective information and matched records across LFS waves in Italy, Boeri (1999) estimates that job-to-job shifts in this country involved in 1992 about 6.5 per cent of employees. This compares with about 15 per cent in Poland.

Table 1.2. Structural change and labour mobility

Country	Year	Measures of structural change				Workers' mobility	
		STD[a]	SR[b]	PR[c]	ΔPS[d]	Across sectors[e]	Across states[f]
Bulgaria[g]	1991-7	5.5	0.43	0.56	0.52	—	—
Czech Rep.	1991–7	11.0	0.72	0.78	0.74	0.08	—
Hungary	1991–7	9.1	0.50	0.66	0.68	0.04	0.08
Poland	1990–7	11.5	0.64	0.66	0.46	0.15	0.16
Romania	1991–7	10.3	0.45	0.85	0.49	0.16	—
Slovak Rep.	1991-7	13.5	0.66	0.67	0.74	—	0.08
Slovenia	1993–7	13.1	0.73	—	0.65	—	—
Other OECD[h]	1990-6	1.7	0.33	0.09	0.02	0.16	0.17

[a] Standard deviation of employment growth rates across nine sectors (average of yearly standard deviations).
[b] Sectoral Reallocation index, calculated over gross employment variations in nine sectors; see the text for details. OECD data 1990–3.
[c] Privatization Reallocation index, calculated over gross employment variations in the public and private sectors; see the text for details. Czech Republic, Hungary and Romania 1991–3.
[d] Average yearly change in the share of private employment in total employment, 1988–97. Bulgaria 1990–7; Romania 1989–98; Slovenia 1994–7, share of firms privatized used instead. OECD displays data for the United States.
[e] Mobility measure for transition matrix across nine sectors (plus unemployment and inactivity); see the text for details. Romania data based on six-status matrix (five main sectors plus non-employment): the one-year index is computed on the basis of the 1993–5 transition matrix, assuming a Markovian process.
[f] Mobility measure for transition matrix between the public and the private sectors (plus unemployment and inactivity); see the text for details.
[g] STD calculated for six sectors only, 1990–6. SR calculated for 1991–3.
[h] Workers' Mobility indexes display data computed for Italy only, April 1995 to April 1996.
Notes: — = not available.
Source: Individual data from National Labour Force Surveys for Central and Eastern Europe; OECD, Labour Force Surveys, for the OECD countries. Boeri and Flinn (1999).

Employers 'poaching' workers from other firms typically have to pay a premium over the wage that they could offer to persons hired from the unemployment ranks. Moreover, individuals without a job can devote more time to searching for one and hence be faster in taking up employment opportunities in the private sector as soon as they arise. Why, then, did all these job-to-job shifts occur?

1.3.4 Overshooting the Target: the Drop in Employment Rates

As a result of the large flows occurring from employment and unemployment to total inactivity, only partly matched by flows occurring in the opposite direction, labour supply has been significantly declining in all the countries of the region. As the former planned economies entered the 1990s with high labour-force participation by Western standards (notably high female participation rates), a decline in labour supply was commonly predicted at the outset of transition and even advocated as a way of preventing employment reductions in state enterprises from translating into large increases of unemployment. However, the decline in employment was much stronger than anticipated.

As is vividly documented by Fig. 1.5, these countries initially had employment rates well above those of countries at comparable GDP per capita levels (at purchasing power parity). The ratio of employment to the working-age population (individuals aged 15 to 64 for the purpose of international comparisons) was indeed well above the regression line (estimated over the panel of middle-income countries, excluding the CEECs, and the OECD countries) that is displayed in Fig. 1.5a, describing the long-run relation between degree of economic development and employment-to-population ratios. Seven years later, most of the former planned economies and all employment-to-population ratios for males had moved below the regression line (Fig. 1.5).

Significantly, the largest drops in employment rates were associated with the strongest declines in labour-force participation (Fig. 1.6a).[29] This suggests that the main vehicle of employment reductions were flows to inactivity, for instance those associated with the forced retirement of working pensioners, early-retirement schemes, undeclared employment, or household production related to survival-oriented activities. Moreover, it was not mainly the participation of women that was seen to fall: in most countries the deepest declines in participation occurred among men (Fig. 1.6b). The *a priori* expectation was that participation of women should have been declining the most because labour supply of women is more elastic and hence could have been more affected by real wage declines—nurseries and childcare facilities previously attached to enterprises were being dismantled, thereby increasing the opportunity

---

[29] See also Boeri, Burda and Köllö (1997), who decompose the decline in employment rates in the shares associated with (1) the growth of unemployment, (2) the increase of inactivity, and (3) the decline in demographic pressures. They find that the strongest employment declines occurred in the countries with the largest falls in inactivity.

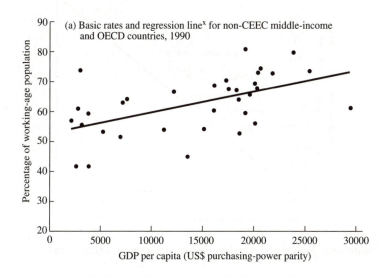

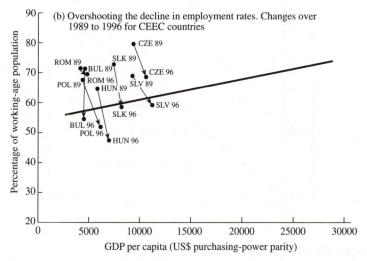

Figure 1.5. Economic growth and employment rates

[x]Estimated equation: ER = 52.59 + 0.006* GDP per capita; $R^2 = 0.25$.

Source: ODCE Labour Market Database, World Development Tables from The OECD National Accounts Report.

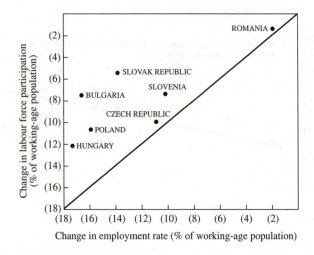

Figure 1.6a. Disemployment and the decline in participation (1989–1996)

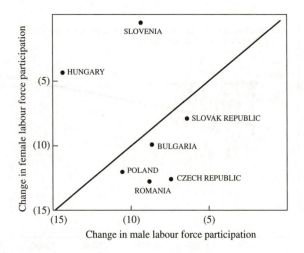

Figure 1.6b. Not only females out of the labour market

Note: The values in parenthesis denote negative numbers.
Source: OECD–CCET Labour Market Database.

cost of employment, and the presumption was that many women had been 'obliged' to work under the previous regime.

1.4 Identifying the Actual Policy Instruments

The OST literature reviewed in this chapter highlights non-trivial inter-actions between the rise of unemployment and the growth of the private sector. It also shows that, if not accompanied by appropriate policies, transition may well go off course. Although providing a useful frame-work to assess some relevant policy trade-offs (e.g., those related to the setting of unemployment benefits), this large and still developing body of literature still leaves many open questions concerning the actual transition dynamics.

The OST models do not yield the U-shaped dynamics of output expe-rienced by some of the countries that were undergoing the most radical transformations. Some additional, and rather ad hoc, assumptions are required to allow these models to replicate the transitional recession. The public–private divide does not often seem to discriminate between output expansion and contraction, or between gross job creation and destruction, as in the OST models.

The adjustment of labour markets during transition has also been quite different from that anticipated by the literature. In particular, it has involved stagnant unemployment pools, large flows to inactivity, and strikingly low workers' mobility, especially when account is taken of the changes occurring in the structure of employment by sector, occupation and ownership of firms.

There are a number of puzzles of transition that are not solved in the literature to date. Among the issues still looking for explanations are the following:

- Why did all countries experience steep declines in output at the start of their transition?
- Why did such a radical structural change occur with such low worker flows?
- Why were there so many job *leavers* as opposed to job *losers* in the years of the steepest employment and output declines?
- Why did private employers recruit their workers mainly from the state enterprises rather than from the large unemployment pools of these countries, which should offer the cheapest labour?
- Why did so many workers, notably among the male population, leave the labour force altogether after the start of transition?

These puzzles are relevant from both a heuristic and a normative stand-point. Understanding why all this occurred can improve our knowledge of economies undergoing major structural change. It may reveal the sources of the limited scope of transition, where the significant drop in employment rates that occurred throughout the region has raised the social security burden on the active population and increased the frictions associated with labour reallocation. Moreover, coping with such puzzles can help us in identifying the relevant policy trade-offs and the actual degrees of freedom of policy makers in economies in transition.

The policy trade-offs embedded in the OST literature relate mainly to the alternative between a big-bang strategy and a process of gradual transition. This amounts to assuming that governments can control the pace of closure of state enterprises. However, the facts discussed in the last section of this chapter suggest that separations from state sector employment were, ultimately, an endogenous variable rather than a policy instrument, because they were to a large extent the by-product of voluntary choices of workers.

It could also be argued that the key (and unconstrained) control variable posited by the OST literature—namely subsidies to state enterprises—did not look at all like a control variable. As discussed further in Chapter 2, subsidies to enterprises in these countries took mainly the form of tax arrears allowed by weak tax collection administrations or by governments fearing domino effects originated by the interlocking of banks and firms.

Thus, it is still necessary to ascertain which policy instruments, if any, can be activated by policy makers in countries shifting from one economic system to another. We argue in this book that the generosity of non-employment benefits is a key variable that governments can rather freely adjust, particularly at early stages of the transformation process, because there are no longstanding entitlements to benefits, and no long transitions involving the grandfathering in of existing claims. This same key variable has the potential significantly to affect the pace and characteristics of labour-market adjustment.

In Chapter 2 we discuss how the initial setting of non-employment benefits and the timing of reforms of unemployment insurance systems has deeply affected the dynamics of unemployment in each country and locked in many non-employed people into inactivity. In Chapter 3 we assess the role played by non-employment benefits in the dispersion of earnings prevailing in the various countries and hence in the skill profile of non-employment and its distribution between unemployment and inactivity. Put another way, Chapter 2 deals mainly with the time-series dimension of labour-market adjustment, whilst Chapter 3 copes with the significant cross-country variation in unemployment and non-employment rates. In passing it should also be noted that such a large variation for countries undergoing quite similar transformations and experiencing the same kind of shocks is another puzzle of transition—and one that we hope to solve, or at least to make a bit less puzzling than it currently is.

Annex 1

A1.1 Building Blocks of the OST Models

A1.1.1 The Scale Effects

A key assumption of the OST literature is that the labour force is fixed to some constant value $\bar{L}$. Thus, the sum of employment in the public sector (E_s), employment in the private sector (E_p) and unemployment (U) can be conveniently normalized to one unit:

$$E_s(t) + E_p(t) + U(t) = \bar{L} = 1 \tag{A1.1}$$

A mechanical model like that outlined in Chapter 1 is a useful starting point in that it highlights the role played by scale effects in the rise of unemployment. In continuous time, this mechanical model of transition can be rewritten as

$$E_s(t) = E_s(0)e^{-st}, \tag{A1.2}$$

where s denotes, as usual, the pace of closure of state sector jobs, and

$$E_p(t) = E_p(0)e^{gt} \tag{A1.3}$$

where g is the (instantaneous) rate at which new jobs are created in the private sector.

It follows that unemployment evolves according to:

$$U(t) = 1 - E_s(0)e^{-st} - E_p(0)e^{gt} \tag{A1.4}$$

The scale effects generate a bell-shaped curve for unemployment. In particular, where $g = s$:

$$\frac{dU}{dt} = s[E_s(t) - E_p(t)]; \tag{A1.5}$$

that is, unemployment grows until employment in the private sector is as large as employment in the state enterprises. After the point where $E_s = E_p$, unemployment starts declining.

A1.1.2 Endogenous Job Creation

There is no economics in the model sketched above because the dynamics of unemployment is entirely driven by mechanical factors, meaning, pure scale effects. In order to assume away scale effects and focus only on the economics, let us define gross job creation and destruction in terms of flows only, i.e.

$$\frac{dE_s(t)}{dt} = -s(t)$$

and

$$\frac{dE_p(t)}{dt} = g(t),$$

from which it follows that

$$\frac{dU(t)}{dt} = s(t) - g(t).$$

Next we endogenize job creation. Along with Aghion and Blanchard (1994) (AB herein for short), we will assume that (private) job creation[30] is governed by

$$g(t) = (1 - e)(1 + \vartheta - w(t) - \tau(t)), \tag{A1.6}$$

where $0 < e < 1$ are entry barriers, ϑ is the productivity differential between the public and the private sectors, whilst w is the (efficiency) wage in the private sector and τ is a (flat) tax *per worker in both public and private enterprises* that is earmarked for the financing of unemployment benefits.[31] In the AB model, private employers recruit only from the unemployment ranks and pay a premium over the reservation wage of the unemployed, which denotes, the unemployment benefit b. Such a premium can be rationalized either as an incentive to prevent shirking—in the style of Shapiro and Stiglitz (1984)—or, alternatively, as a way to increase the workers' loyalty to the firm, as per the 'gift-exchange' in Akerlof (1982). Whatever the interpretation for this premium, private

---

[30] The microeconomic-foundations of the job-creation equation (A1.6) are not spelled out by AB.

[31] Chadha and Coricelli (1994) more realistically assume differential taxation between the state and private sectors, but still maintain the assumption (contrary to experience) that taxation is not proportional to the ongoing wage rate.

wages should be high enough to ensure that the value of being employed in the private sector (V_p) exceeds the value of being unemployed, V_u, by some (exogenous) amount c:

$$V_p(t) - V_u(t) = c. \tag{A1.7}$$

Using then the two asset-value conditions for employment in the private sector and for unemployment,[32] respectively, one obtains that

$$w(t) = b + c\left(r + \frac{g(t)}{U(t)}\right), \tag{A1.8}$$

where r is the discount rate and the last term within brackets denotes hirings over the unemployment stock, that is the job-finding probabilities of the unemployed in this model. Thus, the premium over unemployment benefits should be larger the higher the wedge between the value of being employed in the private sector and the value of unemployment, as measured by the rate at which workers discount future earnings by the probability of being hired once a job is lost. Equation (A1.8) also shows that unemployment exerts moderating effects on wage setting, which in turn, by (A1.6), implies that unemployment boosts job creation in the private sector.

However, there is also a feedback mechanism operating from the fiscal side in the AB model that counteracts the effects of unemployment on job creation via wages, namely the financing of unemployment benefits and associated pressures on unit labour costs. Unemployment benefits are indeed entirely funded out of labour taxation. The budget constraint is therefore given by

$$\tau(t)(1 - U(t)) = bU(t) \tag{A1.9}$$

and hence the tax rate clearing the government budget is given by

$$\tau(t) = \frac{bU(t)}{(E_s(t) + E_p(t))}. \tag{A1.10}$$

---

[32] The asset-value conditions read, respectively,

$$rV_p = w + \frac{dV_p}{dt}$$

and

$$rV_u = b + \frac{g}{U}(V_p - V_u) + \frac{dV_p}{dt}.$$

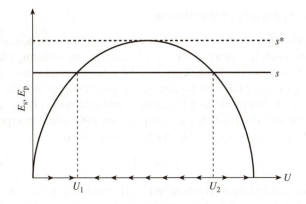

Figure A1.1. Multiple equilibria

This expression together with (A1.6), implies that too high unemployment may also negatively affect private job creation because of the burden on enterprises associated to paying unemployment benefits. This *fiscal externality* clearly becomes less stringent if deficit financing is allowed for, for example by simply adding a new term (d) on the right-hand side of (A1.9), as in Coricelli (1996).

Due to the presence of the fiscal externality, there is a maximum speed at which public-sector jobs can be destroyed. Above this critical level of s, say s^*, transition does not take off because private employers are burdened by too heavy labour taxation. Moreover, for values of s lower than s^*, there can be two equilibria: a low-unemployment equilibrium, like (U_1 in Fig. A1.1) and a high-unemployment equilibrium (U_2), When private employers have static expectations, from any point to the left of U_2 only U_1 can be attained, while if unemployment exceeds U_2, social security contributions are so high that the private sector grows too slowly to prevent a rise of unemployment or it does not take off at all. Thus, the bad equilibrium, U_2, is unstable. When private employers are forward-looking (which amounts to adding expected changes in the value of private-sector jobs on the right-hand side of (A1.6), the economy may settle down at both equilibria. The optimism or pessimism of employers becomes a self-fulfilling prophecy as high job creation reduces labour taxation, and vice versa. This holds even when deficit financing is allowed for.

A1.1.3 Endogenous Job Destruction

The next step is to endogenize job destruction. In these models, separations are entirely demand-driven and dictated by restructuring plans of state enterprises. The latter depend on the extent of employment reductions required to bridge the productivity gap with the private sector. Let $f(E_s)$ denote the production function of state enterprises. It is assumed that at the start of transition everybody is employed in state enterprises[33] and labour productivity therein equals one unit, that is:

$$f(1) = 1. \tag{A1.11}$$

State enterprises are overmanned.[34] The restructuring of state enterprises therefore requires that a proportion $(1 - \lambda)$ of the workforce to be fired, where λ solves

$$\frac{f(\lambda)}{\lambda} = 1 + \vartheta; \tag{A1.12}$$

that is, restructuring makes state firms as productive as private firms. State enterprises are assumed to be controlled by insiders who can block privatization-cum-restructuring plans (Frydman and Rapaczynski, 1994). The part of workers in state enterprises can be considered to be homogeneous and hence, in the case of restructuring, face the same probability of dismissal, $1 - \lambda$. It follows that restructuring can start only if

$$V_s \leq \lambda V_p + (1 - \lambda)V_u, \tag{A1.13}$$

where V_s is the value of being employed in the state sector, V_p the value of being in the private sector and V_u the value of being unemployed. In other words, the expected value of the status quo should be lower than the expected value of restructuring.

As the value of non-employment is always lower than the value of employment (either public or private) in these models, when (A1.13) is not satisfied, managers should be selective in their dismissal policies and exert a 'divide-and-rule' strategy (Dewatripont and Roland, 1992) in order to convince their workforce to accept the restructuring.

---

[33] Actually, employment in the private sector is marginally above zero (and hence E_s only approaches one unit) in order to avoid initial condition problems.

[34] For instance, there can be Leontief-type technologies, and the enterprise may be using more labour than at the corner of the isoquant associated with a given amount of output.

As both V_p and V_u decrease with the size of the unemployment pool (the former because of the fiscal externality and the latter because job-finding probabilities of the unemployed decline), it follows that there is a critical value of U (say U^*) above which restructuring (transition) does not take-off or is blocked by insiders. Below U^*, transition starts and involves increasing unemployment until U^* is reached. If the initial shock to state-sector employment is too large, however, reductions in unemployment are required to set in motion the restructuring process. This is, in essence, the additional feedback mechanism introduced in to the model, coming from the opposition of state sector workers to restructuring.

A1.1.4 The Balanced Path[35]

Normalizing rV_s to equal one unit, and taking into account (A1.7) and the definitions for the value of being employed in the private sector and unemployed, we can rewrite (A1.13) as follows:

$$1 \leq \lambda w + (1 - \lambda)(w - cr). \qquad \text{(A1.14)}$$

When the above condition holds, we have an equality (when we are along the balanced path) that

$$w = 1 + (1 - \lambda)cr, \qquad \text{(A1.15)}$$

which states that there should be a wedge (increasing in the probability of dismissal) between the wage paid in the private and in the state sector in order to induce workers to accept restructuring.[36]

---

[35] This part draws extensively on Blanchard (1997).

[36] Equation (A1.14) may appear in striking contrast to the standard result of the efficiency wage literature (more precisely with the no-shirking condition of the models with imperfect monitoring of workers' effort). The wage premium paid in the primary sector (private firms) over underemployment (employment in the secondary sector) is indeed *decreasing* rather than increasing, in the exogenous probability of dismissal. In the efficiency wage models, a higher probability of layoff forces employers to raise wages in order to increase the punishment (the layoff for disciplinary reasons) of a worker caught while shirking (Saint-Paul, 1996). The fact that here the probability of dismissal decreases the wage premium stems from the fact that OST models deal with 'secondary' workers (public-sector employees) who, by accepting job cuts, may enter the primary sector. In other words, the no-shirking condition here implies accepting having to face a higher (rather than a lower, as in the standard efficiency wage models) probability of being laid off.

We can finally solve for the equilibrium level of unemployment satisfying (A1.14). First, we equate (A1.14) to the wage-setting equation (A1.8). Next, we substitute in this expression the job-creation equation (A1.6) (leaving aside, for simplicity, the fiscal externality effect) and solve for U, obtaining

$$U^* = c(1 - e)\frac{(\theta - (1 - \lambda)cr)}{(1 - b - \lambda cr)}. \qquad (A1.16)$$

The equilibrium speed of transition, s^*, will be such as to maintain unemployment at U^*. In other words, s should be large enough to equate unemployment inflows (s multiplied by the proportion of workers to be laid off) with outflows, when $U = U^*$. Equating then private job creation in (A1.6) to $s(1 - \lambda)$, when (A1.14) is satisfied one obtains

$$s^*\lambda = (1 - e)(\vartheta - (1 - \lambda)cr), \qquad (A1.17)$$

which shows that the equilibrium speed is increasing in the productivity gap and decreasing in entry barriers (exogenous obstacles to gross job creation) and the efficiency wage premium.

Notice that, by (A1.15), equilibrium unemployment is increasing in unemployment benefits. However, too low benefits may prevent the start of transition, especially when the costs of unemployment benefits are only partly internalized by firms (so that, for instance, benefits are paid out of general fiscal revenues,[37] private firms are *de facto* exempted from social security contributions due to weak tax enforcement, or governments receive a gift such as a foreign loan at concessional terms to pay benefits). When a government's budget constraint (A1.9) is not binding, higher benefits increase the asset value of unemployment and hence reduce the opposition of insiders to restructuring. Indeed, we have that

$$\frac{\partial V_{\mathrm{u}}}{\partial b} = \frac{1}{1 + r}\left[1 - \frac{cr(1 - e)}{U + c}\right], \qquad (A1.18)$$

which shows that, on the one hand, higher benefits increase the instantaneous value of unemployment but, on the other hand, reduce the job-finding probability of those without a job. This second effect tends to

---

[37] This interpretation holds if we consider these models as partial equilibrium frameworks.   Under general equilibrium, the way in which unemployment benefits are financed—via payroll taxes or indirect taxation—is ultimately immaterial.

dominate the effect of benefits on the instantaneous utility when benefits are entirely funded via payroll taxation. In the latter case, we find that

$$\frac{\partial V_{\mathrm{u}}}{\partial b} = \frac{1}{(1+r)(U+c)(1-U)} \left[(U+c)(1-U) - cr(1-e) \right],$$

(A1.19)

which becomes negative for large U.

Overall, in so far as benefits can be financed without increasing payroll taxes, high unemployment benefits reduce the resistance of insiders to restructuring and permit the take-off of transition. This is the standard result of the OST literature. However, when higher benefits imply heavier taxation of labour in the private sector, the negative effects of benefits on job generation in the private sector tend to dominate, as the transition proceeds, over those on the (instantaneous) welfare of the unemployed. From this point onward, it is better to reduce unemployment benefits to ease restructuring. In order words, the optimal sequence is (in relative terms) high benefits followed by low benefits.

2
The Timing of Reforms

2.1 Introduction

There are a few myths about the legacy of the Communist regime. Among these is the belief that the old system had developed a highly qualified labour force. Contrary to such belief, the Communists were everything except good 'human capitalists'. They overinvested in narrowly based vocational training, forcing most of those entering secondary education to invest in skills that were not 'fungible', i.e. not transferable across different jobs. Thus, rather than having jobs attributed according to talent—as implied by the Marxist paradigm—there were a lot of bad matches around. Moreover, workers were stuck in these bad matches, not necessarily by coercive power—workers had much more freedom under Communism to change jobs than is usually thought—but because their skills were non-transferable across jobs. Under the radical transformations that occurred in the Eastern European nations at the beginning of the 1990s, it was very difficult for workers, especially those with long tenures in socialist enterprises, to adjust to new production methods and to shift across occupations or even whole industries.

There are also some features of the old system that have been rather neglected by the literature on the economics of transition. Among these, is the formidable lack of product variety characterizing the pre-transition era. Consumers had, *de facto*, no consumption choice under the old system. They could only decide whether or not to buy, not *what* to purchase. Consumption decisions were binary: there was, at best, just one product specification available, one type of bread, one standard shirt. And one of the most visible signs of transition was the appearance on the previously empty shelves of shops of many different types of the same product. This 'shelf-shock' has not been framed in the theoretical models developed in the literature on transitional economies.

Properly identifying the legacies of the old system is important in order to understand the puzzles of transition discussed at the end of Chapter 1, namely the output fall, low worker mobility in spite of the radical transformation occurring in these countries, the presence of many job *leavers* as opposed to job *losers*, the frequency of direct shifts of workers from one job to another without intervening unemployment spells, and the role played by flows to inactivity in the disemployment process. The lack of variety suggests that at the outset of transition there was a large potential for the development of many small-scale activities filling gaps in the provision of varieties to consumers. The overspecialization of the workforce indicates that these shifts towards new gap-filling activities were likely to involve relatively large failure rates because, contrary to Communist propaganda, the workforce could not easily move across occupations and industries. Put another way, the specificity of skills inherited from the previous regime was—and still is, at the dawn of the twenty-first century—a major obstacle to job creation in the new sector in that it makes the matching of workers and jobs more time-consuming and costly for employers.

In order to cope with the puzzles of transition, one has to amend the OST models reviewed in the previous chapter. First, it is essential to allow for frictions in the shift of workers from the old to the new (small business) sector. Second, job-to-job shifts should not be ruled out: employers should be free to choose their recruitment pool, and so be able to hire from the unemployment ranks or among the employees of the old sector. Third, labour supply should play some role in labour-market adjustment. This means abandoning the standard OST assumption of a fixed labour supply and modelling non-trivial participation decisions for those not having a job.

The model used as a background in this chapter and formally developed in Annex 2 extends the OST literature along these lines. Unlike the latter, it shows that transitional unemployment has a high degree of persistence because the unemployed are crowded out by the employed jobseekers. The initial steps of transition are crucial in determining the degree of persistence of transitional unemployment. When the initial market-oriented reforms promote large flows from the old sector to inactivity, it is very likely that employers in the new sector will be reluctant to hire from the ranks of the unemployed, as many of those without a job are not actually seeking. Low job-finding probabilities in turn induce 'discouraged worker' effects, whereby those without a job do not actively seek a job because their outside opportunity looks more appealing than spending a long time in job-search efforts, which have a very low chance of success.

The revised model suggests that the emphasis placed by the OST literature on measures winning the resistance of insiders to restructuring, by buying off workers in the old sector from causing problems, is ill-placed and possibly conducive to wrong policy prescriptions. By putting in place at the outset overgenerous non-employment benefit schemes, conditions are created for having stagnant unemployment pools throughout a transition. Long-duration unemployment made the promises of high non-employment benefits unsustainable because such benefits had been conceived for unemployment of a shorter duration. Moreover, this tightening has not been found to reduce significantly the duration of unemployment. Rather than starting with generous non-employment benefits and then subsequently cutting them down, our framework suggests that the right sequence should have been the other way round.

This chapter will first highlight, in section 2.2, some common misconceptions of the legacies of central planning. Then section 2.3 will put these features into a framework and show that they can help in coping with the puzzles of transition pointed out in Chapter 1. Finally, section 2.4 will present some numerical simulations out of the theoretical model developed along these lines and empirically assess their implications as to the relation between the timing of reforms of non-employment benefits and unemployment dynamics. Details as to the model used in these simulations are provided in Annex 2 to this chapter.

2.2 The True and False Legacies of Central Planning

Perhaps a better title for this section would have been 'Old myths and false initial worries', because common misconceptions about the legacies of the previous regime are a mixture of overoptimistic assessments of some endowments of these countries (for instance their stock of human capital) and of excessive worries (for example the opposition of workers to employment cuts, or their role in the management of firms). We will start by discussing the educational profile of the workforce and end with employment adjustment in state enterprises.

2.2.1 The Specificity of Human Capital

It was widely believed at the outset of transition that former centrally planned economies had a highly qualified labour force compared not only with countries at similar stages of development but also with OECD countries. A main strength of the centrally planned economies was indeed identified in their human capital, which would attract foreign investors and facilitate inter-industry and inter-occupational shifts of workers affected by economic restructuring.

This view was based on aggregate data on the educational attainments of the workforce. The latter pointed to employment shares of workers with only primary or lower educational attainments generally of the order of 25–35 per cent, compared with well over 45 per cent in countries such as Greece and Spain and with an average of 37 per cent in the European Union.

However, a closer look at schooling systems and educational attainments of the workforce in Soviet bloc countries would suggest a less optimistic assessment of the legacies of the previous regime (Boeri and Keese, 1992). The fact of having a relatively high number of workers with educational attainments above elementary schooling was mainly a by-product of the presence in these countries of 'lower vocational' schools offering generally one or two years of training in narrowly defined occupations up to the completion of compulsory schooling. These lower vocational schools were actually part of the basic schools and were indeed not formally considered as a part of the secondary system.[1] Much of this training was also done within the enterprises that the training centres were attached to, and this further strengthened the specificity of the skills being provided.

Moreover, 'upper vocational' schooling, although offering courses up to five years in duration and then the possibility to have access to tertiary schooling, was also *de facto* a dead end. Only a minor fraction of the pupils (generally less than 5 per cent) in upper vocational schools were enrolled in courses offering a school-leaving certificate, while vocational education fields were not covering a broad enough range of new occupations and those contemplated were to a large extent outdated. Finally, secondary education was heavily undersized by OECD standards:

[1] For instance, in the Czech Republic even in the pre-transition phase the *uciliste* (vocational) schools were not formally considered as a part of the secondary-school system.

enrolment to general secondary schools was of the order of 20–30 per cent (of the population of the relevant age group) compared with 60–90 per cent in Western Europe.

Thus, at the outset of transition a far smaller proportion of workers in Central and Eastern Europe than in the West had completed secondary education, and even less had tertiary-level educational attainments. If the quantity of education was far less satisfactory than thought at the outset, the quality of education was even worse. Adult literacy surveys attribute rather low scores to CEECs (generally around 70 per cent of those obtained in Germany) in terms of linguistic, literary, documentary and numerical literacy and an ability to communicate in foreign languages at all levels of the educational ladder.[2]

Those who had gone through vocational training had developed very specific skills,[3] which were not adequate for market conditions and, on top of that, which made workers less transferable across different occupations. This was consistent with the philosophy of central planning, which rewarded physical work in the production sector highly, attaching a very low value to 'mental' work in non-directly productive activities and, consequently, overinvested in vocational training (Flanagan, 1993).[4] The approach was also useful for managers of state enterprises, where they wished to maintain employment levels (in order to be in a stronger bargaining position in the planning process) and reduce the turnover of workers. But it was a recipe for trouble, given the radical structural changes in the composition of employment by sector and occupation that were to follow.

A confirmation of the inadequacy of the education system inherited from the previous regime comes from data on labour-market outcomes of workers with vocational school attainments after the liberalization of markets, and on enrolments in institutes of secondary education since 1989. This data is contained in Table 2.1. The first column provides a

---

[2] Reference can be made to the Second International Adult Literacy Survey (SIALS) run by ETS Princeton and Statistics Canada and to the Third International Math and Science Survey (TIMSS). The two sources are complementary inasmuch as the former covers mainly linguistic, literary and documentary literacy at low educational grades, while the latter targets students in the final year of secondary schools.

[3] An indication of this specificity is provided by the very large number of VOTEC fields existing under the old system. To give an example, in Poland there were more than 700 of such fields, compared with less than one hundred in the German vocational education system.

[4] Significantly, the reformers in the former Soviet Union fiercely opposed this emphasis on vocational education (Fitzpatrick, 1979)

Table 2.1. The over-specialization of the workforce

Country	The fate of workers with vocational education 1994–1997				% Enrolment rates[e] 1989–1996	
	Share in total unemployment[a]	Differential probability of job loss[b]	Differential job-finding probability[c]	Wage premia wrt general secondary[d]	Vocational education	General secondary education
Bulgaria	11.1	9.3%	−6.4%	—	−10.2	5.0
Czech Republic	42.5	10.5%	−2.9%	−21.4	−24.1	23.9
Hungary	36.4	2.7%	−6.6%	−21.7	−5.7	13.2
Poland	43.6	0.7%	−13.5%	—	−6.5	45.2
Romania	32.1	3.2%	−4.8%	—	−35.2	75.9
Russia	28.6	3.1%	−8.1%	−25.2	−22.9	3.8
Slovak Republic	63.3	0.6%	−5.6%	−19.9	−5.5	34.0
Slovenia	36.2	1.0%	−4.4%	−24.4	—	—

[a] Share in unemployment of workers with vocational education, average data for 1994–7.   [b] Difference between the probability to be laid-off for a worker with vocational education and for a worker with general secondary education.   [c] Difference between the probability to find a job for an unemployed with primary vocational education and for an unemployed with general secondary education.   [d] Percentage difference of wages for workers with secondary vocational education relative to workers with general secondary education (from estimates of Mincer-type wage equations).   [e] Enrolment as a percentage of the 15–18 population age group. Vocational education includes here technical secondary and vocational secondary.

'—' = not available.

Notes: See Table 3.3, Chapter 3, for details on estimates of Mincer-type earnings functions.

Source: OECD/CEET Labour Market Database for data on unemployment by educational attainments. UNICEF (1998) for data on enrolment rates. Probability of job loss and job finding calculated on the basis of individual data. For Bulgaria data are drawn from Kotzeva-Worgotter in OECD (1997), for Romania from J. S. Earle (1997), for Russia from the Russian Longitudinal Monitoring System, for Slovenia from Abraham and Vodopivec (1993). Nestorova and Sabirianova (1999), for estimates on transition probabilities and earnings functions. For the other countries are our own calculations: Bulgaria data from LFS (March 1996) for vocational compared with secondary; Czech Republic data from LFS (2Q-3Q 1996) for primary vocational compared to secondary general; Hungary data from LFS (3Q-4Q 1996) 'certificate of vocational school' compared with 'other secondary school'; Poland data from LFS (3Q-4Q 1995) for technical training compared with general secondary; Slovak Republic data from LFS (4Q95-1Q96) for skilled compared to secondary with leaving examination.

measure of unemployment incidence for this group, that is, the share in unemployment of workers with (primary and secondary) vocational education. The next two columns tabulate the probabilities of job loss and of finding a job as a deviation from the same rates for individuals with general secondary education, in order to better appreciate differences in labour-market outcomes of VOTEC workers *vis-à-vis* individuals with broadly the same years of schooling but a less specialized education. Such flow data are estimated on the basis of retrospective information from Labour Force Surveys. In particular, the probabilities of job loss are obtained by taking the number of persons declaring to be non-employed because of a layoff as a percentage of the employees with the same educational attainment; the job finding probability is obtained by taking as numerator the number of hirings from non-employment of individuals with vocational education and as denominator the population of origin. The fourth column in Table 2.1 provides information on wage reductions associated with having, other things being equal, vocational education rather than general secondary education. These negative 'wage premiums' are obtained on the basis of estimates of Mincer-type earning functions, such as those presented in Chapter 3.

Four facts are striking. First, workers with vocational training account in countries such as the Slovak Republic for more than 60 per cent of the unemployed and elsewhere for no less than one-third of total unemployment. Second, the probability of job loss is up to 10 per cent (e.g. Czech Republic) higher for workers with vocational education than for those with general secondary attainments. Third, job-finding rates for unemployed individuals who underwent vocational training can be (e.g. Poland) even 15 per cent lower than for jobless people with general secondary education. Fourth, wage premiums of workers with general secondary education compared with workers with vocational schooling (fourth column of Table 2.1) range between 20 and 25 per cent—that is to say, other things being equal, that a worker with a general secondary education earns about one-quarter more than a worker with vocational (secondary) education. It should be stressed that before the transition these wage premiums were of the order of 8–10 per cent only[5] and that,

[5] See Sakova (1996) for estimates of pre-transition earnings functions in the Czech Republic, Rutkowski (1996) for Poland, and Kertesi and Köllö (1997) for Hungary. Based on household income data, Vecernik (1996) shows that income inequality across households having as head individuals with different educational attainments have significantly increased in CEECs since the start of transition. Significantly, there is a large income inequality (at least judging from decompositions of Theil indexes of disposable

according to trade theory, integration in the Western markets should have led to a relative (if not absolute) increase in the price of the abundant factor, so that relative wages of people with vocational education should have gone up.[6]

The best indication of the fact that the previous system had overinvested in educational training comes, however, from the changes which occurred in enrolment rates at secondary education institutes (fourth and fifth columns of Table 2.1). Just as human capital theory would have predicted, there has been a veritable boom of enrolments for general secondary and a strong decline of inflows into vocational education. This happened even in a country like the Czech Republic, which had in place at the outset the best apprenticeship system in Central and Eastern Europe (heavily influenced by the German *Lehrausbildungs* system) and where since 1990 significant effort had been put into the modernization of vocational schooling.[7]

2.2.2 The Shelf-Shock

Surprisingly enough, the literature on transitional economies has overlooked a crucial dimension of structural change, namely the appearance of product variety.[8] Under the previous system consumers had no choice in the same class of goods; there was just one type of goods, a single 'homogenized' (and often low-quality) article. (I distinctly remember spending almost half a day in Warsaw in 1986 desperately trying to find something to buy with my remaining zlotys, which I was forced to use up before leaving the country. Coming back in 1990 I was struck to observe that shops have started to fill up their previously empty shelves with items varying only by brand name, design and 'look', rather than by their intended use).

incomes) also *within* the group of families headed by individuals with vocational education attainments. Flanagan (1993) comparing earnings structures in the Czech Republic before and after the 'Velvet Revolution' of 1989 finds a decrease of the returns to vocational education and an increase of the returns to university education.

[6] This effect may be partly offset by capital and labour mobility but, as discussed in Chapter 4, both foreign direct investment and East–West migration have so far been fairly small.

[7] In the Czech Republic at the outset of transition it was necessary to reform about 70 VOTEC fields per year in order to make curricula better related to the targeted professions.

[8] To be fair, Jeffrey Sachs (1993) made reference to increasing product diversification in Eastern Europe, but only as a way to underplay the consequences on social welfare of the severe (but measured) output losses experienced by Poland under the shock therapy.

Why was variety lacking before the start of transition? Under central planning, resources were systematically diverted away from goods for final consumption, and countries maintained very limited trade relations with Western countries, which were confined to exports of raw materials or intermediate goods. Moreover, the increase in the amount of variety available to consumers requires two things that were very much lacking in these countries. First, it requires a multiplication in the number of firms, and there were practically insurmountable entry barriers to enterprise creation in these countries.[9] And, second, it required a diversification of production in the existing state firms, while the absence of consumer sovereignty and an administered price regime did not create any incentive for firms to do this. The most efficient managers were primarily interested in attaining economies of scale;[10] the average number of employees per manufacturing firm was about 1,000 compared with 20–30 in the United States and Japan. A futher characteristic of the socialist firms was a high degree of vertical integration, which naturally (even under market conditions) does not favour the development of product variety.[11] In summary, we have that the absence of consumer sovereignty meant a lack of varieties, rationing not only the quantity available to consumers of the same item but also the range of choices available.

One of the first steps of the transition towards a market economy was the opening up to trade, and hence the lifting of restrictions on the purchase of differentiated goods by domestic consumers. Accordingly, a large number of varieties were imported. Domestic production of more varieties also began, but only gradually. The increasing diversification of domestic production is reflected in a gradual, but steady, increase in intra-industry trade. Although still of the vertical type (that is to say, the

---

[9] Hungary is a partial exception in this context. Entry was allowed, but only for relatively large firms.

[10] The absence of varieties under the old system can be rationalized by the presence of a (malevolent) social planner minimizing costs in an increasing returns-to-scale industry. Let n define the number of varieties of product x and L_x be the amount of the primary input (for example energy or raw materials) allocated to the sector. Further let a and a_l denote, respectively, overhead and unit input requirements in the production of varieties. The choice of n will solve:

$$\max_{n} nx \text{ subject to i } n \geq 1, \text{ and (ii) } n(a + a_l x) \leq L_x$$

This is a simple linear programming problem with a corner solution at $n = 1$

[11] See Feenstra *et al.* (1997) for evidence on the effect of vertical integration on product differentiation in the case of Korean and Taiwanese exports.

trade of low-quality varieties for high-quality ones, rather than the trade of goods at comparable quality standards), intra-industry trade by CEEC countries significantly picked up over time, notably with countries in the European Union.[12] Moreover, the strongest increases in intra-industry trade were recorded in the early starters, such as Poland or Hungary (Brenton and Gros, 1997), which may suggest that a crucial dimension of restructuring is the development of new varieties.

In so far as new products are produced by new firms (and available evidence suggests that this is indeed the case),[13] the large increase in enterprise density (number of enterprises per inhabitant) observed in these countries and the strong employment performance of new firms compared with continuing units are further indications of the importance of this variety effect.

The increase in enterprise density throughout the region has been documented by Eurostat (1996). From having between 15 and 30 firms per one thousand members of the non-farming population at the beginning of the 1990s, by 1996 these countries had reached an average enterprise density of 83 firms compared with 113 in the European Union.

Table 2.2 groups figures on gross job flows in different kind of firms gathered from surveys of enterprises carried out in several countries of Central and Eastern Europe and Russia. As usual in the literature on job turnover, POS stands for gross job *creation* (the sum of net employment variations in expanding units), NEG stands for gross job *destruction* (the sum of net employment variations in declining units), NET stands for net employment growth (the difference between POS and NEG) and all magnitudes are normalized by employment in each class in the base year.

A striking fact highlighted by Table 2.2 is the remarkably better employment performance of new firms (units started after 1989) in comparison with continuing units. In all countries, only new firms are contributing to net job creation (third column of table). This is due not only to larger gross job creation among new firms (something that is

[12] Aturupane, Djankov and Hoeckman (1997) calculated adjusted Grubel and Lloyd indexes (in order to disentangle horizontal from vertical intra-industry trade) on three-digit level data on trade between the Central and Eastern European countries and the European Union. They found that intra-industry trade was significantly picking up over time, but it was mainly of the vertical type.

[13] In the context of enterprise surveys carried out in several countries of Central and Eastern Europe by the Leuven Institute for Central and East European Studies (LICOS), managers of firms were asked about changes recently introduced in their product lines. The results suggest that changes in product lines are concentrated in new firms, meaning units started after the beginning of transition.

Table 2.2. New firms starting after 1989 outperforming state-owned and privatized units

Country	Year (%)	POS[a] (%)	NEG[b] (%)	NET[c]	Increasing productivity[d]
Bulgaria	1997				
State		1.0	7.0	−6.0	29
Privatized		1.8	9.9	−8.1	29
New		13.0	4.7	8.3	32
Hungary	1994				
State		0.1	5.0	−4.9	—
Privatized		1.0	7.0	−6.0	—
New		6.0	5.0	1.0	—
Poland	1991				
State		1.0	18.0	−17.0	—
Privatized		10.0	22.0	−12.0	—
New		17.0	1.0	16.0	—
Romania	1997				
State		0.2	8.0	−7.8	46
Privatized		2.0	3.0	−1.0	68
New		22.0	4.8	17.2	60
Russia	1996				
State		1.0	6.3	−5.3	—
Privatized		2.0	9.0	−7.0	—
New		25.0	6.0	19.0	—
Ukraine	1996				
State and Privatized		2.0	16.0	−14.0	23
New		22.0	7.0	15.0	43

[a]POS = gross job creation (sum of net employment changes in units increasing their workforce).

[b]NEG = gross job destruction (sum of net employment changes in units decreasing their workforce).

[c]NET = POS − NEG.

[d]Percentage of firms in the sample and category of the ownership type reporting increases in productivity.

Notes: '—' = not available.

Source: Bilsen and Konings (1997) for data on Bulgaria, Hungary and Romania. Konings, Lehmann and Schaffer (1996) for data on Poland. Richter and Schaffer (1996) for data on Russia. Konings and Walsh (1998) for data on Ukraine.

generally observed also in OECD countries), but also to lower job destruction rates for new firms relative to the other types of firms. In
OECD countries young firms have the highest probability to fail. Even
though no information is available on the output of firms, managers were
in some countries asked qualitative information about the productivity
performance of their firms. Significantly in all countries for which this
information is available (Bulgaria, Romania and the Ukraine), gains in
productivity were generally reported in the new firms.[14] Put another
way, new firms perform better than other units in terms not only of
employment (which may be partly explained by the effects of regression
to the mean, as new firms tend to be smaller than other units)[15], but also
of output. As stressed above, the introduction of new products tends to
be concentrated in new firms. Thus, the contribution of (genuinely) new
firms to net job creation *and* productivity growth would seem to be the
by-product of the filling of market niches and investment opportunities
opened by the transition to a market system.

Table 2.2 also indicates that, contrary to popular wisdom and the
transition mechanics embedded in the OST models, the ownership of
enterprises, by itself, does not discriminate between job creation and
job destruction. While the bulk of job creation is concentrated in the
new small-business sector, enterprises being privatized do not seem to
behave very differently from enterprises still in state hands, in terms of
both employment and output performance. Estimates of employment
equations on the basis of large enterprise panels in several countries
confirm this finding in that they do not point to significant differences
in employment-to-output elasticities between state firms and privatized
units (Basu *et al.*, 1997; Estrin and Svejnar, 1998) and point to a superior
investment and productivity performance of new versus existing units,
even in private hands, inherited from the previous system (Estrin, 1998).

Overall, various pieces of evidence, including those of the anecdotal
type, suggest that improvements in firms' performance are mainly associated with the development of new goods, rather than with the downsizing of overmanned state enterprises and their privatization. This leads

---

[14] Data on Bulgaria and Romania—the only two countries where such an information
is available—suggest that new firms are not more likely to experience financial difficulties
than state and privatized units. In Western Europe, new (and small) units are, by and large,
those most likely to fail.

[15] There is ample evidence of a negative relation between, on the one hand, plant size
and, on the other, net employment growth and job turnover (the sum of POS and NEG) in
OECD countries (OECD, 1987 and 1996b).

us to the third misconception, namely the constraints facing employment reductions in state enterprises.

2.2.3 'Soft' Constraints to Downsizing

A dominant concern of policy makers, advisors and academicians at the outset of transition was how to win the resistance of workers to staff reductions.[16] The prevailing view was one where workers maintained substantial veto power over managerial decisions in state enterprises and were strongly opposed to staff reductions. In order to overcome resistance to restructuring, it was therefore necessary to 'buy them out', that is, to grant rather generous transfers to the workers involved in layoffs. A major rationale for the introduction from scratch of unemployment benefits systems, the wide-scale use of early retirement, and the granting of a rather liberal access to invalidity pensions at the outset of transition was indeed the need to reduce opposition to the downsizing of state enterprises and relieve the managers of these firms from their social responsibilities.

In retrospect, it is possible to argue that these concerns were somewhat overstated. Too much emphasis was put on the demand side, as if workers were desperately attached to the enterprise without having any outside opportunity. A closer inspection of employment dynamics in the years immediately preceding the transition would have revealed that there was a significant portion of the state enterprise workforce that had one foot outside the firm. Already, before 1989, Hungary and Poland in particular had experienced significant employment reductions associated with *voluntary* decisions of workers—dismissals were, after all, still legally forbidden at that stage. The supply-side determinants of these pre-transition staff reductions are also highlighted by the fact that they were unrelated to the dynamics of sales at the firm level (Köllö, 1997). But why were workers so prone to leave the firm they were attached to?

First, there was a significant shadow economy in existence in these countries, deemed to have a high potential to develop further in the

---

[16] This concern is heavily reflected in the papers presented at the OECD–World Bank 1990 Paris Conference on 'The Transition to a Market Economy in Central and Eastern Europe' (OECD, 1991). The models reviewed in the previous chapter are also largely inspired by this view, taking account as they do of workers' opposition to the restructuring of the firms they are attached to. For instance Dewatripont and Roland (1992) extensively discuss strategies to buy out workers in state enterprises.

disorganization following the systemic transformation.[17] Recent studies aimed at measuring the size of the hidden economy in CEECs, based on patterns of electricity consumption, point to about 30 per cent of GDP being produced in the informal sector even at the outset of transition (Lacko, 1999). Before the systemic transformation, activities in the informal sector were combined with formal-sector job attachments, but since the beginning of the 1990s it was no longer necessary (because work was no longer considered as a duty to the state) nor possible (because, for instance, the tightening of budget constraints induced a stronger monitoring of workers' productivity) to combine formal with informal job attachments. All the measures of the informal-sector activity that could possibly be devised as a result show that the informal sector has grown during the 1990s.

Second, as argued above, there was a formidable lack of small entrepreneurship, notably a gap of basic activities to be filled, especially in the retail sector, which required in many cases rather low initial investment. In other words, it was tempting for many to leave the state firm and start up their own business.[18] By walking round the centre of Budapest in the early 1990s it was easy to see several plates announcing the presence in the building of some sort of consulting firm. Strangely enough, the denomination of these new activities always contained the word 'market'.

Third, the climate of uncertainty surrounding the initial steps of transition and the unpredictability of future events were inducing workers heavily to discount the future and make decisions on a day-by-day basis.[19] The short time-horizon of workers in post-Communist transition is revealed by the failure of many programmes providing one-off lump-sum payments to workers made redundant. One of such examples (discussed further in Chapter 4) is that of the miners in Romania. Generally, workers in CEECs would seem to have rapidly eaten up, these sums rather

---

[17] Disorganization in the network of firms' providers arising in the aftermath of economic transformation is, according to the model by Blanchard and Kremer (1997) reviewed in Chapter 1, a main explanation for the transitional output fall. Disorganization is, perhaps, a more convincing explanation for the flourishing of many informal-sector activities at the margins of state enterprises rather than for the transitional recession.

[18] Based on evidence from the records of jobseekers, Socha and Sztanderska (1993) report that a significant share of Polish unemployment was voluntary.

[19] In some respects the situation in these economies at the beginning of the 1990s resembled one of Knightian uncertainty, where individuals do not have prior knowledge as to the (probabilistic) distribution of future events. Under these conditions, it is optimal to adopt static decision rules.

than using them to invest in new activities or to pay the costs of migration to areas offering better employment opportunities. Public-opinion polls carried out at the outset of transition also show that there was much optimism as to the implications of moving to market conditions.[20] This faith in the market created a window of opportunity not only to governments, but also to managers wishing to reduce their workforce.

Finally, as work was no longer considered a duty and social assets such as kindergartens and nurseries were being detached from enterprises, the value of time allocated to household work was getting increasingly important. Activities such as child-rearing and, more broadly, responsibilities within the family and family networks became a powerful factor stimulating non-participation decisions.

In addition to being easier to achieve than anticipated at the outset, employment reductions were neither always necessary nor sufficient for restructuring.

They were not necessary because overmanning was somewhat overstated. It is true that aggregate estimates of 'labour hoarding' were pointing to large shares of employment in excess of that needed to achieve any given output level (OECD, 1993a). However, these estimates were largely affected by the presence in state enterprises of a large number of supporting activities (related to their social functions, for example). As these activities were not directly productive, they were, by definition, independent of output in the short run if not negatively associated to it (because firms typically divert labour from productive to non-productive activities during downswings).[21] Moreover, common measures of labour hoarding were not taking into account that significant real wage losses were being experienced in state firms, making it more profitable to keep low-productivity labour in the firm. Put another way, labour hoarding was overemphasized and could have been significantly reduced by simply unbundling state enterprises—separating supporting activities from the core business—without necessarily entailing outright employment losses.[22]

---

[20] Typical is the case of a poll carried out in Bulgaria at the beginning of 1990. A large majority of individuals stated that they would be prepared to sacrifice something in the transition to a market economy. The same poll was carried out two years later, and the consensus around a policy of trading short-run costs for long-term benefits—the window of opportunity offered to by reformers at the outset of transition—had been eroded away.

[21] This point is made by Fay and Medoff (1985) with reference to the United States.

[22] See Lizal *et al.* (1997) for evidence on the Czech Republic that enterprise breakups were mutually profitable for both the spinoff subsidiaries and the mother company.

Employment reductions were also not sufficient for restructuring. Staff cuts in the core business were by themselves unlikely to improve the viability of firms, and could even cause it to deteriorate. There was evidence that under socialism enterprise efficiency and size were closely related as if existing technologies were of the increasing-returns type (Ickes and Ryterman, 1993). Moreover, the presence of 'ratchet effects' under central planning has been documented, whereby the most efficient firms were not producing at their full capacity because managers feared that their output targets would be revised upwards by central planners (Milgrom and Roberts, 1990).

Factors other than employees' resistance to staff cuts were seriously obstructing the restructuring of state enterprises. More than a problem of unused capacity, managers were facing an *unusable* capacity issue. State enterprises needed desperately to renew their machinery, without necessarily shedding labour. Empirical evidence suggests that new capital equipment, whenever available, was a complement to labour, rather than a substitute for it.[23] Fresh capital was hardly reaching worthwhile projects because there were marked informational asymmetries. In addition to managers of state enterprises, only state bureaucrats knew the quality of the firms. Private investors could not rely on capital markets conveying information on the quality of projects. Under such conditions, private productive investment was lacking and support from the state was hardly selective.[24] Actually, as state subsidies were mainly taking the form of tax (and social security) arrears (Schaffer, 1998), they were often benefiting mainly the enterprises that had not yet started restructuring.

Summarizing, we should note that three legacies of central planning should be taken into account when assessing developments since 1990. The first is the presence of a highly specific human capital. The

---

[23] Boeri, Burda and Köllő (1997) document the coexistence of employment growth and gross capital formation over a large sample of Hungarian firms. Labour demand equations estimated on the basis of employers' surveys (e.g. Konings and Walsh, 1998) also point to a positive and statistically significant coefficient of new capital on employment.

[24] See Maskin and Xu (1999) for a survey of models explaining the persistence of a 'soft budget constraint' (Kornai, 1979, 1980 and 1988), whereby the state bails out loss-making state firms even in reforming economies. In one of such models—the work of Bai and Wang (1998)—the principals of state enterprises (or state agencies) are supposed mainly to pursue efficiency goals. In Bai's and Wang's model, the thinness of capital markets does not allow the state to acquire information on the quality of projects, which is private information for the bureaucrats. In order to induce the bureaucrats to put more effort into the screening (beforehand) of projects, it is optimal for the state to penalize bureaucrats who terminate (after the event) all the projects that turn out not to be viable.

second is the presence of many market niches and an overall lack of variety, waiting to be filled. The third is the existence of repressed 'non-participation', whereby many workers have been prone to leave the formal sector as soon as an opportunity—for example, the provision of open-ended non-employment benefits—arises.

2.3 Putting the Legacies of Central Planning into a Framework

A better perception of these legacies of central planning is essential to understand the mechanics of transition for at least three reasons.

First, because they point to labour-supply determinants of the job-reallocation process and permit a better understanding of the fate of those leaving state enterprises. A focus on labour supply is indispensable in order to interpret the large output losses occurring in these countries at the outset of transition and the strikingly low mobility of workers, in spite of the radical transformations in the structure of employment that took place.

Second, these features are important because they suggest that down-sizing is not a sufficient condition (and, in some cases, not even a necessary one) for restructuring. The lack of product variety, in particular, indicates that there was a lack of enterprises—a gap in enterprise density to be filled—and that successful transition would involve a rapid increase in the number of firms.

Third, these neglected legacies of the past are important because they highlight inertial forces and risks of failure of the transition process. In particular, the drive to non-employment, the associated fiscal burden on the active population, and more recent phenomena such as the failure of reforms of unemployment benefit systems in boosting flows from unemployment to employment—which will be discussed later on in this chapter—can be rationalized when we take into account the quality of education under central planning and the incentives to stay out of the formal sector.

2.3.1 A Simple Model

A simple model is offered in Annex 2 that has been developed out of these ideas. Like all models, it oversimplifies reality, but it is useful for evaluating the interactions between the various factors qualitatively discussed above, as well as their combined effect on the speed and scope of transition (that is, the amount of the workforce succeeding in moving from an old to a new sector). Technically speaking, the model adds to the two-sector, Harris–Todaro type of framework of the OST literature matching frictions, accrued by specific human capital,[25] and non-participation decisions. The model takes into account costs in the reallocation of labour from an old to a new sector, and it captures sources of unemployment persistence at the micro-economic level. The details of the model and its algebra are presented in Annex 2. Here, I shall confine myself to discussing its building blocks and presenting some numerical simulations of the model, which draws on three basic assumptions that have been taken from the above discussion of the legacy of central planning.

The first assumption is that restructuring means not only downsizing but also changing the product specialization of firms. Jobs in the production of the homogenized goods of the previous regime are bound to become obsolete and hence be destroyed. New jobs are created which more closely correspond to the diversified preferences of consumers. This also means that privatization is not, in itself, conducive to improved economic performance in this model, which is as much as to say that the public sector/private sector divide does not discriminate between job destruction and job creation. Indeed, there is an 'old sector' and a 'new sector' in the model, rather than the 'state sector' and 'private sector' of the OST models reviewed in Chapter 1. The distinction is not semantic: the old sector is bound, sooner or later, to disappear, while the state sector remains an employer (and not a minor one!) in market economies.

The second assumption is that separations from the old sector can be either to private (formal) employment or to non-employment, rather than only to unemployment (as in the OST models). Non-employment encompasses unemployment (that is, the state of being without work, actively searching for a job and available to take up job offers) and inactivity (or informal-sector attachment in survival-oriented, home production and consumption activities). This means that there is a non-trivial participation decision involved in economic transition. Persons decide to be 'in' or 'out' and, although individuals can change their mind in the process, the non-participation decision is practically irreversible

---

[25] See Caballero and Hammour (1995) for another model where specific investment leads to a sluggish emergence of a new sector.

because, once out of formal employment, it is very difficult to regain access to it.

The third assumption is that employers offering jobs in the new sector can recruit either from the non-employment ranks or from the pool of workers in an old sector. This decision is made *before* notifying vacancies and starting to interview applicants. This is consistent with the presence of significantly different wage-offer distributions for state sector workers and the unemployed, as well as a high degree of segmentation in the allocation of job offers across different pools of jobseekers (Boeri and Flinn, 1999). Although employers in most CEECs were at the outset of the transition compelled to report all vacancies to labour offices, only a fraction of job openings were, and still are, notified to public placement agencies. After all, even in OECD countries compulsory notification of vacancies was (when legally binding) not enforced and vacancy coverage rates have rarely exceeded 30 per cent.[26] Furthermore, in the CEECs and in many OECD countries, vacancy registers of the labour offices are not used by on-the-job searchers; labour offices concentrate their activities on the population of unemployed jobseekers. Thus, reporting vacancies to labour offices and screening the records and the candidates sent by public placement agencies is a different, and often alternative, strategy to recruiting among the ranks of state firms.[27]

Productivity in the new jobs of workers coming from either one or the other pool is equal. However, employers are not indifferent in their choice between the two pools because non-employment contains a larger proportion of individuals with a relatively high reservation utility, who are thus unlikely to be engaged in active job searches. This means that, even when non-employment is large enough to provide a wide pool of applicants to be screened by employers, it may be more difficult to fill vacancies with unemployed jobseekers rather than with workers 'poached' from the public sector, because some of the non-employed applicants (referred by labour offices as a requirement to receive unemployment benefits) may turn out not to be available. This is consistent with remarks frequently made by private employers in CEECs, that many

[26] Unfortunately, there are no such figures for the CEECs. It is possible, however, to derive the share of placements by the labour offices in total hirings. This ranges between a low 8 per cent in Slovenia to a high 37 per cent in Slovakia (Boeri, 1997a).

[27] See Pissarides (1979) for a model where firms can either advertise vacancies privately and screen applicants calling at their gates or, alternatively, find potential workers via the network of labour offices. Search equilibrium is characterized as a matching function defined over one or the other stock of vacancies and jobseekers.

of the persons referred to them by the public employment service were not actually attending for interview or were not motivated; they were just trying not to lose their rights to unemployment benefits.[28]

Why does a non-marginal component of the non-employed population decide to leave the labour force altogether rather than seek a job, or at least a job in the formal sector? Unemployment benefits or, more precisely, the whole battery of non-employment benefits (encompassing early retirements, disability pensions loosely granted also to able-bodied individuals, sickness benefits, and social assistance) need not be particularly generous to induce people to stay out of the (formal) job market. Actually, the replacement of previous earnings offered by non-employment benefits may even fall significantly below OECD levels without inducing people to search for jobs.

This phenomenon is because of a combination of three factors. First, the excessive specialization of the workforce inherited from central planning makes the matching of jobs and workers more difficult.[29] As job search has a cost in terms of foregone reservation utility, low matching probabilities discourage a segment of the population from actively searching for jobs. Second, uncertainty as to the outcomes of transition induces decisions based on short time horizons. Workers heavily discount the future, preferring to receive a guaranteed, albeit low, non-employment benefit (plus enjoying their reservation utility or productivity in home production) to a time-consuming and highly uncertain job search. Third, recruitment takes place in a non-sequential fashion, which means that employers have to first choose the recruitment pool (the range of likely applicants) and then (and only then) the workers to be hired. This magnifies compositional asymmetries between the two pools.

2.3.2 Calibrating the Model

The way in which the various factors mentioned above interact in the midst of transition can be better grasped by calibrating the model against real data and then producing some numerical simulations (and like most

[28] Most countries make the provision of unemployment benefits dependent on the acceptance of 'suitable' job offers. The notion of 'suitability' is, however, arbitrary and this requirement is rarely enforced in practice.

[29] Business surveys carried out in most countries of Central and Eastern Europe suggest that even at times when transitional unemployment was at its peak, a significant proportion of employers (e.g. more than 20 per cent in high-unemployment Poland) were reporting shortages of skills and difficulties in recruiting workers with suitable qualifications.

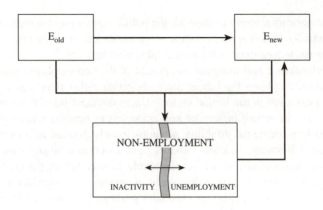

Figure 2.1. Labour market flows in the model developed in Annex 2.

dynamic optimization models, ours does not have an analytic solution) under different assumptions concerning the level of exogenous parameters such as non-employment benefits.

The model endogenously generates at each point in time the flows described in Fig. 2.1. As can be seen from the diagram, all kinds of flows are admitted except those entering employment in the state sector (if we associate it to the 'old' sector of my model). This means that more than 75 per cent of the flows across the relevant labour market states are framed by this model, compared with slightly more than 10 per cent in the OST literature. In the model there are 'old' and 'new' jobs (rather than 'public' and 'private' jobs), and consequently it is implicit within the nomenclature that the 'old' sector is fading away. No hiring occurs in the 'old' sector as not even the workers who leave these firms voluntarily are replaced.

The direct flows from the old sector to the new sector occurring in our model are entirely the by-product of voluntary decisions of workers to leave the job held under the previous regime in response to offers coming from the new sector. A quit occurs whenever the worker matches a job in the new sector. Hence, the number of quits from the old sector occurring in each period can be predicted by simply simulating a matching process between the vacancies, which are directed to the pool of *employed* jobseekers, and the workers in the old sector. The nature of this matching process will depend on the way in which the labour market operates and the characteristics of labour supply, and it can be summarized by an aggregate matching function (Blanchard and Diamond, 1992; Pissarides, 1990), whose arguments are vacancies and jobseekers. I assume that the technologies for matching are the same for employed and unemployed jobseekers.[30] Thus, the key parameters of the matching process (namely the two elasticities of job finding with respect to vacancies and jobseekers respectively) can be estimated from unemployment outflows via regressions that have been run on monthly, district-level, data for a number of countries in transition (Burda, 1993; Boeri, 1994, 1996; Munich *et al.*, 1999).

The technologies for matching also generate flows from non-employment to employment. The latter depend on the proportion of active jobseekers present in the non-employment pool. Hence, in order to estimate outflows from non-employment to jobs in the new sector, one has to simulate participation decisions by assertaining how many non-employed are genuinely unemployed. The decision to withdraw from the labour force originates from a dynamic optimization problem that yields a critical value of the reservation utility $\tilde{u}$: workers with reservation utility lower than $\tilde{u}$ will search, while those with a higher satisfaction in household-based work will not. Clearly, $\tilde{u}$ will depend on the probability of finding a job in the new sector (hence in the number of vacancies targeting the unemployed) and in the level of non-employment benefits. It is therefore endogenously generated in the model.

The last set of flows in the model are shifts of workers from employment to non-employment. It is proved in Annex 2 that if non-employment benefits are not increased over time, quits from employment in the old sector to non-employment (as opposed to quits from the old sector to employment in the new sector) can only occur at the outset of transition. Intuitively, the fewer the workers in the old sector, and the higher the probability that each of them can find a job in the new sector, the higher the option value of staying in comparison with the value of non-employment. Conversely, the build-up of a large unemployment pool, and one where there are many individuals who are not actually seeking jobs, reduces the value of non-employment. Thus, quits from the old sector to non-employment occur only in the first year of transition and are endogenously given once the level of non-employment benefits

---

[30] I preferred not to assume that matching technologies are different for employed and unemployed jobseekers because I wished to confine all asymmetries between the two pools to the (endogenous) choice of an individual within the non-employed population not to actively seek jobs.

and an initial value for each of the state variables is specified.[31] The other flows from employment to non-employment come from genuine job destruction.

As is customary in the matching literature (Pissarides, 1990), it is assumed in the model that a constant fraction of the jobs in the economy is hit each period by some adverse shock, reducing the value of the match below the outside option. The fraction of jobs destroyed each period in the old and new sectors are two exogenous parameters (job destruction is endogenized in Annex 3, *q.v*) which can be recovered from labour turnover data. The latter series is available in the initial years of transition but is limited to state-sector employment only. The scant evidence on labour turnover in the private sector does not point to significant differences in (total) separation rates, but the composition of separations varies across the two sectors because there is a higher incidence of layoffs in the private sector. This can be partly explained by the lower average size of business units in the private sector, given that job destruction bears a strong and negative relation with plant size (OECD, 1996b).

In the numerical simulations, I assume that 3.5 and 4 per cent of jobs are destroyed each year in the old and new sectors respectively. The first number is obtained by simply averaging out[32] layoff rates data (which mostly cover state sector firms) for the period 1990–3 for all countries for which such data are available. The layoff rate for the new sector is then obtained by multiplying 3.5 by the ratio of private to public layoffs rates in the countries and time periods covered by data.[33] Clearly the fact that layoff rates are lower in the state sector does not mean that overall separation rates are also lower. Quite the opposite: the baseline scenario yields higher separation rates in the old sector in the first period, owing to the effects of the introduction of non-employment benefits, and, later on, a significant number of voluntary separations

---

[31] In the numerical simulations, I always assume that initially 79 per cent of employment is in the old sector, while 1 per cent is in the new sector (a positive value for the latter sector is specified in order to avoid problems with initial conditions). The overall initial employment rate is therefore 80 per cent, which is broadly in line with the conditions prevailing in CEECs in the mid-1980s.

[32] This amounts to assuming that job destruction has a stochastic component that is symmetrical around zero.

[33] I have also produced simulations imposing an identical layoff rate in the two sectors, namely 3.5 per cent. The only significant difference with the baseline scenario is that, clearly, the decline in old-sector employment is slower.

originated by transitions from the old to the new sector.[34]

Wage formation in the new sector is governed by a Nash bargaining rule, splitting the surplus from the match (the total value of the match minus the foregone value of continued job search) in fixed proportions between the worker and the employer. The stronger the bargaining power of workers, the higher the share of the surplus going to them. The parameter assigning a fraction of the quasi-rents to the worker is taken from the labour cost share in total added value, which was roughly of the order of 40 per cent throughout CEECs in the 1990s.

As mentioned above, several estimates have been provided of matching functions against regional data on unemployment, stocks and flows of vacancies at monthly frequencies in CEECs. Results are fragile in so far as they depend on the functional form being used and on the lag structure allowed for in the response of unemployment flows to vacancy formation. However, all estimates point to a rather low elasticity of outflows to jobs with respect to vacancies. In the model, matching technologies are assumed to be the same for the two recruitment pools, and in the numerical simulations I take an average over the vacancy elasticities estimated by the earlier studies, namely 0.3. Given the assumption that matching takes place at constant returns to scale, the elasticity of job finding with respect to the stock of jobseekers is thus 0.7.

There are still three parameters that need to be specified before evaluating the model, and these have to do mainly with vacancy formation. In particular, we have the (fixed) cost of issuing a vacancy for the employer (c), the parameter capturing the degree of fungibility of the workforce (σ),[35] and the discount factor. In the baseline simulation, c equals a yearly wage in the old sector, which is broadly the amount offered as a startup loan within active labour-market policy schemes aimed at supporting self-employment in transitional economies. The degree of fungibility of the workforce is calibrated so as to generate flows from the old sector to the new sector comparable to the shifts from public sector to private sector jobs observed in those countries for which such data are available. In the model, σ equals 0.2, so that, other things

---

[34] The fact that, in our simulations, separation rates are higher in the old sector may seem to be at odds with the evidence discussed here. However, the dividing line between private and public firms does not correspond to the distinction between old and new sectors in our model.

[35] If you assume that the skills required in the new sector are uniformly distributed over a unit circle, then σ can be thought of as the arc distance round the circle given by workers' qualifications. If workers are fully transferable in their skills, σ will be one unit.

being equal, matching probabilities should be reduced by a factor of five. As discussed below, some simulations allow σ to (slowly) increase over time, for instance as a result of improvements in the quality of human capital and/or simply in the information available to employers on the actual skills of the applicants. Finally, the discount factor is taken in the model to be 0.8, allowing for the relatively short-time horizons prevailing especially at early stages of transition. Simulations with higher discount factors yield more or less the same results as those with the fungibility parameter increasing over time: as there are more non-employed individuals actively seeking jobs, more matches, and hence more outflows from non-employment, occur.

2.3.3 Evaluating the Model

Figure 2.2 displays numerical simulations of the model under different values of the non-employment benefits. One period before the start of transition (at time −1), 80 per cent of the working-age population is employed almost entirely in the old sector. At t = 0, the transition starts: a non-employment benefit is introduced and, as a consequence, some workers quit the old sector to draw benefits and gain from their reservation utility (household production). Then workers start moving from the old to the new sector, either directly or indirectly (meaning, via intervening non-employment spells); non-employment and unemployment initially build up and are then partly reabsorbed by the growth of the new sector. The system eventually settles down with positive non-employment and unemployment and with the disappearance of the old sector. The *speed* of transition is, in this context, the number of periods required for the process to converge.[36] The *scope* of transition is the share of employment in the new sector (the complement to non-employment) resulting at the end of the process.

I consider three scenarios. In the low-benefit scenario (continuous thin line), the non-employment benefit (perceived by workers as open-ended[37] in that it encompasses social assistance of the last resort, bridg-

---

[36] The simple convergence criterion being used herein is that all labour-market aggregates should not deviate by more than one percentage point from their steady-state equilibrium.

[37] In most countries, unemployment benefits introduced at the outset of transition involved nominal replacement rates declining over time rather than remaining flat, as is assumed in the numerical simulations. However, under rapid inflation and indexation only

ing schemes to retirement, and various kind of disabilities) is 0.25, so that the benefit replaces one-quarter of the wages earned in the old sector. In the high-benefit scenario (continuous thick line), b is set to 0.35. In the third scenario (dotted lines) benefits are initially high, but one year after the start of transition, as in most CEECs, the replacement rate is reduced by ten percentage points (from 35 down to 25 per cent of the old sector wage).

The general results with the foregoing parameters are given in Fig. 2.2a. Under low benefits, the speed of transition is of the order of eight years (30 quarters), while its scope (the steady-state employment rate) is almost 70 per cent, meaning that seven able-bodied individuals out of ten are employed at the end of the process compared with eight at the outset. The unemployment rate is roughly 6.5 per cent and the economy recovers in about six quarters from the transitional recession,[38] originating from the initial flows to inactivity of workers on low-productivity jobs, not yet offset by flows into more productive posts. Under the high-benefit scenario, non-employment and unemployment continue to grow (albeit at a rather low pace) even ten years down the road of transition (see Fig. 2.2b).

Output falls are in this model induced by the initial large drop in employment in the old sector, which is not matched by the increase in the number of high-productivity jobs because of the significant frictions induced by skill specificity and an increase in non-participation. The latter was repressed under the previous regime, which maximized output in inefficient units.[39] The continuous thick line in Fig. 2.2c shows that in the high-benefit scenario output initially recovers from the 'transitional recession' but later on it starts declining again, as soon as the economy gets onto a low-participation high-labour-taxation path. Such

of the benefit minima, unemployment benefits systems have in practice collapsed to a flat rate in most countries. Moreover, after the exhaustion of the unemployment (insurance) benefits, so-called unemployment assistance benefits (if not general social assistance) are offered in most countries and the amount of transfers in this segment of non-employment benefits is (even in nominal terms) independent of previous earnings. Micklewright and Nagy (1994) neatly document this convergence of the structure of unemployment benefits to the minima in the case of Hungary.

[38] Output is, in this context, simply given by employment in the old sector (labour productivity is therein normalized to equal one unit) plus employment in the new sector times (one plus the positional rent between new and old jobs), which is constant throughout the transition.

[39] This explanation for the output fall has something in common with the 'classical' explanation offered by Bofinger (1994). In his model, a switch of firms from output to profit maximization leads to an immediate reduction of output.

(a) General results

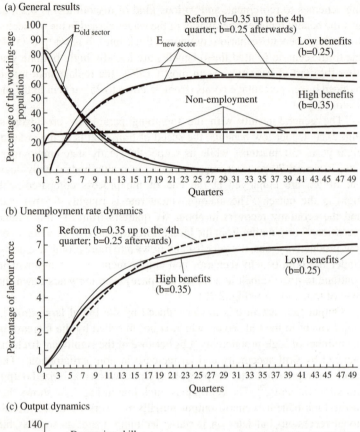

(b) Unemployment rate dynamics

(c) Output dynamics

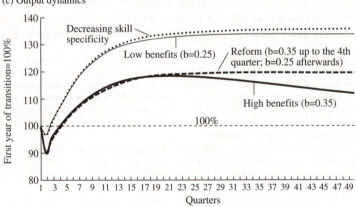

Figure 2.2. Numerical simulations of the model developed in Annex 2

Notes: See Annex 2 for details on the simulated model.

an outcome is avoided when benefits are tightened (thick dotted lines), but the effects of reforms are initially very mild and their impact on unemployment is likewise limited. Actually, in the quarters immediately after the tightening of benefits, unemployment grows faster than in the absence of reforms because a larger number of non-employed people start actively seeking jobs.

Simulations of the model in which the degree of fungibility of workers is allowed gradually to increase over time, where σ converges to unity in about 20 years, yield lower non-employment rates and larger employment in the new sector throughout the transition, while unemployment rates are only mildly affected (because the positive effect of larger σ on outflows from unemployment are partly offset by encouraged participation in the labour force). Clearly, convergence is achieved only after σ stabilizes, and then output continues to grow up to the 80th quarter (dotted thin lines in Fig. 2.2c), unlike the baseline simulations. Simulations with lower values for c (representing lower entry barriers) also yield higher employment rates at the steady state. Significantly in this case, intensive margins play a major role in the reduction of non-employment: almost the entire increase of employment in the new sector is brought about by a decline of the unemployment rate.

The effects of reforms on employment and output are significantly affected by the timing of reforms. If the benefits are low from the start, there is a visible improvement with respect to the high-benefit scenario in terms both of job generation in the new sector and of unemployment. If the reform is implemented at $t = 4$, the change in the time path of non-employment and employment in the new sector is much less marked, especially in the quarters immediately following the policy change. Simulations of reforms intervening at $t = 1$, 2 and 3 produce the same results: the earlier the change in the benefits system, the faster the transition and the lower is non-employment generated throughout the transition and prevailing at the steady state.

These timing effects originate from two factors. The first is that reductions in benefit generosity implemented before quits from the old sector have occurred induce a switch from non-participation to participation for a larger number of individuals when they are introduced later on. This is because the initial distribution of reservation utilities in the old sector is uniform, unlike that prevailing in the non-employment ranks, which is skewed to the right. Only unemployed individuals with a low reservation utility search for jobs and eventually leave the non-employment pool, while for those with the highest reservation utility, non-employment is an absorbing state—they do not search and hence have probability zero of finding a job in the new sector.

The second factor is the social security burden. If cuts to benefits are implemented after a large non-employment pool is in place, the reform cannot generate the same employment rate as if benefits had been low from the start because there is a higher social security bill to be financed via taxes on the payroll throughout the transition. Both effects are neutralized when reforms bring the level of benefits down to zero. At that level everybody seeks jobs, and there is no fiscal externality associated with unemployment. However, a zero-benefit scenario is just not realistic and hence of no interest when interpreting the dynamics of unemployment in real-life CEECs. Moreover, Chapter 3 provides solid grounds for deeming that a no-benefit scenario would be harmful to transition.

The economics behind these timing effects of reforms of non-employment benefits is that when a large pool of non-employed individuals is in place and a significant portion of them is not actively seeking jobs (that is, people are registered at labour offices just to draw some sort of non-employment benefits, such as free medical insurance), it is improbable that reforms can induce employers in the new sector to increase significantly the number of vacancies issued for the non-employed segment of the population. As most applicants are likely not to be motivated in any event, employers may prefer to continue recruiting most of their workers among the ranks of the old sector workers.

At the steady state, the old sector is no longer in place and hence there is no longer substitutability between the two recruitment pools. However, the system settles down at a level where labour taxation is high and outflows from non-employment are too low to induce all the non-employed people to take up job offers, thereby giving up their reservation utility. In other words, labour force participation decisions become more and more important in preventing the absorption of non-employment. Barriers to job creation coming from the demand side, however, are still present because the fiscal burden associated with non-employment benefit payment can no longer be shifted onto the old sector. In the baseline model, the equilibrium statutory contribution rate (the payroll tax that clears the social security budget) is 35 per cent; in the high-benefit scenario, the budget-clearing payroll taxes get as high as 65 per cent, which represents the upper bound of actual statutory contribution rates in transitional economies.

It should be stressed that unemployment persistence is generated in the model even if there is no human capital loss associated to long spells of unemployment and no ranking of workers on the basis of unemployment duration occurs. Were these effects present in the model, its implications as to the importance of a good timing of reforms could only become stronger.

Thus, unlike the OST models, the stylized representation of transition offered in this chapter suggests that *late reforms of the benefit systems are largely ineffective in reducing non-employment*. Although OST models have suggested that it was preferable to have initially relatively high benefits in order to ease restructuring, and then lower them in order to reduce the fiscal burden on the emerging private sector, in this model the optimal sequence goes just the other way round. High non-employment benefits at the outset do not speed up transition but simply induce a large number of quits to inactivity, thereby making the absorption of non-employment more difficult. When non-employment benefits exceed approximately 70 per cent of the old-sector average wage, transition does not even take off. Under these circumstances, transition can start (in the sense that some positive employment is generated in the new sector) only if governments can borrow (or, taking a partial-equilibrium view, non-employment benefits are paid out of general government revenues).

As in the OST literature, borrowing is, however, treated as a gift in the simulations, which consider only a static budget constraint. In the absence of borrowing, non-employment benefits command high social security contributions, especially at the outset; tax rates imposed later on in the process can be lower. This is because the new sector pays higher wages than the old sector, and hence lower tax rates are required to ensure a given amount of revenues from payroll taxation. Hence, governments facing tight borrowing constraints (dealing in practice with a static social security budget) should keep non-employment benefits low at the outset and, if anything, raise them at later stages—rather than doing just the opposite, as actually happened in all CEECs.

2.4 Unemployment Persistence and the Policy Experiments

A key implication of the developed model is that a tightening of non-employment benefits is effective in reducing unemployment only if such a reform is made before a large pool of non-employed, able-bodied, individuals has built up.

Table 2.3. The tightening of unemployment benefits: The design of unemployment insurance

Country	Maximum duration months	Unemployment benefit levels (expressed in % of the minimum wage)		Gross replacement rates[b]			Cove ra
		minima	maxima	First 3 months	First year	Second year	
Bulgaria[f]							
before	12	100[g]	none	93	91	0	5
after	12	90	140	60	60	0	3
Czech Republic							
before	12	none	none	65	58	0	7
after	6	none[h]	150-180%[i]	60	30	0	4
Hungary[j]							
before	24[k]	100	300	75	59	34	8
after	12	70	150	58	51	0	4
Poland							
before	open-ended	100	average wage	70	53	40	7
after	12	none	none	45	45	0	5
Slovak Republic							
before	12	none	none	65	58	0	8
after	6	none[l]	150	60	30	0	2

[a]Data before the reforms refer to the period 1/91 to 12/91. Data after the reforms refer to the 1/92-period unless otherwise specified. Further (marginal) adjustments were made to the UB systems in 19

[b]Gross benefit income in unemployment as a percentage of gross wage in previous employment single worker, aged 40, who has been working continuously since age 18 with no interruptions and was earning the average of replacement rates at two levels (average earnings and two-thirds of av earnings).

[c]Unemployment benefit recipients as a percentage of registered unemployment. Figures befor change refer to December 1991. For figures after the change: Bulgaria, December 1995; Czech Rep December 1996; Hungary, December 1997; Poland, April 1998 and Slovak Republic, December 199(

[d]Average time-dummies in matching functions estimated at monthly frequencies before and afte reforms.

[e]Elasticity of outflows to jobs with respect to unemployment before (U_1) and after (U_2) the break. R standard errors (with respect to heteroskedasticity and serial correlation) of U_1 and (U_1-U_2) in parent One asterisk denotes significance at 5% level, two asterisks at 1% level.

[f]Data on flows refer to the period October to December 1991.

[g]Since October 1990.

[h]70% of the minimum living standard (MLS) if not employed before.

[i]The recipient receives 180% of the minimum wage if enrolled in a training course.

systems before and after the January 1992 reforms[a]

Monthly outflow rates	Monthly outflow to job rates	Outflows to jobs on total outflows	Matching function estimates	
			time-dummies[d]	OJ to U elasticity[e]
6.8	4.5	35.5	–	–
9.5	1.5	15.8	–	–
15.1	10.3	68.1	−0.01	0.40 (0.08)**
21.3	15.4	72.8	−0.56	0.51 (0.04)*
6.2	3.6	55.9	−0.20	0.78 (0.09)**
8.1	2.1	26.4	−0.50	0.78 (0.00)
–	2.5	–	0.05	0.28 (0.16)*
5.8	2.9	51.3	−0.05	0.31 (0.05)
5.4	3.2	52.1	0.09	0.67 (0.13)**
8.7	3.4	38.3	−0.01	0.70 (0.07)

[j]In Hungary benefit maxima and minima are not expressed as a percentage of the minimum wage, but are fixed in levels. The figures reported in the table refer to the relativities between benefit floors and ceilings and the minimum wage in 1995. Unemployed who were previously earning less than the benefit minima are entitled to 100% of the previous earnings. In 1997 the benefit minima and maxima were calculated as a percentage of pension minima (min = 90% & max = 180) and the gross replacement rates were 48, 48, 0 for the durations considered. Data on flows prior to January 1993 refer strictly to unemployment benefit recipients.

[k]One year until January 1990 when it was extended to two years.

[l]Net monthly wage if lower than the minimum pension.

Notes: Further marginal changes were made to the unemployment benefits systems after 1995, which are characterized in Table 3.2 of Chapter 3.

Source: Boeri and Edwards (1996); Employment Observatory no 8, OECD Short-term Economic Indicators. Sources and Definitions, National Labour Ministries; Rutkowski (1996); Micklewright and Nagy (1996); Terrell, Erbenova and Sorm (1996), Vodopivec (1996), Lubyova and van Ours (1996).

2.4.1 The Tightening of Unemployment Benefits

This implication of the model is consistent with the effects of the tightening of unemployment benefits systems and early retirement schemes implemented in most CEECs as a component of broader fiscal consolidation plans. The quite radical changes in the design of unemployment benefits, which occurred in most of the Central and Eastern European countries at the end of 1991, are outlined in Table 2.3. The maximum duration of unemployment benefits was halved in the Czech and Slovak republics and in Hungary, and a maximum duration of one year was set in Poland (which had initially adopted an open-ended system). Gross statutory replacement rates were also decreased in Bulgaria, in the former Czechoslovakia and in Poland, where the earnings-related system was turned into a flat-rate scheme and minimum employment-record conditions were introduced for eligibility to benefits. The lifting of benefit minima or the introduction of benefit ceilings ranging between 140 and 150 per cent of the minimum wage also contributed to reducing benefit levels. In the Czech and Slovak republics, regulatory changes were enforced *retroactively*, while in Bulgaria, Poland and Hungary existing entitlements were grandfathered in. Needless to say, in OECD countries cuts in the generosity of benefits are rarely made and, even when they are, they are much less radical and are diluted over a longer time period.

The impact of the tightening of benefits was made even more dramatic by the spread of long-term unemployment. The combined effect of a rising percentage of unemployed for more than one year and of a decreased duration of benefits was a large decline in the proportion of registered jobseekers receiving unemployment benefits (see the coverage rates reported in the middle of Table 2.3).[40]

Although the reforms in unemployment benefits systems were mainly inspired by budgetary restraint, policy makers expected that the tightening of such systems would boost outflows from unemployment to employment. Economic theory also suggests that reductions in the generosity of a benefits system should induce more matches between employers and jobseekers by reducing the 'reservation wages' of the unemployed. Job creation should also

---

[40] It should be stressed that unemployment benefits for school-leavers were not discontinued, although in some countries benefit levels for this group were reduced. This means that the decrease in coverage rates documented in Table 2.3. cannot be attributed to inflows of large cohorts of jobseekers not eligible for unemployment benefits.

be boosted by benefit cuts because of the stronger competition for jobs—and hence lower wages—between unemployed and employed jobseekers, and because of the reductions in statutory contribution rates on top of the payroll, which could accompany expenditure savings.

However, aggregate data on unemployment outflows and micro-economic evidence on hazards from unemployment do not point to a significant increase in exits from unemployment to employment after the tightening of unemployment insurance systems.[41] In the last five columns of Table 2.3, information on labour-market flows is provided for both the period before the reforms (the year 1991) and the four years after the tightening.[42]

With the important exception of the Czech Republic, unemployment outflows to jobs as a proportion of the population of origin have not significantly reacted to benefit cuts. Total outflows have often increased, but it is outflows to destinations other than employment that have picked up and, indeed, the share of outflows from unemployment to jobs in total unemployment outflows has declined everywhere except in the Czech Republic. The limited effects of policy changes on aggregate outflows to jobs can be econometrically assessed by testing the stability of matching functions, relating outflows to jobs to the stocks of unemployment and vacancies in the various countries. The last two columns on the right-hand side of Table 2.3 report such tests. In particular, the stability of 'time dummies' (reflecting a sort of 'disembodied progress' in matching technologies) and of the elasticity of job finds with respect to the number of jobseekers are assessed, taking as a structural break the 1992

---

[41] This is consistent with micro-economic studies analysing the role played by benefit generosity on individuals' unemployment durations in these countries. Ham, Svejnar and Terrell (1998), on the basis of data from the unemployment register in the former Czechoslovak Federal Republic, found very low elasticities of exits to jobs with respect to unemployment benefit levels and duration. Micklewright and Nagy (1996) compared empirical hazards from unemployment to employment before and after the tightening of benefits in Hungary; they report that the cuts do not seem to have substantially increased re-employment probabilities. Similarly, multinomial logit estimates of transitions from unemployment to employment in Bulgaria (Jones and Kato, 1993; Kotzeva *et al.*, 1996) do not suggest that there was any increase in outflows to jobs after the tightening of benefits has occurred, while they signal a strong increase in flows from unemployment to inactivity. Finally, Lubyova and van Ours (1997) found that the reform had a modest impact on outflows to inactivity and no impact on outflows to jobs.

[42] Later on, further (mostly marginal) changes of the benefit system were made and thus it is safer to confine the impact analysis to the period ending in 1995.

reforms.[43]   These tests seem to confirm that policy changes have not significantly boosted outflows to jobs, except in the case of the Czech Republic.[44]

The asymmetries between the Czech Republic and the other CEECs in the effects of the tightening of benefits on outflows from unemployment to employment can be visually appreciated by looking at the (seasonally adjusted) monthly outflows to job rates displayed in Fig. 2.3. The vertical line marked on all four graphs (Figs 2.3a–d) in this case denotes the time at which the reforms of unemployment benefit systems occurred. While outflows to jobs increased immediately after the reforms in Hungary[45] and Slovakia (see Figs 2.3b and 2.3d respectively), they rapidly returned to their levels before the tightening. The Czech Republic has maintained, since the beginning of 1992, outflows to job rates twice as large as the other countries in the region (see Fig. 2.3a).

2.4.2 Behind the 'Czech Unemployment Miracle'

Why did the Czech Republic experience a larger turnover of its unemployment pool than other countries in the region? The answer is hinted at in Fig. 2.4: unlike the other countries, unemployment benefits were tightened in the Czech nation when unemployment was still rather low (although on a steeply rising trend, as in the other countries). This effect of the timing of reforms on unemployment is in line with the implications of the model laid out in the previous section of this chapter. There are

---

[43] Consistent with a large body of empirical literature, the functional form used in the estimates of the matching function in CEECs is a Cobb-Douglas. In particular, I have estimated against monthly, district-level, data for each country, the following equation:

$$O_{it} = c + T_i + \beta u_{it-1} + \gamma v_{it-1} + \varepsilon_{it},$$

where o, u, and v denote the natural logarithms of outflows from the live register to jobs, stocks of registered unemployment and unfilled vacancies, respectively, while T stands for time dummies and c for regional dummies. Subscripts i and t denote regions and time respectively, ε is the error term, and β and γ are the key parameters (the respective elasticities of job-finding with respect to unemployment and vacancies) that have to be estimated. Tests of the stability of β and the average time dummies before and after the tightening of the benefits regime are reported in Table 2.3.

[44] This is consistent with earlier results obtained by Burda (1993) and Boeri (1994, 1996).

[45] The large spike observable in the case of Hungary can be explained by the fact that unemployment outflows data for Hungary refer only to unemployment benefit recipients (rather than to all those registered as unemployed). Given that the reforms reduced the duration of benefits, they induced a large number of outflows from unemployment compensation rolls. For more details on this, see Boeri and Pulay (1998).

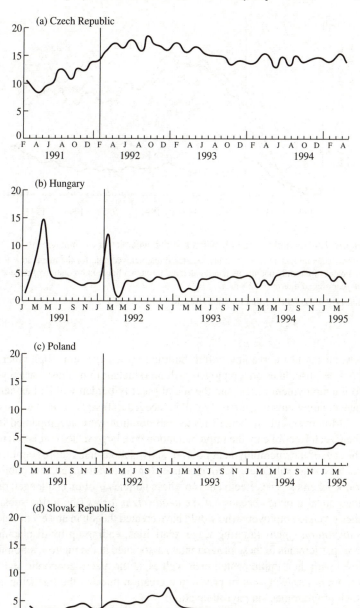

Figure 2.3. Outflows to jobs as a percentage of registered unemployment (seasonally adjusted series January 1991–April 1995)

Notes: The vertical line indicates the time at which the tightening of unemployment benefits occurred.

Source: OECD-CEET Regional Labour Market Database.

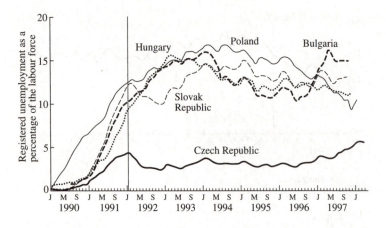

Figure 2.4. The tightening of benefits and the dynamics of Unemployment

Notes: Unemployment rate: monthly registered unemployed data for the numerator; the estimates of monthly unemployment are derived through a linear interpolation of the end-of-year official figures or LFS data.

Source: OECD-CEET Labour Market Database.

advantages in intervening before building up a large non-employment pool because, later on, employers will be reluctant to increase vacancy-to-unemployment ratios, and the social security burden will be heavier; hence, larger cuts in generosity will be needed to foster outflows to jobs.

Moreover, cuts in benefit levels and duration were accompanied in the Czech Republic by the implementation on a large scale (in relation to the size of the unemployment pool) of active labour-market programmes such as wage subsidies, training courses for the unemployed, and public work schemes. The effectiveness of these policies is often challenged on theoretical grounds because of the *deadweight losses* (the hiring subsidies given to employers who would have created the job in any event) and *substitution effects* (altering wage relativities, ending up by displacing non-participants in these programmes) associated at the micro-economic level with their implementation as well as, at the macro-economic level, the *fiscal crowding-out* of private job creation through the financing of such programmes via payroll taxation.

Ongoing evaluations of active policies in the CEECs would seem to underplay the importance of such distortionary effects of active policies in transitional economies, not least because an overall lack of vacancies makes deadweight losses quite unlikely to occur.[46] Moreover, there is one thing that active policies are usually successful in obtaining, independently of their impact on net job creation: they allow the public employment service to separate those who are actually searching for jobs from those who are not. Active policies, particularly in conditions of severe labour slack, are, in other words, a powerful device to enforce work tests, and the Czech Public Employment Service (PES) has been relatively tough in enforcing such tests. Available data suggest that one in ten exiting the live register in 1992–4 at the end of each month were persons struck off the registers (Terrell and Munich, 1996).

The possibility of distinguishing jobseekers from inactive people is equivalent, in the model under consideration, to an increase in the probability that an employer can fill a vacancy that targets the non-employed population. This is because, after such a screening, only those who are actually searching are referred to employers for interviews and, hence, posting vacancies targeting the unemployed yields almost the same probability of success as posting vacancies for workers from the old sector. The combined tightening of unemployment benefits and the use of slots in active policy programmes in order to enforce work tests can significantly increase the proportion of the unemployed actually seeking work.

While in the Czech Republic active policies have had a significant and strong *net* effect on outflows to jobs,[47] they seem to have been much less successful in the country's former federal partner, the Slovak Republic, after the split (Burda and Lubyova, 1995). This is perhaps because the use of active policies as a work test (which requires, after all, that slots in active policies are tailored to the characteristics of the unemployed, so that jobs offered are 'suitable' for them) is very difficult to achieve when there are few PES staff members per registered unemployed in the republic. Hence, we have a second channel—in addition to the asymmetries in the recruitment pool—whereby a better timing of reforms allowed the Czech nation to experience one of the lowest unemployment rates in the OECD arena in spite of the radical transformations and large changes in the composition of employment that were occurring.[48]

[46] See, for instance, the studies collected in the 1999 Symposium issue of the *Journal of Comparative Economics*.

[47] This is revealed by estimates of 'augmented' (that is, including active policy expenditure or intakes) matching functions (Boeri and Burda, 1996).

[48] There are, clearly, also other reasons—including historical ones, such as those related to initial conditions—as to why the Czech Republic has experienced lower unemployment

2.5 Final Remarks on Timing

Failure to take stock of the actual legacies of central planning in terms of human capital specificity, low enterprise density, and repressed voluntary non-employment has seriously biased the modelling of transitional dynamics and, more importantly, policy advice inspired by the OST literature towards measures buying out workers of state firms. Policies reducing labour supply and overgenerous non-employment benefits at the outset of transition have favoured the large drive to non-employment documented in Chapter 1. There would be no problem if this transitional non-employment could be quickly reabsorbed at later stages, as implied by the nice, bell-shaped, unemployment paths of the optimal speed of transition literature. However, there are powerful inertial factors at work that make it more difficult to push unemployment downhill.

The model developed in this chapter points to two such factors, namely the presence at the outset of *two* recruitment pools for the new sector, and a vicious circle of low re-employment probabilities and non-participation decisions. Another factor is the fiscal burden placed on gross job creation in the emerging sector by the financing of non-employment benefits. This 'fiscal externality' was present also in the OST literature, but it operated mainly at the end of the process rather than at its beginning. Indeed, the optimal timing of policy reforms implied by the OST models is one where non-employment benefits are initially relatively generous (in order to win workers' resistance to restructuring) and are subsequently reduced (or governments commit themselves beforehand to doing so in case of excessively high social security burdens). The model developed in this chapter prescribes a sequence that goes the other way round. Non-employment benefits should be low to start with, in order to prevent large labour supply reductions. They can be raised only when the new sector is large enough to make the benefit system sustainable with relatively low statutory contribution rates (given that wages in the new sector are higher than in the old sector).

CEECs have, for the most part, followed the high–low sequence, introducing grossly over-generous benefits at the outset (for example, open-ended commitments in Poland in 1990) and cutting them down after reaching two-digit unemployment rates. As has been documented, these reforms did not boost outflows from unemployment to jobs and

rates than the other CEECs throughout the transition period. See OECD (1995a) and Boeri and Burda (1996)) for reviews of the literature on the 'Czech unemployment miracle'.

ended up by shifting non-employed people to other social transfer schemes. Hence, the high–low sequence does not seem to have been working too well. Unfortunately, we do not have the opposite experience of a country following the low–high sequence; the only experiment we can draw upon is that of the Czech Republic, the only country in the region that reformed its unemployment benefits system when unemployment was still relatively low—a policy that has paid off with one of the lowest unemployment rates in the OECD area throughout transition, although it has increased somewhat in the most recent years after the hiatus of the 1997 currency crisis. In addition to providing insights as to the right sequence of reforms of unemployment benefits, the model also suggests that high unemployment and low participation can go hand-in-hand. Put another way, policies which reduce labour supply, like those documented in Chapter 1, cannot be expected to reduce unemployment for long. Rather economies may well get mapped in low participation and high unemployment equilibria, such as those currently prevailing in Southern European countries.

Another case of low non-employment benefits and low transitional non-employment that we have not discussed in this chapter is that of the former Soviet republics. I will devote attention to this case in the next chapter, because from it one can learn much about the interactions between labour-market outcomes and distributional issues. In order to analyse these interactions, we will have to extend the model used so far because the only dimension along which earnings were allowed to vary in this chapter was the divide between old and new jobs.

Annex 2
A Simple Model of Transition

The purpose of this annex is to illustrate the transition model whose numerical simulations are discussed in Chapter 2.

A2.1 Building Blocks

As in the literature on the optimal speed of the transition (developing Harris–Todaro types of models), we have two sectors endowed with different technologies. In particular, we have an 'old' sector (firms inherited from the previous regime) and a 'new' sector (newly created firms).

'Old' and 'new' are used as descriptors, rather than the usual 'public' and 'private' divide, because neither privatization nor downsizing are sufficient for a firm to move from one sector to another. Only new firms can have access to new technologies and products.

Unlike the models reviewed in Chapter 1, here workers are heterogeneous. In particular, they differ along two dimensions: they have different skills (horizontal differentiation), and they have varying reservation utilities (productivity in the subsistence sector). It is posited that both skills and reservation utilities are uniformly distributed over the relevant spectrum. Workers' skills matter only in the new sector. The old firms use standardized production techniques: for them all workers are alike. New firms, instead, can produce only if the workers have a given range of skills. For simplicity, we assume that all workers within this range are equally productive; outside this range, their productivity is zero. The extension of this range can be interpreted as a measure of the fungibility of the workforce,[49] in turn associated with the specificity

---

[49] One may think of a ring of skills, and of new firms being located along this ring. The more specialized the workforce, the shorter the arc distance between the upper and lower boundary of the 'skill-area' covered by the firm.

of skills developed by the nations education system. As discussed in Chapter 2, transitional economies have in general inherited from their previous system a low level of flexibility of the workforce, due to their overinvestment in vocational education.

The presence of different skills implies that there is a non-trivial matching that has to occur between firms' jobs and the workers.[50]

Individuals can be either employed in one of the two sectors, or non-employed. Both employed and non-employed individuals can search for work. Hence, employers when issuing a vacancy have also to choose a recruitment pool: they can either advertise the vacancy among the pool of workers in the old sector or can go through the network of labour offices registering the unemployed. Searching is non-sequential, as is suggested by an increasing body of empirical evidence:[51] employers fill a vacancy only after having interviewed *all* applicants rather than stopping the interview process after finding the first workers with the right skills.

A2.2 Values

All persons in working age (their total being normalized to one unit) have a reservation utility (productivity in the informal sector) u, which is deemed to be distributed uniformly along the unit interval. Workers know their own reservation utility, while employers know only the distribution of u.

The value added of old-sector jobs is also normalized to unity (so that this rules out cases where, *in the absence of unemployment benefits*, workers are better off being non-employed than in an old enterprise) and is entirely appropriated by the workers.[52] Let δ denote the discount factor. The asset value of being employed in the old sector (subscript 'o') is then given by

$$W_o = 1 + \delta \{\pi_o W_n + \lambda(1 - \pi_o)W_u + (1 - \pi_o - \lambda(1 - \pi_o))W_o\},$$
(A2.1)

where λ is the (exogenous) layoff rate, π_o denotes the probability of

---

[50] In the optimal speed of transition literature, workers are homogeneous and hence the 'matching' process is only a by-product of transaction costs.

[51] See, in particular, van Ours and Ridder (1992).

[52] The model can be readily extended to allow for only a proportion of the surplus going to the workers, as assumed in the case of the private sector.

moving to the new sector, and subscripts n and u denote, respectively, the new sector and non-employment.

The value of being employed at wage w_n in the new sector is given by

$$W_n = w_n + \delta \{(1 - \lambda_n)W_n + \lambda_n W_u\} \qquad (A2.2)$$

where λ_n is the probability of dismissal in the new sector.[53]

Non-employed individuals can be actively seeking a job or not searching. If they are seeking, they receive a non-employment benefit (encompassing unemployment benefits, social assistance, early retirements, liberal access to invalidity pensions, etc.) and face a probability π_u of finding a job in the private sector. If they are *not* seeking work, they continue to receive the non-employment benefit[54] and, on the top of that, they can draw their reservation utility (or productivity in the subsistence sector). Hence, the value of being non-employed for an individual with reservation utility u is:

$$W_u(u) = b + \max \{\delta[\pi_u W_n + (1 - \pi_u)W_u(u)], u + \delta W_u(u)\},$$
$$(A2.3)$$

where $0 < b < 1$.

The above equations define a cutoff reservation utility level, $\tilde{u}$, at which the non-employed are indifferent between searching and being available for jobs or not searching (being inactive). In particular, $\tilde{u}$ is defined by

$$\tilde{u} = \delta \pi_u (W_n - W_u(\tilde{u})). \qquad (A2.4)$$

By substituting (A2.2) into (A2.4), it can be readily shown that the cutoff reservation utility is decreasing with the probability of being laid

---

[53] Empirical evidence suggests that separation rates from state and private firms are roughly comparable; however, there are more quits in state firms than in private units. Differences between old and new firms are marked on the hiring side: new firms display higher hiring rates than the other firms. In this model we have two different parameters for job destruction (λ and λ_n) and we only allow firms in the new sector to hire workers.

[54] Although some countries have norms conditioning the provision of unemployment benefits for able-bodied individuals to the passing of a work test, such rules are rarely enforced, not least because of an overall lack of vacancies. Only countries with a low unemployment rate, like the Czech Republic, have been able to use the offer of slots in active labour-market programmes as a way to test the actual willingness of the registered unemployed to take up the job opportunities offered to them. Other kinds of non-employment benefits (e.g. disability benefits) are not conditional on passing a work test.

off in the new sector, while it is increasing with w_n and the discount factor. In other words, for any given π_u, the lower the discount rate, the larger the share of the unemployed not engaged in job search, because seeking jobs involves a trade-off between forgone income from informal (or subsistence) activities and future gains from employment in the new sector.[55]

In summary, at any point in time, persons of working age can be either employed in the old sector (in pool E_o), employed in the new sector (in pool E_n) or non-employed (in pool N). In the latter case, they can be either inactive or 'ILO-type unemployed' (i.e. actively seeking and available to take up jobs offered to them), the latter denoted by E_u.

A2.3 Matching Technologies

Employers in the new sector can recruit either from the unemployment ranks or from the pool of workers in the old sector. In both cases, they have to issue vacancies at a fixed cost per period and get applicants only from the pool to which vacancies are addressed.[56] This is consistent with evidence of significant segmentation of job-offer arrival rates in countries such as Poland (Boeri and Flinn, 1999).

Matching technologies are identical for both kind of pools; we assume for simplicity that they are of the constant-returns-to scale type.[57] Hence, the two job-finding probabilities, for old sector workers and for the non-employed seeking jobs, respectively, are given by

$$\pi_i = m\left(1, \frac{v_i}{E_i}\right) = \theta_i q(\theta_i), \text{ with } i = \text{o, u respectively,} \qquad (A2.5)$$

where θ_i is the vacancy to jobseekers ratio (market tightness) for the pool

[55] Under the conditions of Knightian uncertainty prevailing at the outset of transition, static decision rules may have been extensively followed. This may also contribute to explaining why a large drop in participation occurred at the start of transition.

[56] This is an easily altered assumption. Our results still hold as long as the majority of applicants come from the pool to which vacancies are addressed.

[57] Our results would be strengthened were we to assume that there is a higher efficiency in matching when employers recruit from the old sector. Evidence from transitional economies points to decreasing returns to scale in unemployment outflows. Theoretical arguments are often made in favour of increasing returns. Matching functions estimated over a wide range of OECD countries do not falsify the assumption of constant returns to scale, which is also consistent with a constant unemployment rate along a balanced growth path.

i, $q(\theta_i) \equiv m\left(\frac{E_i}{v_i}, 1\right)$, with m representing a matching function and, by
the properties of matching functions, $q' < 0$.

Filled vacancies from any of the two pools (see wage determination
below) are jobs with a value J. We have, therefore, the two 'free-
entry conditions' for vacancies issued in the old sector and for the non-
employed, respectively

$$\delta\frac{J}{\theta_o} = c \quad \forall\, 0 < \theta_o < \infty \qquad (A2.6)$$

and

$$\delta\phi\frac{J}{\theta_u} = c \quad \forall\, 0 < \theta_u < \infty, \qquad (A2.7)$$

where c denotes the (fixed[58]) cost of issuing vacancies and ϕ is the
proportion of non-employed individuals who are seeking jobs (E_u/N).
This is because, from the pool of the non-employed individuals, only
those actively seeking come for interviews and we assume—as seems
more realistic—that employers screen all the potential applicants before
making a decision.

The above conditions imply that when vacancies are issued for both
old sector workers and non-employed jobseekers, the following arbitrage
condition holds:

$$\frac{\phi}{q(\theta_u)} = \frac{1}{q(\theta_o)},$$

which implies (since $0 \le \phi \le 1$ and $q' < 0$) that $\theta_u \le \theta_o$. Notice that,
for given θ_u, an increasing proportion of non-employed people seeking
jobs involves a decline in θ_o. By appropriate choice of the parameters
(it suffices to assume that c is sufficiently small) we will always impose
that, at the beginning of transition, vacancies are issued for *both* pools
of jobseekers. In so far as there are initially more employed in the old
sector than non-employed jobseekers (that is, at time 0, $E_o > E_u$), we
will also have that, at the outset, $v_o > v_u$.

---

[58] We could allow c to vary with the size of the pool of potential applicants, which
is consistent with a non-sequential matching process. This would, however, complicate
the algebra without adding further insights to the model (because it would increase the
asymmetries between the two recruitment pools). There is just too little empirical evidence
on vacancy formation to offer any guidance on modelling the relation between the costs of
posting vacancies and the size of the recruitment pools.

A2.4 Wage Determination and Job Creation

Let ρ be the positional rent enjoyed by new posts relative to those located in the old sector. Clearly, the rents will be increasing in matching frictions and in the costs of issuing vacancies. The value of a new job in a firm for the employer is then given by

$$J = 1 + \rho - w_n + \delta(1 - \lambda_n)J. \tag{A2.8}$$

In fact, when a job is hit by an adverse shock, its value reduces to that of a vacancy, which is always zero by the 'free entry' condition. As is customary in the matching literature, we assume that wages in the new sector are set according to a Nash bargaining rule[59] having as threat point for the worker the value of non-employment (which holds also for workers from the old sector because the latter is bound, sooner or later, to disappear[60]). Only one wage is set. Despite the distribution of the reservation utility of workers being non-degenerate, the threat point for those seeking work is unique because it is not possible to seek jobs and get the reservation utility at the same time. Put another way, the threat point relevant in wage bargaining (that of the unemployed person rather than the inactive individual) always coincides with that of the worker with zero reservation utility ($W_u(0)$, or W_u for short), i.e.:

$$W_n - W_u = \gamma(J + W_n - W_u), \tag{A2.9}$$

where $0 < \gamma < 1$ denotes the bargaining power of workers.

A2.5 Market Tightness

In order to derive the laws of motion of the state variables E_o, E_n, N and E_u, we proceed as follows. First, we characterize non-participation decisions and quits from the old sector.[61] This yields the relevant transition

---

[59] The latter maximizes $J^{(1-\gamma)}(W_n - W_u)^\gamma$, yielding

$$W_n - W_u = \frac{\gamma}{1 - \gamma} J.$$

where γ is as defined in the main text.

[60] Empirical evidence, after all, suggests that the mean of the distribution of job offers for employed and unemployed jobseekers are almost identical in countries such as Poland. See Boeri and Flinn (1999).

[61] In the new sector, wages are set according to a sharing rule and jobs are destroyed only when the total surplus of the match becomes negative. It follows that quits from the new sector are not distinguishable from layoffs, not only empirically but also from a theoretical standpoint.

probabilities as a function of market tightness, that is, the vacancy-to-unemployed ratio. Then, we characterize the asset values of jobs and employment (in the new sector) as well as unemployment as a function of market tightness. Finally, we can derive a law of motion for θ_u.

We begin by using (A2.4) and the Nash-bargaining solution (A2.9) to express the cutoff reservation utility $\tilde{u}$ as a function of the share of the surplus going to employers and of the job-finding probability of unemployed jobseekers:

$$\tilde{u} = \frac{\delta \pi_u \gamma J}{(1 - \gamma)}. \qquad (A2.10)$$

Substituting into this expression the free entry condition, we obtain

$$\tilde{u} = \frac{c\gamma}{(1-\gamma)} \frac{\theta_u}{\phi} = \frac{c\gamma}{(1-\gamma)} \frac{\theta_u N}{\mu(\tilde{u})}$$

where $\mu(\tilde{u})$ is a measure of the non-employed with reservation utility less than or equal to $\tilde{u}$. By the implicit function theorem, it is straightforward to show that the cutoff utility level is increasing in θ_u. Next, we equate (A2.1) to W_u and solve for the threshold reservation utility $\tilde{u}_o$ holding for the old sector workers: workers whose $u > \tilde{u}_o$ choose to quit into non-employment when b is offered to them.[62] As argued above, job-finding probabilities of the non-employed jobseekers cannot be larger than those of the individuals employed in the old sector. It follows that, at the outset, $\tilde{u}_o > \tilde{u}$, indicating that those quitting their job in the old sector do not engage in a job search. Hence, we have:

$$\tilde{u}_o = \frac{(1 - \delta)(1 + \delta \pi_o W_n)}{(1 - \pi_o - \lambda(1 - \pi_o))} - b, \qquad (A2.11)$$

which, for reasonable values of the parameters[63] is increasing with π_o and W_n, with the latter effect outweighing the former. I show below that ϕ is non-decreasing along the transition path, which implies (by the arbitrage condition in vacancy formation) that π_o is non-increasing over time. Moreover, W_n is constant along the transition path. Hence, workers

---

[62] Job leavers were eligible for unemployment benefit systems introduced at the beginning of the 1990s in transitional economies, in some cases after only a relatively short waiting period.

[63] All what we need to assume is that $\lambda < 1/3$. As discussed in Chapter 2, yearly layoff rates rarely exceed 5 per cent of dependent employment and are lower in the old than in the new sector.

in the old sector can only quit to non-employment in the first period. This is consistent with evidence, displayed in Chapter 1, that quit rates were large at the outset of transition and with the observation in most CEECs of lower re-employment probabilities for job leavers compared with job losers.[64]

Notice further that $\tilde{u}_o > \tilde{u}$. In fact, we show below that θ_u is constant along the transition. Hence also $\tilde{u}$ is constant over time. By using the properties of geometric series, we can rewrite (A2.4) as

$$\tilde{u} = \frac{\delta\pi_u[(1-\delta)W_n - b]}{1 - \delta(1-\pi_u)},$$

which indicates that the greater the job-finding probability and the lower the unemployment benefit, the larger $\tilde{u}$ and hence the smaller the proportion of the non-employed (and of the working-age) population that are inactive. Subtracting this result from (A2.11) and upon some manipulations, we obtain:

$$\tilde{u}_o - \tilde{u} = \frac{1 + \delta W_n(1-\delta)\left[(\pi_o - \pi_u) + \lambda\pi_u(1-\pi_o)\right]}{(1 - \delta(1-\pi_u))(1 - \pi_o - \lambda(1-\pi_o))}$$
$$- \frac{\delta\left[(1-\pi_u)(1 - \delta(1-\lambda\pi_u b)) + b\pi_u(1+\pi_o)\right]}{(1 - \delta(1-\pi_u))(1 - \pi_o - \lambda(1-\pi_o))},$$

which is positive because, by free entry condition, $\pi_o \geq \pi_u$. It is straightforward to show that both $\tilde{u}_o$ and $\tilde{u}$ decline with b. Moreover, by taking the derivative of the above expression with respect to the unemployment benefit, we obtain

$$\frac{\partial(\tilde{u}_o - \tilde{u})}{\partial b} = \frac{-\delta\pi_u(1 + \pi_o - \delta\lambda)}{(1 - \delta(1-\pi_u))(1 - \pi_o - \lambda(1-\pi_o))} < 0$$

We show below that θ_u (hence also W_n, π_u and π_o) are constant along the transition path.[65] Thus, we have from the above that those initially quitting the old sector will never be seeking re-employment and that higher unemployment benefits decrease the proportion of those who, if dismissed from the old sector, will not be seeking jobs. Put another

[64] See the estimates of hazard functions reported for several CEECs in the January 1999 Symposium issue of the Journal of Comparative Economics. These estimates point to re-employment hazards for job leavers significantly lower than those estimated for job losers in all samples for both sexes.

[65] Clearly, θ_o, and hence π_o, are positive only when E_o is positive.

way, ϕ is non-decreasing along the transition path; and the higher is b at the outset, the further ϕ moves from its steady-state equilibrium level.

Next, we can use (A2.2) and (A2.3) to express the asset value of non-employment and of employment in the new sector as a function of market tightness. This yields

$$W_u = \frac{1}{A}[b(1 - \delta(1 - \lambda_n)) + \delta\pi_u w_n] \qquad (A2.12)$$

and

$$W_n = \frac{w_n}{1 - \delta(1 - \lambda_n)} + \frac{1}{A}\left[\delta\lambda_n b + \frac{\delta^2\lambda_n\pi_u w_n}{(1 - \delta(1 - \lambda_n))}\right], \qquad (A2.13)$$

where $A = (1 - \delta - (\delta - \delta^2)(1 - \lambda_n - \pi_u))$. Now, we can use the Nash bargaining rule (A2.9) to rewrite the asset value of a job in the new sector (for the employer) also as a function of θ_u:

$$J = \frac{(1 - \gamma)}{\gamma}\left[\frac{w_n}{1 - \delta(1 - \lambda_n)} - \frac{b(1 - \delta)}{A}\right]. \qquad (A2.14)$$

Next, we equate (A2.14) to the free-entry condition (solved for J) in order to obtain an equation for the equilibrium transition path of θ_u:

$$\frac{cq(\theta_u)}{\phi(\theta_u)\delta} = \frac{(1 - \gamma)}{\gamma}\left[\frac{w_n}{1 - \delta(1 - \lambda_n)} - \frac{b(1 - \delta)}{A}\right]. \qquad (A2.15)$$

As can be shown, the term on the left-hand side of (A2.15) is always decreasing with θ_u, whilst the term on the right-hand side is monotonically increasing. Moreover, for $\theta_u = 0$, the term on the right-hand side is negative and the term on the left-hand side is zero, whilst for $\theta_u \longrightarrow \infty$, the right-hand side is larger than the left-hand side. It follows that there must be a θ_u^* satisfying (A2.15); further, this θ_u^* must be unique.

Finally, we can obtain the wage equation by substituting the free-entry condition (A2.7) into (A2.9) and carrying out some manipulations:

$$w_n = (1 - \gamma)b + \gamma(1 + \rho)(1 + c\theta_u). \qquad (A2.16)$$

A2.6 Steady–State Equilibrium

At the steady state, E_o is zero as all jobs in the old sector have been destroyed. Employment (concentrated in the new sector) is given by

$$E_n = \frac{q(\theta_u)\theta_u\phi(\theta_u)}{(\lambda_n + q(\theta_u)\theta_u\phi(\theta_u))}, \qquad (A2.17)$$

whilst 'ILO–OECD unemployment' (the number of those without a formal job and seeking employment) is given by

$$E_u = \frac{\phi(\theta_u)\lambda_n}{(\lambda_n + q(\theta_u)\theta_u\phi(\theta_u))}, \tag{A2.18}$$

and the total number of those without employment (equal to the non-employment rate, given that the total population of working age is normalized to one unit) is given by

$$N = 1 - E_n. \tag{A2.19}$$

Finally we have $\theta_u = \theta_u^*$.

Comparative statics of the steady-state equilibrium reveals that $\frac{\partial \theta_u}{\partial b} < 0$. By (A2.17–19), it then follows that the steady-state equilibrium employment (non-employment) rate is declining (increasing) with the level of non-employment benefits, whilst the steady-state proportion of the non-employed seeking jobs, ϕ, declines with b.

A2.7 Transition Paths

As is apparent from (A2.15), along the saddle path, θ_u is constant with value θ^*. It follows that also w_n and $\tilde{u}$ jump immediately to their steady-state equilibrium.

For the remaining state variables of the model, dynamics are induced by matching technologies (which are a function of the past realizations of the state variables), associated with N, E_u and J in the previous period. In the numerical simulations displayed in Chapter 2, the following system of difference equations is used:

$$E_o^{t+1} = (1 - \lambda - \pi_o^t)E_o^t, \tag{A2.20}$$

$$E_n^{t+1} = (1 - \lambda_n) E_n^t + \pi_o^t E_o^t + \pi_u^t E_u^t, \tag{A2.21}$$

$$E_u^{t+1} = E_u^t(1 - \pi_u^t) + \lambda \frac{\tilde{u}^t}{\tilde{u}_o} E_o^t + \lambda_n \mu(\tilde{u})E_n^t, \tag{A2.22}$$

where $\mu(\tilde{u})$ is the proportion of people employed in the new sector with reservation utility less than or equal to $\tilde{u}$. Clearly, $\mu(\tilde{u})$ approaches unity as the transition proceeds, given that inactivity is an absorbing state.

I specialize in matching technologies of the Cobb-Douglas type. Let $0 < \alpha < 1$ denote the elasticity of job finds with respect to vacancies.

Given the assumption of constant-returns-to-scale matching technologies, $(1 - \alpha)$ is then the elasticity of job finding with respect to the pool of jobseekers.

The specificity of skills of transitional economies is embedded in a parameter, $0 < \sigma \leq 1$, hitting matching technologies in a multiplicative fashion. This parameter can be interpreted as a measure of the fungibility of the workforce; in other words, we have

$$\pi_i E_i = \sigma v_i^{\alpha} E_i^{(1-\alpha)}, \qquad (A2.23)$$

where $i = \text{o, u}$. Over time we can expect σ to increase to unity. Estimates of matching functions in transitional economies reveal an upward trend of time dummies, which may indeed point to (disembodied) technological progress in job matching. Hence, we can also carry out simulations with σ slowly (but steadily) increasing over time.

A2.8 Fiscal Externality

The numerical simulations commented on in Chapter 2 also include a 'fiscal externality' effect. This involves adding a governmental budget constraint to the model, related to the payment of non-employment benefits out of payroll taxation. Unlike the OST models reviewed in Chapter 1, we also allow payroll tax rates to differ between the old and the new sector. This means that subsidies offered to firms in the old sector (in the form of negative taxes) can be taken into account.

In particular, the (static) social security budget constraint is given by

$$bN = \tau_n w_n E_n + \tau_o E_o, \qquad (A2.24)$$

where τ denotes the statutory contribution rates.

In the light of the discussion in Chapter 2, it is reasonable to assume that the only control variable of governments is the contribution rate on the old sector, τ_o, while τ_n adjusts at each point in time in order to clear the social security budget:

$$\tau_n = \frac{bN - \tau_o E_o}{(w_n E_n)}. \qquad (A2.25)$$

This shows that, when $w_n > 1$, an increased employment share in the new sector (for any given N) involves lower statutory contribution rates.

3
Safety Nets, Earnings Inequalities and Reallocation

3.1 Introduction

The previous chapter shed some light on the factors leading to the stagnancy of transitional unemployment, on the failure of the policy experiments carried out with the reforms of non-employment benefits, and hence on the appropriate timing of these reforms. An attempt was made to develop some theory framing (and possibly explaining) the time-series properties of job reallocation in each country under consideration, as well as the evolving borderline between unemployment and inactivity. This chapter is more on the cross-sectional dimension of transition. We hope at least to convince the reader that there is much to learn by comparing the many high-unemployment outcomes with the few success stories in labour-market adjustment. Hence, not only will the 'Czech miracle' be revisited but also more prosaic cases will be considered, such as the explanations for low unemployment in the former Soviet republics. The regional dispersion of unemployment within each country will also be addressed, so that distributional considerations will play a major role in this chapter.

The three key messages of this chapter are that

- governments in transitional economies could do much at the outset to affect the dispersion of earnings;
- much of the disparity in the incidence of transitional unemployment amongst the CEECs has to do with the degree of earning dispersion allowed in the various countries; and
- the presence in some countries of a 'safety net', imposing a floor to wage setting, has fostered the reallocation of labour from declining to expanding industries.

It may be argued that wage inequalities have only partly to do with governments. Most typically, earnings dispersion is the result of the way in which wage-bargaining institutions operate (notably of their degree of centralization and coordination), of the degree of unionization of the workforce, and of the relative strength of the 'solidarity principle' that unions attach to wage negotiations. It also has to do with the presence of marginal groups in the labour market, notably ethnic minorities such as those characterizing most of the countries in the region. These are all things that governments typically can do little about, at least in advance. If anything, governments may intervene afterwards, for instance by introducing cash transfers to low income earners and by adjusting tax brackets in order to make taxation more or less progressive.

In transitional economies, however, governments could do much more than in most Western countries to affect the degree of earnings dispersion. And they could intervene beforehand, that is to say they could intervene on wage levels *before* tax is deducted, or distribute rather than simply *re*distribute.

In the initial phase of the transition period, a large component of the workforce in CEECs was employed in state firms, which were still subject to the tariff wage system that was inherited from the previous regime and that was heavily affected by political decisions. Also (and foremost), contrary to popular belief, trade unions in these countries were weak and the monopoly power of the old unions was rapidly eroded by the appearance of new workers' organizations and the growth of a private and largely non-unionized sector.

A veritable explosion in the number of firm-specific (or sector-specific) workers' organizations marked the first years of transition. This important, and all too often neglected, phenomenon highly complicated the task of coordinating wage bargaining. While this made it easier for some segments of the workforce—typically those most educated—to extract higher rents for their specific skills, it made those less educated significantly worse off. This worsening of the relative position of the less educated people is particularly marked in the new-firms sector, where trade unions are still, ten or so years later, almost non-existent.

Why were unions so weak? It was widely believed at the outset that the weakness and short history of entrepreneurial organizations in these countries (the virtual absence of organizations whose interests were vested in standing against wage increases) would enhance the power of the unions in wage setting. In reality, the monopoly power of unions was weakened by not having an organized counterpart to deal with. According to the theory of coalitions, the presence of a monopolistic counterpart provides stronger incentives for unions to join their forces. In transitional economies, there were no bilateral monopoly conditions, except perhaps in the case of state enterprises located in rural areas and of the so-called 'one-company towns' of the Russian industrial landscape. However, state enterprises were experiencing relatively high employment and real wage losses—things that certainly do not make it easier to organize the workforce.

Thus, governments could do much to influence wage setting, and even more so the dispersion of earnings.

CEEC governments actually intervened in wage setting by introducing unemployment benefits systems in which only social minima were fully indexed to inflation. As already discussed in Chapter 2, this transformed nominally earnings-related systems (neutral with respect to the dispersion of earnings) into *de facto* flat rate systems. Even more than a minimum wage—also present in most of these countries—and more relevant for the setting of cash transfers than wages, these benefit minima or safety nets, as provided to non-employed individuals, put a floor to wage setting. Tax-based income policies were also introduced at the outset of transition, which were likely to have played an important role in influencing wage *dispersion*, notably in state enterprises, rather than aggregate wage *growth*.

In the former Soviet republics, however, governments abstained from intervening in wage setting. Unemployment benefits were in real terms replacing between 5 and 10 per cent of previous earnings and, in any event, in nominal terms the benefits maintained a strong link with previous earnings, thereby being neutral with respect to the wage distribution. Tax-based income policies were not introduced or not enforced; and minimum wages were not adjusted to galloping inflation and, as a result, they soon fell below minimum living standards.

Summing up, wage dispersion in the CEECs was somewhat contained by redistributive policies, while in the CIS there were *de facto* no constraints to the spread of the earning distribution. Although these two extreme characterizations of labour-market adjustment should not conceal differences in the scope of redistribution within the two groups of countries, they do explain much of the different paths of labour-market adjustments in the two geopolitical regions. In the CEECs, unemployment grew rapidly but, at the same time, significant job reallocation from declining to expanding sectors occurred within a relatively short amount of time. In the former Soviet republics, notably in Russia, unemployment built-up very slowly as wages rather than employment bore the weight of adjustment. However, job reallocation did not occur because workers, especially those with lower levels of education, were trapped in the old sectors.

From a normative standpoint, both adjustment trajectories have pros and cons. On the one hand, the CEEC experience shows that non-employment benefits can reduce earning inequality and contribute to job reallocation, but at a high price in terms of increasing unemployment, notably among the less educated people. On the other hand, the Russian experience indicates that wage flexibility is not always desirable or, at least, is not desirable *per se*: when there are important barriers to adjustment via quantities—for example, the narrow base (and hence specificity) of skills developed under the previous system, which has been characterized in the previous chapter, and a significant portion of the population being located in rural areas while the new sector is concentrated in urban centres—too much wage flexibility may actually end up delaying economic restructuring.

In order to highlight the interactions between non-employment benefits, wage dispersion and unemployment incidence, as well as between wage dispersion and job reallocation, we need to extend further the model introduced in Chapter 2. In particular, a vertical dimension will be added to the (so far horizontal) heterogeneity of workers: they will no longer vary only by their reservation utility (unobservable by employers) but also by their productivity in the new sector. This heterogeneity will be observable by workers and employers, which means that labour markets will be segmented along observable dimensions, for instance by the educational attainments of individuals. Differences in the productivity in the new sector will clearly affect the distribution of reservation utilities. This extension of the model partly endogenizes the heterogeneity in the reservation utility levels that, so far, have been taken as given.

The plan of this chapter is as follows. Section 3.2 tries to convince the reader that governments in the region could do much to affect the wage distribution. Thus, wage bargaining institutions and the way in which governments have interacted with them in the midst of transition are described. Next, section 3.3 provides a framework enabling discussion of the interactions between wage setting, unemployment incidence, job reallocation and non-employment benefits. Finally, section 3.4 interprets, against the background provided by the above model, the differences in unemployment rates across countries, the reasons for low unemployment in the former Soviet republics, and the wide regional disparities in the incidence of unemployment within each country. As usual, an annex (Annex 3.) contains the more technical parts related to the extensions of our model.

3.2 Wage Setting in the Midst of Transition

Surprisingly, little attention has been given to the development of modern collective-bargaining institutions throughout transitional economies. However, this has been one of the most important changes that have occurred in these countries in the 1990s, and one that is likely to shape their future.

The neglect of this very important aspect of economic transformation is perhaps the by-product of another prejudice that was deeply rooted in the early literature on transitional economies, namely the belief that the countries under consideration lacked everything but unions and that workers' representatives were all-powerful in these countries. After all, the legacy of the previous regime was one where unions were running the funds administering sickness benefits, family allowances and other social benefits. At the firm level, unions were in charge of important social assets of enterprises and workers' councils in some countries had been empowered—in the course of the partial reforms of the 1980s—to appoint and remove managers.[1] Unions were deemed to dominate the initial phases of the transition, ultimately decide upon the speed of restructuring, and benefit from the dismantling of state enterprises in order to extract a larger share of the added value. There was indeed a high risk of wage-push inflation episodes, and the task of governments—it was claimed—was to prevent unions from fully exerting this power.[2]

---

[1] The right of workers' representatives to hire and fire managers was introduced in Poland by the 1982 law on workers' councils. In Hungary, unions had the power of veto when managers took decisions 'offending socialist morality'. See Petkov and Thirkell (1991) and Burawoy and Krotov (1993) for a discussion of the control exerted by workers over the management of firms at the end of the 1980s. They convincingly argued that middle-managers were especially subject to the conditionality of workers' councils.

[2] Quoting Paul Marer's opening speech at the November 1990 OECD Conference on 'The Transition to a Market Economy':

> 'In several countries, earlier reforms had devolved certain business decisions from the state bureaucracy to newly formed enterprise councils or workers councils that are run jointly by managers and workers. Arrangements under which workers rather than real owners 'control' managers is a recipe for wage-push inflation, unless the government administratively

3.2.1 The Tale of the Omnipotent Unions

The view of unions being omnipotent in Eastern bloc countries was wrong from both a historical and theoretical perspective.

It was wrong in that it overlooked the complete disorganization of workers' associations at the outset of transition. Even in Poland, the country in which unions had played the biggest role in the move to a democratic and free-market system, unions were, at the beginning of the 1990s, in complete disarray. Solidarnosc was still trying to choose between being a political party or a union. The majority of workers were still affiliated to the old unions, the Association of Polish Trade Unions (OPZZ), which had lost credibility and most of its leaders, and a lot of new local, branch-level workers' associations were springing up. On our first mission to Romania, in early 1991, we asked for a meeting with representatives of unions operating at a nationwide level, because we wished to hear their views about the transformation process; we acutely embarrassed the Minister of Labour, who was organizing this meeting, because, he said, there were to his knowledge about 3,500 unions claiming to represent the Romanian workforce.

The disorganization and segmentation of workers' organizations was not only a by-product of a lack of credibility of the old unions, which had been supporters of the Communist regime; it was also resulting from the fact that the old unions were actually not rooted at the workplace.[3] Unions under the old system were 'transmission belts' for authorities rather than voices for workers. They were nourished by soft budget constraints and were largely unprepared for wage negotiations and any opposition to staff cuts. Wage bargaining at the enterprise level had been partly liberalized already before the start of transition (for example, in Russia under *perestroika*), with the dismantling of the old tariff system, but the total wage bills of enterprises were still in most cases centrally determined. As regards employment protection, one of the unions' main functions under the old systems was actually to discourage workers from

> controls wage increases. .... *The threat of wage-push inflation is substantial* [italicized by this author] unless the government intervenes. (P. Marer, 'Pitfalls in Transferring Market-Economy Experiences to the European Economies in Transition', in OECD (1991, pp. 41–42)).

[3] For instance, IG Metall, the powerful West German metalworkers' union, had originally planned to merge with its Eastern German counterpart. It had to give up this idea as it found that the Eastern German union was in fact an organization subordinate to the central Communist federation, not rooted at the workplace.

voluntarily leaving a firm by providing them with fringe benefits that they would have lost by moving to another enterprise—certainly a very different task from preventing workers' jobs from being lost. There was also no tradition and union culture for protection of real wages against price inflation. It is true that in countries like Poland and Hungary unions had already experienced some erosion of real wages under the partial price reforms of the 1980s, but this was nothing compared with the explosion of repressed inflation to come.

Thus, the old unions were forced to undergo radical changes at the outset of transition. They were deprived of the administration of social benefits, which were being detached from employment status. Neither could they oppose the extension of eligibility for social benefits from just employees to all those of working age, as the build-up of unemployment (and of self-employment) called for the provision of cash transfers irrespective of whether workers held jobs in unionized firms or not. The old unions were also forced by law to return assets and properties that could potentially be used by the former Communist *nomenklatura*. Social assets were also being detached from business enterprises in the context of privatization plans, and this also contributed to reducing the power of unions and their appeal to workers.[4]

The new unions lacked resources, experience and professional staff.[5] They were often coalitions of a large body of independent unions—as in the case of the Hungarian Democratic League of Independent Trade Unions (LIGA), Support (Podkrepa) in Bulgaria, and the 'Brotherhood' National Free Trade Union (Fratia) in Romania—and often far from attaining internal cohesion. There were also powerful centrifugal forces pushing towards greater union segmentation, such as those arising from the desire of groupings that were given preferential treatment under the old regime not to lose their privileges in comparison with the rest of the workforce, and the legitimate aspirations of the most educated workers to see a better recognition of their skills. The external environment was

---

[4] The provision of social assets within an enterprise and, more broadly, the provision of jobs as a sort of benefit in kind is, in my view, the strongest theoretical justification for the presence of 'soft budget constraints' in state enterprises *under the old regime* (and explanations for their persistence even during the transition are discussed in Chapter 2). The soft budget constraints were due to the fact that assets were a 'sunk cost' for enterprises: the investment could not be recouped because enterprises had to maintain their social obligations in respect of their workers and the social community.

[5] An indication of the lack of resources facing the new unions is that the big rival of Solidarnosc, the OPZZ, tried with all the means at its disposal to prevent assets that had been taken away from Solidarnosc under martial law from being returned to it.

certainly not favourable to the extension of the coverage of the new unions: in many countries there was plummeting real wages, steep price inflation, major redundancies being planned, and the development of many small businesses, where it is difficult for workers to be organized.[6]

Union membership declined very sharply at the start of transition in the countries under discussion. Although official union figures are not reliable, and are inflated by membership among pensioners, they generally point to 10–15 per cent declines of union membership. Data from ad hoc surveys carried out in various CEECs seem to indicate that union membership may have fallen to about 35 per cent of the workforce, a fraction that is well within the OECD range and marks a decline of nearly 50 per cent of membership with respect to the pre-transition phase.[7] Union coverage—that fraction of workers receiving wages negotiated in the context of collective agreements—has been estimated to be of the order of 30 per cent in the Czech Republic and Hungary (Rusnok and Fassman, 1995). Macro-economic data on the functional distribution of income also point to a deterioration of the bargaining position of workers: wage shares in GDP markedly declined at early stages of transition to about 30 per cent of GDP (compared with the 'rule-of-thumb' wage share of 70 per cent in OECD countries) and only partly recovered the ground lost afterwards; in the Baltic and Slavic countries, they actually continued to decline (Milanovic, 1999). While these aggregate income statistics are subject to a number of measurement problems and do not necessarily capture income losses suffered by the workers (inasmuch as cash transfers may partly, or even totally, offset wage losses), they nonetheless are indicative of a weak bargaining position of workers.

The omnipotent unions syndrome is ill-founded also from a theoretical perspective. Unions were stronger in state enterprises, which were, for the most part, bound to be split up in the context of privatization plans, if not liquidated altogether. As documented in Chapter 2, job creation was concentrated in the non-unionized segment, specifically the emerging small-business sector. Thus, union members were threatened

---

[6] Grosfeld and Nivet (1997) document the inability of unions to extract rents in Polish private firms: their estimated wage equations do not display any positive relation between wages and labour productivity in the private sector. Evidence from surveys of enterprises in Bulgaria, Hungary, Romania undertaken within the LICOS (Louvain) programme indicates that only about 20 per cent of employers in the new firms recognize trade unions as a bargaining partner in wage negotiations, compared with more than 90 per cent in state or privatized units.

[7] Trends in unionization in several CEECs and the former Soviet republics are reviewed in EC–ILO (1995).

by layoffs, pulled by wage offers coming from the private sector, or 'bought off' in the context of privatization plans. Needless to say, these are not the conditions in which models of union behaviour[8] would predict that unions will push for strong wage rises: there were no strong insiders, and some of the workers with the longest tenures—those who normally fight the most for wage rises and are less concerned about employment protection[9]—had left or were about to leave the firm with one of the rather generous early-retirement schemes introduced at the outset of transition. There were also strong pressures (coming from union members) for greater wage differentiation, and this is typically something that unions are less keen to accommodate, partly because increasing wage differentials make it more difficult to create coalitions of workers, and partly because increasing wage inequality is antithetic to the wage-smoothing, wage-insurance functions fulfilled by unions.[10]

Summing up, we can state that, at the outset of transition, unions were weak, disorganized and highly segmented across sectors, regions and firms. Not surprisingly, the resulting pattern of collective bargaining was one favouring bargaining at the enterprise level with respect to branch-level or nationwide wage negotiations.[11] This was happening also in the smallest CEECs and in those countries where the new laws on collective bargaining had a strong bias in favour of centralized wage setting, for example, the former Czech and Slovak Federal Republic. Here, the new regulations adopted as early as February 1991 forbade lower-level bodies from agreeing wages in excess of those settled at the central level, and granted the Labour Ministry the right to impose national agreements such that it could extend its coverage to enterprises not involved in centralized wage bargaining, regardless of whether or

---

[8] See Booth (1995) for a survey of models of union behaviour.

[9] Median voter models of union preferences (e.g. the seminal model by Farber (1978) suggest that the larger the percentage of workers with long tenures in a firm, the stronger the bias of unions in favour of wage rises (and the lower the weight attached to employment in union strategies). This is because labour shedding typically has a 'last in, first out' character. Moreover, employment-protection regulations make it more costly for firms to lay off the workers with the longest tenures.

[10] See Agell and Lommerud (1992) and Hibbs and Locking (1995) for a rationalization of the solidarity principle as an insurance against the risk of income losses.

[11] According to a survey conducted by the ILO (ILO, 1998), 96.5 per cent of negotiated wage agreements in Poland in 1996 were based on enterprise-level bargaining. The corresponding figures for the Czech Republic, Hungary, and Slovakia were 72 per cent, 65 per cent, and 60 per cent respectively. And it should be stressed that, more generally, only a minor fraction of workers is covered by some sort of collective wage agreement.

not they were members of the employers' associations that signed the agreement. In spite of all this, industry-level wage bargaining seems never to have taken off, at least outside the so-called 'budgetary sphere' (i.e., education, health and public administration, where wages where set directly by the state), in both the Czech lands and the Slovak Republic (EC–ILO, 1995).[12]

Tripartite structures—involving representatives of workers, employers and government, along with neocorporatist principles—that were established in most countries at the national level also had a hard life.[13]   After all, international experience suggests that these structures typically work best under conditions of moderate inflation and where interest groups are not fragmented (Pencavel, 1991)— both aspects that were very much lacking at the early stages of transition.

Trade unions and employers' associations and, more broadly, collective bargaining institutions have only more recently started coming into play, at least in Central Europe, thanks not only to a stabilization of macroeconomic conditions, but also to a necessarily long process of build-up from scratch of employers' associations, and to the creation of decentralized union structures. But this is another story, and one that is very different from the 'omnipotent union' tale appearing in literature early in the transition.

3.2.2 Administrative Ceilings and Floors to Wage Setting

The other side of the coin to the fears over wage-push inflation is the introduction of tax-based income policies (TIPs), namely penalties on firms granting wage increases above a given norm. A wide variety of schemes were adopted, which more or less linked wage norms to indicators of productivity at the enterprise level. Some of these schemes were grossly ill-designed. Typical is the case of the original *popiwek* introduced in Poland in 1990, which targeted the total wage bill of enterprises

---

[12] This is supported by evidence from enterprise surveys of a large wage dispersion across firms within well-defined (four-digit SITC) industries. See for example, Djankov and Pohl (1997).

[13] Tripartite structures were created in Hungary as early as in 1988, while in Bulgaria and the former Czechoslovakia, tripartite commissions were established in 1990. Poland and Russia embarked on tripartism in 1991–2. See Kyloh (1995) for a review of tripartism in individual countries of Central and Eastern Europe.

with the implication of being strongly biased against employment.[14] It also allowed enterprises to carry forward any 'unused' potential for wage increases, because only the *cumulative excess* of wages over the norm was subject to penalty taxes, but the employers could use these 'credits' only up to the end of the calendar year, with the result of incentivizing wage concessions in the fourth quarter. Owing to these shortcomings, the *popiwek* was revised only one year after its introduction, establishing among other things the norm in terms of the *average* wage, as opposed to the *total* wage bill (which, actually, may have biased hiring and firing policies of firms against the most skilled, and hence best paid, workers). Trials and errors characterized the experience also of other countries with TIPs, one of which was the Albakin tax (from the name of the former Deputy Prime Minister of the USSR), introduced into the Soviet Union in 1989, which indiscriminately taxed (and on a steeply progressive basis) any increase in the wage fund beyond 3 per cent. Again, the law had to be rapidly revised (as early as 1991).

Thus, there were not only many national variants of TIPs, but also many different versions within the rather short history of these schemes in each country. Two key parameters, however, were common to all versions of TIP: the first was the warranted wage-price indexation admitted by the norm; the second was the progressivity of the tax-rate scale used in defining penalties for firms violating the norms. Both parameters were subject to frequent revisions and negotiations on the part of tripartite bodies, and quite considerable energy and time was put into this process.[15] Forgiveness measures and exemptions were also granted in many cases, with the result of undermining the credibility of the relevant government's commitments to enforce penalties, and of making the policies time-inconsistent.

TIPs were either explicitly or *de facto* applicable only to state en-

---

[14] The wage norm under the original *popiwek* was established for each firm as follows:

$$\sum_i w_{i\tau+1} L_{i\tau+1} = \sum_{t=0}^{\tau} \sum_i (w_{i0} L_{i0})(1 + \mu \dot{p}_i),$$

where w and L denote nominal wages and the number of workers receiving wage i, respectively, while $\dot{p}$ is the change in the retail price index and μ is the indexation coefficient, establishing the targeted ratio between wage and price changes (initially set at 20 per cent and subsequently increased).

[15] Often, the tripartite commissions could not reach an agreement on these parameters. Typical is the case of the Czech Republic, where failure to reach an agreement at the beginning of each year (as envisaged by the law) often left wages unregulated in the first half of the year and then regulated again in the second half.

terprises; private units were exempted from the sphere of application of these regulations (as in Albania, Bulgaria, Poland, Romania, and in the more recent versions of the Slovak TIPs). In any event, enforcement of these regulations with private firms would have been dauntingly difficult, as proved by the experience of the countries and time periods (e.g. the Czech Republic after 1993) in which TIPs were not confined to state enterprises. The fragility of tripartite structures discussed in the previous section was, in any event, a serious obstacle to the enforcement of tax-based income policies.

In a context where real wages were experiencing declines of the order of 25–30 per cent, wage norms have rarely been binding on the aggregate, so long as the norm was established in terms of the *average* wage (as has become common practice since 1991 in most countries), TIPs were, however, a constraint on increased wage differentiation in state enterprises, notably an impediment to offering high wages to the most productive workers. Some firms asked for exemptions from the application of the TIPs in order to meet the requests of these workers, but getting administrative authorization was, in any event, time-consuming; meanwhile the best workers had gone.

Surprisingly enough, TIPs were abandoned just at the time when they could have been most useful. In more stable environments, with unions having recovered from the transition shock and a workforce feeling less exposed to the threat of dismissals typical of the early stages of transition, conditions of bilateral monopoly could materialize in some surviving state enterprises. There is indeed some evidence of significant insider power, where workers captured most of the productivity gains, in Polish state enterprises as soon as economic recovery had begun (Grosfeld and Nivet, 1997). Microeconomic data on Hungarian enterprises also point to state sector workers capturing almost 60 per cent of productivity increases, against less than 10 per cent in private firms (Boeri *et al.*, 1997). Lastly, wage increases above productivity are reported in several large state enterprises surviving the initial phases of transition in the CEECs (Pohl *et al.*, 1997). The decision of the Czech government to reintroduce TIPs as late as at the beginning of 1997 may also be an indication of the presence of significant wage pressures in the remaining large state enterprises. As discussed in Chapter 4, some risks of wage-push inflation are emerging within the EU Eastern enlargement process.

If TIPs were not, for the most part, a cap on wage growth, other administrative controls on wage setting were put in place from below. The dismantling of the tariff wage system was in most countries associated with the introduction of statutory minimum wages. The latter were set by governments—generally in consultation with social partners—at frequencies that were not legally compelling. Thus, they were often kept unaltered for several years in spite of two-digit inflation rates. For instance in the Czech Republic the minimum wage was kept at 2,200 crowns from 1992 to 1996, implying a decline of about 50 per cent in real terms. Inevitably, minimum wages became increasingly irrelevant in wage setting. The enterprise-level or branch-level agreements that were signed generally specified contractual minima above the statutory minimum wage level. Several international studies carried out at the International Labour Office point to a modest fraction of the labour force being paid in the vicinity (some even below) of the minimum wage in CEECs.[16] Minimum wages had by 1999 fallen below 40 per cent of the average wage in all countries under consideration (in Russia even below 10 per cent), which is significantly lower than the level typically observed in European OECD countries with minimum wage legislation (where minimum wages range between 50 and 60 per cent of the average wage).[17]

Perhaps the best indication of the increasing irrelevance of minimum wages (at least to wage setting) comes from the fact that minimum wages were no longer binding even in the budgetary sphere. We can give an example: in Russia in 1995, the lower wage rate for workers in public administration was established at a level that was almost 10 per cent higher than the statutory minimum wage (60,000 rather than 55,000 roubles).

Minimum wages have continued to play an important role as a social policy parameter as many benefit floors, such as social pensions, unemployment benefit minima and some family allowances, are often established as a multiple (or fraction) of the minimum wage. Thus, the question arises as to whether minimum wage legislation has, at least indirectly, affected wage setting, for example by modifying the reservation wages of individuals receiving cash transfers. But this is, after all, an issue concerning the role played in wage setting by non-employment benefits, rather than the minimum wage itself.

Summing up, we have established that, contrary to what is commonly believed, unions were weak at the outset of transition and the risks of wage-push inflation spirals (or leapfrogging wage increases across state

---

[16] See EC–ILO (1995), and Standing and Vaughan-Whitehead (1995).

[17] See OECD (1998), Chapter 2.

enterprises) were largely overestimated. The policies adopted to reduce the presumed omnipotence of unions—namely the introduction of tax-based income policies—would seem to have constrained the attainment of increased wage dispersion in state enterprises, rather than aggregate wage dynamics. While real wages dropped significantly in all transitional economies, managers of state enterprises were often constrained by these norms from hiring skilled workers or granting to those already in the firm wages that matched the levels they could get in private firms.

Paradoxically, TIPs could be more useful today—to face conditions where bilateral monopoly prevails in wage bargaining—than at the outset of transition. The weakness of unions and the decentralized patterns of collective bargaining that prevailed early on gave governments the possibility to affect wage setting by imposing wage floors that were uniform across the board. Statutory minimum wages were introduced but not adjusted for inflation, and hence they gradually lost importance in wage setting. Non-employment benefits have exerted a much more significant effect on wage setting than minimum wages. The way in which this happened is discussed below.

3.3 Wage Dispersion, Unemployment and Non-Employment Benefits

As argued above, transition began with young and weak bargaining institutions, a lack of unionization in the private sector, and a virtual absence of minimum wages. In such an environment, wage floors in the private sector were driven mainly by *individual*, as opposed to collective, labour supply decisions, represented by the reservation wages of individuals. Evidence is provided below that reservation wages were determined also by factors independent of labour demand conditions, and that they were at least partly exogenous with respect to wage setting. In particular, the lowest wage at which those seeking a job were willing to accept a job offer did not depend only on the way in which the market rewarded individuals' characteristics like education and age. Reservation wages of Polish workers, in particular, were sensitive to whether or not jobseekers were receiving non-employment benefits and were located in rural or urban regions.

Thus, governments had, *de facto*, quite a powerful tool in their hands to affect the distribution of earnings in the private sector, and in most CEECs non-employment benefits played an important role in shaping the distribution of earnings in this rapidly growing segment of the economy. In Poland, the initial earnings-related unemployment benefits system was soon turned into a flat-rate system assigning the same benefit level to everybody independently of her/his previous earnings.[18] In other countries, the unemployment benefits system was allowed to collapse (by letting only benefit minima be indexed) into a *de facto* flat-rate system.

The positive association found between the levels (or generosity) of non-employment benefits and the reservation wages of individuals does not come as a surprise, because it is consistent with standard models of labour-force participation decisions. Less obvious is the link between the *structure* of non-employment benefits and wage setting. In general, we would expect that the less dispersed the structure of non-employment benefits, and the lower the relation of benefits with past (and prospective) earnings of individuals, the less neutral benefits are with respect to the pay structure and hence the stronger the effects of benefits on the wage distribution. This is because flat-rate benefits are likely to increase the opportunity cost of employment disproportionately across workers with different productivity levels, notably increasing the wage aspirations of the least productive workers proportionally more than the wage claims of those who are more productive (and get the highest wages to start with). This means that the distribution of reservation wages of individuals will not increase uniformly as a result of the introduction (or increase) of non-employment benefits, but will rise mainly at its lower end, increasing the chance that the unskilled are out of employment.

3.3.1 Characterizing Worker Heterogeneity

The links between non-employment benefits, wage setting and unemployment can be better appreciated by extending futher the model developed in Chapter 2. In particular, (observable) sources of heterogeneity across individuals and segmentation in job-offer arrival rates need to be accommodated in the model.

The framework developed in the previous chapter does not say anything about how the fate of transition is shared across workers. In particular, it provides no information as to which workers are successful in moving to the new sector and which ones are more prone to become

---

[18] Actually, some differences in benefit levels and maximum duration persisted, mainly related to workers' tenure. Such differences are described in detail in Boeri and Steiner (1998), where the effects on job search associated with the exhaustion of the entitlement to unemployment benefits are also characterized.

inactive; the model focuses, after all, on the transitional dynamics of the main labour market aggregates. In order to analyse the interactions between wage-setting institutions, non-employment benefits and transitional unemployment, the model has to be made suitable for distributional analyses. This requires adding new dimensions of worker heterogeneity to those introduced in the basic model and, above all, offering some explanation—for this heterogeneity.

As argued in Chapter 2, educational attainments at the outset of transition were not particularly informative as to the workers' actual productivity in the new sector. Yet the difference between primary and secondary education and—within secondary schools—the dividing line between vocational and general secondary education is likely to have offered employers and workers themselves some clues as to the adaptability of labour to the continuously changing tasks involved by work in the new sector. Evidence from OECD countries points to a positive association between the educational attainment of the workforce and enterprise tenure, which is robust across all countries and age groups for which data are available. In particular, the average tenure of those with a university education is about 30 per cent longer than that of workers with a high-school diploma in both the United States and Japan—two countries with very different workforce tenure profiles.[19]

The reservation utility of individuals is also likely to be correlated with educational attainment. Jobseekers define their search strategies on the basis of the wage offer distribution that they face, and more educated people generally receive better wage offers than those having spent less years in formal education. Hence, well-educated people are likely to be more choosy in screening job offers than those with lower levels of education. The way in which individuals can use the time out of employment in home production is also likely to depend on educational attainments. In this respect, less time spent in schools may involve greater ability in the many manual occupations that are involved in production by household members.

Some indication of this relation between educational attainment and reservation utility of workers comes from data on the so-called 'reservation wage' (the lowest wages at which individuals would take up job offers) of unemployed individuals in Poland. A Labour Force Survey (LFS) carried out in that country at quarterly intervals since 1992 indeed contained a question on the lowest pay that the interviewee was willing

---

[19] See, in particular, Table 4.6, p. 136 of OECD (1993b).

to accept when offered a job. The average reservation wage reported has been consistently about half the actual average wage and nearly one-quarter larger than the minimum wage. It should be stressed that the question on the reservation wage is formulated in such a way as to find out whether or not the jobseeker has in mind posts outside the place of residence (likely to involve some compensation or premium for the costs of mobility) or involving reduced working time (and so covering part-time jobs). Hence, by checking all these factors, it is possible to get some comparable information about the reservation wage of individuals.[20]

Indications as to the reliability of such data come by matching observations on the same individual over time and comparing reservation wages stated when still searching a job with the actual accepted wages. Significantly, for those finding a job shortly (within two months) after the interview in which they stated their wage aspirations, the ratio of the accepted wage to the reservation wage is close to unity. This is consistent with the presence of a fairly compressed distribution of wage offers for the unemployed compared with on-the-job seekers.

According to job-search theory, the optimal stopping rule of a rational jobseeker is to continue searching until receiving an offer that lies above a given threshold, capturing the opportunity costs of employment and matching the reservation utility of the individuals. If we believe that individuals are rational in their job-search activities, then the stated reservation wage of workers should coincide with their reservation utility.

Table 3.1 shows the results obtained by running a regression of the reservation wage of Polish unemployed individuals against data from the fourth quarter of 1996 from LFS.[21] In particular, I ran the following Mincer-type earning equation:

$$\ln(w_i^*) = \alpha + \beta_0 GENDER + \beta_1 AGE_i + \beta_2 AGE_i^2 + \gamma_1 EDU_i$$
$$+ \gamma_2 EDU_i^2 + \phi UBREC_i + \varepsilon_i,$$

where w_i^* denotes the reservation wage of individual i, AGE counts the years since her/his birth (and is entered both linearly and with a quadratic term, as I suspect that age does not bear a linear relation with

---

[20] It should be stressed that the question in the survey is posed only to individuals who declare they are seeking a job, rather than to all non-employed (or employed, job-seeking) individuals.

[21] I carried out the same analysis with previous quarters and obtained results not significantly different from those shown in Table 3.1.

Table 3.1. Determinants of the reservation wage of Polish workers[a]

Variable	Urban areas		Rural areas[b]	
	coeff.	|t-stat|	coeff.	|t-stat|
Constant	5.65	46.98**	5.80	82.65**
Gender[c]	−0.15	7.76**	−0.14	13.42**
Age	0.02	2.769**	0.01	4.27**
Age^2	−0.0002	2.34*	−0.0002	3.87**
Education[d]	0.03	1.90*	0.02	1.60
Education^2	−0.0001	0.07	−0.00002	0.04
UB recipient	0.07	3.73**	0.04	4.00**
Adjusted R^2	0.14		0.12	
No. observations	768		1886	

[a]Regression results from 4Q 1996. See the text for details on the equation being estimated. One asterisk denotes significance at 90, two at 99 significance level.
[b]Districts with less than 50,000 inhabitants.
[c]0 male, 1 female.
[d]Years of schooling imputed on the basis of data on educational attainment as follows: not completed primary = 2, primary = 5, lower vocational = 8, upper vocational = 10, general secondary = 13, post secondary = 17, university = 19.
[e]1 if benefit recipient, 0 otherwise.

Notes: The (t) test of homogeneity of the education coefficients among urban and rural areas is 2.28. Thus the null hypothesis that the coefficient for education is the same in the two areas can be rejected at 98% confidence levels.

Source: Primary data from the Polish Quarterly Labour Force Survey.

w_i^*), EDU is the numbers of years of schooling of individuals, attributed on the basis of data on educational attainments and ranging from 2 (not completed primary) to 19 (tertiary education)[22]—and also entered with a linear and a quadratic term—and $UBREC$ is a dummy variable taking a value of unity when the jobseeker is receiving unemployment benefits and value zero otherwise.[23]

The inclusion of AGE is aimed at capturing the effects of the previous work experience (under the previous regime everybody was em-

[22] I prefer to use years of schooling as this eases comparisons with the (actual) earnings function estimates reproduced in Table 3.3. I tried also with educational attainment dummies, obtaining consistent results: the reservation wage–education profile in rural areas is always flatter than in urban areas.

[23] There is no need to include in the set of regressors the unemployment benefit *level* as in Poland this is a flat rate, so that the amount of the subsidy does not vary across individuals.

ployed, and hence the age of individuals is a good proxy for the length of their work record) on the wage aspirations of individuals, as well as factors likely to affect the reservation wage, such as the proximity of individuals to retirement age. The $UBREC$ variable is included in order to distinguish the actual reservation utility of individuals (or productivity in the subsistence sector) from benefits paid to the non-employed. This regression was run separately for urban areas (districts with more than 50,000 inhabitants) and for rural areas, because the effects of education on the reservation wage of individuals may vary depending on the location of jobseekers. There is evidence that enrolment rates are significantly lower in rural areas compared with urban areas (UNICEF, 1998) and, according to human capital theory, this may be an indication of lower yields from education that can be obtained outside the large towns.[24] By allowing for separate coefficients for education, I do not want to rule out the possibility that returns from education do indeed differ in the two types of regions.

All variables are signed in line with the wage distribution (see, for instance, the wage functions estimated and commented upon in section 3.4 below), suggesting that wage aspirations are consistent with actual market wage premiums. There are also marked differences in the reservation wage function between urban and rural areas. The econometric results for the urban areas point to a strongly positive and statistically significant effect of education on the reservation utility of Polish workers. The fact of having a university degree is associated in the large towns with an increase in the reservation utility of about 50 per cent with respect to individuals with only primary education.

The wage–education profile is much less marked when the focus is on rural areas. The coefficient for education is not even significant at conventional levels in this case.[25] Figure 3.1 visually characterizes the differences in the reservation-wage–education profile between the two kinds of regions. Reference is made to two male jobseekers, aged 25, resident in urban and rural areas respectively. For low levels of education, the reservation wage of the individual living in rural areas is larger

---

[24] There is some evidence of a widening gap in the quality of education between urban and rural areas. Tests of reading and mathematics conducted in 1991 and 1995 in Hungary point to a major fall in test scores of students in smaller towns and villages, compared with Budapest and the county capitals (Köllö, 1999).

[25] Unsurprisingly, standard tests of the heterogeneity of the education coefficients between rural and urban areas point to rejection of the homogeneity hypothesis. (The t-test is 4.29, which is significant at 99 per cent confidence levels.)

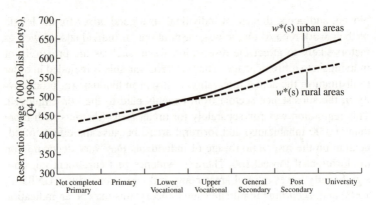

Figure 3.1. Reservation wage and education

Notes: Education-reservation wage profile estimated on the basis of the Mincer-type earnings function, as displayed in Table 3.1.: Reference is made to 25-year-old men not receiving unemployment benefits, in both urban (continuous line) and rural (dotted line) areas.

than that of the urban jobseeker, while for educational attainments above the primary level the opposite holds true. For individuals aged more than 50 of both sexes and not having completed primary education, the difference between reservation wages in rural and urban areas is almost negligible, and the urban reservation wage lies above that in rural areas for any (completed) educational attainment. However, in real terms the two curves in Figure 3.1 may still intersect, especially when one takes into account differentials in the cost of living between urban and rural areas, which may reach 30 per cent. This means that, at urban prices, the reservation wage of a male rural worker aged 50 and with only primary education could be of the order of 600,000 1996 Polish zlotys, compared with roughly 460,000 for an urban worker with the same level of education.

In both, rural and urban areas, the fact of receiving unemployment benefits involves an increase in the reservation wage. However, the labour supply shift associated with unemployment benefit receipt is larger in urban areas (where reservation wages increase by 3 per cent as a result of the subsidies) than in rural districts (where the increase in wage aspirations is of the order of 1 per cent). Thus, unemployment benefits would seem to be less important in conditioning wage claims of jobseekers in this second type of region.

What does all this tell us? There are indications that job-search strategies (optimal stopping rules) are not independent of the area of residence of individuals. Since changing residence is costly, the regional distribution of labour supply may significantly affect aggregate labour market outcomes. Put another way, reservation wages are at least partly exogenous with respect to wage setting. Factors other than the wages potentially offered to jobseekers affect the reservation wages of individuals. This is important in order to rule out reverse-causation mechanisms whereby it is actual wages, rather than reservation utilities, that influence labour-supply decisions. The way in which non-employment benefits interact with a regionally differentiated labour supply is discussed below.

3.3.2 Labour Market Transitions

The above argument suggests that it may not be unrealistic to assume that the adaptability of workers, and hence the stability of job matches in the new sector, increases with educational attainment. There is scant evidence of the relation between duration of a match and educational attainment in transitional economies (and, in any event, available data are not easy to interpret, given the short history of the new sector in these countries and the occurrence, at the outset of transition, of many voluntary quits from the old sector). Controlling for other factors, like age and gender, the workers with the lowest levels of education have the shortest tenure—this is consistent with evidence from OECD countries (OECD, 1997), although the relationship between tenure and education is flatter in the CEECs than in OECD countries. For instance, in Poland in 1996 the share of workers with primary or lower educational attainments with tenures less than one year (roughly 20 per cent) was only slightly larger than the same share for workers with tertiary education (18 per cent). Interestingly, the largest share of workers with short tenures is observed in the case of workers with vocational education. This seems to support the notion, embedded in the model discussed in Chapter 2, that vocational education in these countries had a particularly narrow base.

The evidence presented in the previous section also suggests that there are significant differences in the shape of the relation between reservation utility and education between urban and rural areas. While it seems legitimate from the foregoing results to model reservation utilities of urban workers as increasing in educational attainments, labour supply in rural areas can be more safely modelled as if it were independent of the years spent by individuals in formal education.

As spelled out in Annex 3., even without making strong restrictions as to the shape of the relation between educational attainment, job tenure and the reservation utility of workers, there are quite a number of results that can be obtained about the way in which transition affects the various groups and the aggregate labour-market outcomes.

The fact that workers' fungibility (and hence the stability of job matches) is associated with observed characteristics of individuals creates a segmentation of the labour market along these dimensions. Employers will issue vacancies not only by recruitment pool, as was the case in the model presented in Chapter 2, but also by educational attainment of workers: that is to say, jobs will only be offered to workers with a given educational attainment. Similarly workers with a university degree will only look for jobs corresponding to their qualifications. Thus, wage bargaining and job matching will be differentiated by educational attainment of the workforce.[26]

For the old sector, it is another story. Here, tasks are standardized, and hence it is unlikely that educational attainments can affect workers' tenures. Nor does education influence the wage of individuals: there is evidence of significant wage compression in state firms.[27] Put bluntly, in the model in Annex 3. employers of the old firms do not have a distinction between highly educated and less educated people: they pay all workers alike.

The final assumption concerns the location of the new jobs. I assume that wage setting in the new sector takes as reference the reservation utility of the urban workers. This is consistent with evidence from all transition countries, pointing to a concentration of new jobs and vacancies in urban areas, where new service activities are developed.

How does all this affect labour-market outcomes? They will clearly vary by region and educational attainment of individuals. Moreover, they will be affected by the structure of non-employment benefits, notably their relation with previous earnings. We will first consider the main

[26] Wage setting, however, is not allowed to vary across regions. Vacancies are issued nationwide, irrespective of the area of residence of applicants (any variation from this being in conflict with basic constitutional principle in the countries under consideration).

[27] This is consistent with the observation of highly compressed wage structures in state enterprises, especially at the outset of transition (Svejnar, 1999). The fact that wage premiums on education are virtually absent in the old sector may also have to do with other factors, such as the role of unions, the relevance of fixed, non-monetary, components of the compensation package (for instance, access to social assets of the enterprise), and the possibility for the unskilled to combine work in the state sector with secondary (often) informal jobs.

results of the model as to labour-market outcomes by region and level of education. Later on, we will summarize these results by highlighting the role played by earning-related versus flat non-employment benefits.

Let us consider first urban areas. We already know from Chapter 2 that only the workers with the highest reservation utility will quit into non-employment at the outset of transition. Coupled with the education–reservation-wage profile documented above, this means that the most educated people are more likely to quit from the old sector into non-employment than the least educated ones:[28] if anybody leaves the old sector to become inactive, these will not be the unskilled. More precisely, this will happen when non-employment benefits set at the outset of transition (remember that all quits to non-employment occur the first period in the model) are earning-related, as was the case of early-retirement schemes proposed in the initial years of economic transformation.

This goes contrary to the inspiration of the policies carried out in many CEECs, which were aimed at reducing labour supply among the less educated (and oldest) segments of the working-age population. The unskilled workers in urban areas are actually those most attached to the old-sector jobs, partly because of the fact that wage compression therein rewards those less educated,[29] and partly because, if they become unemployed, they would have a rather low probability of finding a job in the new sector (and it is likely that they will search for one since they have a low productivity in home/informal production).

Hence, the model suggests that the observed relatively large flows from the old sector to unemployment of low-skilled individuals in urban areas are mainly a by-product of self-selection, where workers of this type stay attached to their previous jobs as long as they can while those more educated quit either to the new sector or to inactivity. Moreover, as quits to the new sector occur via a time-consuming matching process, the proportion of the unskilled in the pool of old sector workers gradually increases (and, consequently, the proportion of unskilled workers involved in layoffs from the old sector steadily increases over time).

All this is consistent with the observation in many transitional

---

[28] Interestingly, this holds even if the probability of finding a job in the new sector increases with the educational attainment of individuals. One may have thought that the effect of education on the value of non-employment (and hence on the decision to quit into non-employment) could be offset by a greater chance to find a job in the new sector for those staying.

[29] See Rutkowski (1997) for evidence that less-educated and low-paid workers are better off in the state sector than in the private sector.

economies of unemployment pools with a relatively high proportion of educated people at the outset of transition, especially in urban areas, and an increasing proportion of unskilled people at later stages of the transformation.[30] In urban areas, generous non-employment benefits tend to increase flows of highly educated people to inactivity (especially if benefits are earning-related) and make it more difficult for the unskilled unemployed to find a job, notably when non-employment benefits are flat or, in any event, strongly progressive.

The relation between education and labour-force participation will be significantly different in rural areas. While, in urban areas, for low levels of education (low reservation utility) searching is more rewarding than inactivity, and hence the unskilled can only be either employed or unemployed, under flat benefits in rural areas the decision to become inactive will be made mainly by those with low levels of education because of the higher reservation utility (associated with home production in the context of family-run agricultural business and casual working on family plots) that less-educated people enjoy in rural areas compared with their urban counterparts. Put another way, in rural areas either non-employment benefits should decline or wages should increase in order to stimulate larger participation (larger flows from non-employment to the new sector) of less-educated workers.

Summing up, we can see that our model predicts that in urban areas there should be a higher number of less-educated people among the unemployed, while in rural areas unemployment should be more evenly distributed across education groups because of decisions to withdraw from the labour force (or at least from formal employment-unemployment) made therein at the lower end of the education distribution.

Another interesting, and quite unorthodox, implication of the model is that non-employment benefits, by setting a floor to wage setting in the new sector, may actually end up fostering the reallocation of labour from the old sector to the new sector. In the absence of such a floor to wage setting in the new sector, unskilled workers in the old sector will have everything to lose by moving to the new sector, which offers lower

[30] Typical is the case of Bulgaria, where the unemployment pool was initially dominated by persons with a secondary or tertiary education. Cazes and Scarpetta (1998) also report increasing proportions of less-educated people in inflows into unemployment in urban areas. For instance, in Warsaw, the proportion of workers with primary or lower levels of education in total inflows increased from 16 per cent in 1990 to 37 per cent in 1993.

wages and less job security. This unorthodox implication of the model originates from the compression of wage structures in the old sector. Were wages allowed to vary by skill level (with productivity significantly varying by level of education) also in the old sector, there would be no need for a wage floor in the new sector in order to induce voluntary shifts of the unskilled workers from low-productivity to high-productivity jobs.

These effects of low benefits on structural change are magnified when a large fraction of the population is located in rural areas or when urban–rural migration is accounted for. When benefits are negligible for the unskilled, there are strong incentives for the unskilled to migrate to rural areas because therein they can live on family plots devoting their time to home production. These incentives are stronger when the cost of moving from urban to rural areas is smaller than the cost of moving the other way round and the real value of benefits is higher in rural areas.

Overall, the model suggests that, in the design of non-employment benefits, there is a trade-off involving unemployment, earnings inequality and structural change, and that both high *and* low benefits for the unskilled may generate locking-in effects at the microeconomic level. High benefits will generate persistence of unemployment, notably in rural areas, while low benefits will discourage shifts from the old to the new sector, locking in many unskilled individuals in unproductive employment.

Under *flat benefits*, relatively generous transfers provided to those without a job tend to bias job creation against the unskilled. In so far as the less-educated workers are the majority, generous benefits increase non-employment throughout the transition period. In rural areas, non-employment among the unskilled mainly results in non-participation, while in urban areas it leads to long-term unemployment. Moreover, a flat benefits system compresses the wage distribution from below, both by putting a floor to wage setting in the new sector and by reducing the number of less-educated individuals in employment (either unemployed, in urban areas, or inactive, in rural areas).

Under an *earnings-related benefit system*, the wage distribution will be compressed only from above, owing to the self-selection of the better educated, who are induced to become inactive. Thus, contrary to the goals of policies to reduce the labour supply, which have been pursued in many CEECs, the rather generous (and often earning-related) bridging schemes to retirement provided at the outset may end-up reducing participation of highly educated individuals in urban areas. While earning-related benefits reduce differences in the duration of unemployment by level of education, they will also reduce the amount of job-to-job shifts occurring from the old to the new sector because unskilled workers will find it more profitable to stay as long as they can in the old sector. Put another way, earning-related systems may negatively affect the speed of reallocation, because they increase the value of the 'wait-until-you-lose-your-job' option for the less-educated individuals—who are, after all, the larger fraction of the workforce in all countries. When benefits replace only a very small fraction of previous earnings, unskilled workers will try as much as they can to remain attached to the old sector (just like the Russian workers remaining in state enterprises in spite of mounting wage arrears). If they become unemployed, they will, whenever possible, move to rural areas, drawing on rural family networks.

In conclusion, the model spelled out in Annex 3. suggests that non-employment benefits having the chance to maximize employment (reducing both unemployment and inactivity) should be earning-related at the lower end of the wage distribution and flat (though by establishing appropriate benefit ceilings) at the upper end. However, if the objective of policy makers is to foster job reallocation from the old to the new sector and the non-employment generated in the process is not a major concern, then a flat-rate system—or an earning-related system with binding benefit minima—may be more adequate. We find both kinds of non-employment benefits in transitional economies. Therefore these implications of the model can shed some light on the wide cross-country variation in the levels and growth of unemployment, and hopefully on differences in the speed of reallocation as well. This will be attempted in the next section, where the model will also be used to understand the reasons for the regional unemployment disparities present in the countries under consideration and their underlying dynamics.

There are design features of non-employment benefits that can make this trade-off between, on the one hand, high non-employment and fast structural change and, on the other hand, high earning inequality and low structural change somewhat less stringent. Such features will be discussed in Chapter 4. The task set out for this chapter is to characterize the different adjustment trajectories prevailing in transitional economies. Hence, the focus will be only on the positive implications of the model.

3.4 The Large-Scale Unemployment Differentials across Countries and Regions

Can the above framework shed some light on the wide differences in the incidence of unemployment that we notice both *across* transitional economies and *within* each formerly planned economy? This section starts by empirically assessing the relation between the structure of non-employment benefits and earnings dispersion, which is at the core of the model. Then the specific features of labour-market adjustment in Russia and the former Soviet republics are compared with developments in the CEECs. Finally, regional labour-market imbalances and their persistence over time are analysed.

3.4.1 Unemployment Benefits and Cross-Country Differences in the Distribution of Earnings

The model outlined in the previous section builds on the assumption that non-employment benefits are the single most important factor imposing a floor to wage setting throughout transition. An implication of the model is that rather generous and flat benefits, unrelated to previous earnings, compress from below the wage distribution and reduce employment rates for the unskilled. While an increase in earnings inequality was expected to occur everywhere in the countries under consideration, given the relatively low degree of dispersion of the pay structures inherited from their previous systems, it is interesting to evaluate the extent to which the shift towards more dispersed wage structures has occurred in the various countries and its relation to available measures of the dispersion of the distribution of non-employment benefits.

Table 3.2 produces evidence of the structure of non-employment benefits and of the dispersion of earnings in the CEECs and Russia. Two kinds of benefits are taken into account: unemployment benefits, and social assistance of the last resort provided to able-bodied individuals of working age. The distinction between unemployment benefits and social assistance is blurred by the presence in many countries of so-called 'unemployment assistance' schemes, which are a cross between unemployment benefits (in so far as eligibility is conditional to being unemployed) and social assistance (because they are, in frequent cases, subject to a means test—a check that the household has income and assets below a given 'minimum living standard'). In Table 3.2. only the dividing line between means-tested and non-means-tested cash transfers

Table 3.2. Non-employment benefits and the distribution of earnings (1992–3 for all countries)

Country	Summary generosity measure[a]			Minimum benefit[b] (% average wage) 1995	Measures of earning dispersion[c]		
	A) at 2 times the average wage	B) at 2/3 of the average wage	A/B		ΔGini (%) 1990-3	Δdecile ratio 1990-3	ΔLow-pay[b] 1990-3
Bulgaria	27	68	0.40	20	0.04	0.56	4.6
	18	*47*	*0.38*	*17*	—	—	—
Czech Republic	23	59	0.39	no minimum	0.06	0.69	1.9
	21	*52*	*0.40*	*30*			
Hungary	27	55	0.49	35	0.02	0.27	0.8
	18	*50*	*0.36*	*25*			
Poland	16	51	0.31	36	0.03	0.39	1.6
	14	*46*	*0.30*	*28*			
Romania	30	54	0.56	23	0.05	0.62	7.4
	16	*40*	*0.40*	*16*			
Russia	24	28	0.84	no minimum	0.25	—	—
	8	*11*	*0.73*	*no minimum*			
Slovak Republic	23	57	0.40	10	—	—	—
	22	*53*	*0.42*	*32*			

[a] Average of the (gross) nominal replacement rates inclusive of social assistance (SA) for one-person households in the first two years of unemployment. In italics are the measures obtained by applying benefit indexation mechanisms (if any) to actual inflation rates 1992–3.
[b] Statutory minimum benefit. Normal characters denote unemployment benefits (UB), italicized figures SA. As minima are either set in terms of the minimum wage, minimum pension or arbitrarily fixed by governments, the data displayed in the table are actual average 1992–3 minima.   [c] ΔGini = first difference in the Gini coefficient; Δ Decile ratio = first difference in upper decile to bottom decile ratio; Δlow-pay = first difference in the % of workers receiving wages lower than two-thirds of the median wage (for Czech Republic, Poland and Romania the base year is 1989).

Notes: See Boeri and Edwards (1998) for details on unemployment-benefit and social-assistance schemes in the various countries. '—' = not available

Source: For data on earnings dispersion, Milanovic (1997); Rutkowski (1996) and Vecernik (1996). For data on non-employment benefits, Boeri and Edwards (1998).

is emphasized, because it is important in terms of work incentives let alone considerations relating to the distributive effects of income support schemes for the unemployed. In particular, the term 'unemployment benefit' is used in the table to characterize only the *non-means-tested* segment of schemes offered to individuals seeking a job. Reference is made to social assistance (SA) as inclusive of all *means-tested* income support schemes of the last resort offered to the non-employed having exhausted the maximum duration of benefits or, if necessary, to 'top up' the incomes of unemployment benefit recipients not reaching a given income threshold, in the countries where a 'guaranteed minimum income' scheme is in place.[31] Provision of SA to able-bodied individuals is often conditional upon their registration at labour offices as unemployed and the passing of a work test (a check of their willingness to take up job offers, for instance through a slot on some public works scheme).

As discussed in Chapter 2, unemployment benefits have undergone major reforms in these countries, notably after the first big shock of transition at the end of 1991. Because it is likely that the impact of benefit structures on earning distributions is felt with some lags, Table 3.2 refers to the structure of non-employment benefits prevailing after the 1991–2 reforms. The compression of the benefits structure and its relation with previous earnings is evaluated on the basis of a battery of indicators. Some of them are supplied by the regulations themselves, and hence are truly exogenous in the sense that they are not affected by the incidence of unemployment at different wage levels. Others, instead, are based on actual cash transfers being provided to households, and hence are influenced by the composition of the pool of benefit recipients (for example, overrepresentation of the unskilled). The two kinds of indicators are complementary in so far as regulations by themselves cannot highlight the impact on inflation of the compression of benefits, while actual payments suffer from the selectivity problems (the fact that benefits are compressed simply because only the low paid are unemployed) that we discussed above.

The first two columns of Table 3.2 provide summary 'generosity' measures (an average of the degree of replacement of the previous earn-

---

[31] In principle, a further distinction should be made between social assistance offered *only to the unemployed* (mainly to unemployment benefit 'exhaustees') and *general* social assistance offered to all poor households, irrespective of whether or not they include unemployed individuals. A common denominator between the two kinds of schemes is that both depend on an income and asset test, and hence almost by definition target the household as opposed to the individual.

ings offered by benefits over the first two years[32] of an unemployment spell) at different income levels. The figures in roman type describe the (nominal) replacement rates prescribed by the regulations, which would prevail in the absence of inflation; the data in italics are estimates of the actual replacement rate obtained by applying regulations concerning the indexation (if any) of benefits to actual data on changes in consumer prices. This is because I have made an attempt at capturing the effects of the benefits indexation mechanism on the actual compression of non-employment benefits. The third column is simply the ratio between benefit generosity for the high-wage cases (those paid twice the average wage) and the summary replacement rates for low-paid individuals (those with previous earnings corresponding to two-thirds of the average wage).

As shown by Table 3.2, in *nominal* terms the benefits system offering the largest replacement of previous earnings to those at the top of the wage distribution is the Romanian system, followed by the Hungarian unemployment-benefit-cum-social-assistance schemes. However, when account is taken of inflation, the picture changes significantly. Hungary now appears—together with Bulgaria, Romania and Poland—to have a benefits system that replaces no more than 20 per cent of the earnings of those located at the top of the wage distribution, whilst the Czech and Slovak systems appear to be more generous with respect to those who were earning twice the average wage in their previous job. The system that in nominal terms would appear to be more generous in relation to low-income earners is the Bulgarian one. Although inflation significantly erodes replacement rates also in this case, it does so to a lesser degree than in the case of high wage earners. The indexation mechanism present in countries such as Bulgaria, Hungary and Romania is indeed one that promotes redistribution in favour of low-income earners.

An indicator of the extent to which non-employment benefits maintain a link with previous earnings is provided by the third column of Table 3.2, which provides the ratio of the generosity measures for high-income earners to that of low-wage individuals. Rather strikingly, there is a significant variation across countries in the way in which non-employment benefits preserve the dispersion of earnings, rather than redistributing in favour of the low-income earners. The country whose

---

[32] In most of these countries the average duration of unemployment is longer than one year. Thus, generosity measures are computed with reference to unemployment spells lasting more than 12 months.

system best preserves wage relativities is Russia, followed by Romania and the Czech and Slovak republics, while a strong redistribution occurs in Poland and Hungary (especially when account is taken of inflation). In Hungary, the ratio of the generosity measure for those earning twice the average wage and two-thirds of it is not much higher than in Poland, the only country in the table having an *explicit* flat-rate system in place (and, given that the latter is almost fully indexed,[33] not experiencing benefit compression as a result of inflation). Clearly the indicator displayed in the third column of the table is designed in such a way as to capture the relation of benefits with previous earnings no matter how generous the system is as a whole: the Russian non-employment benefits system appears, by and large, the least generous one, because replacement rates are, for low-income earners, only of the order of 10 per cent in real terms.

The fourth column offers a measure of the generosity of the benefit floor in the various countries, in other words the ratio of this benefit to the country-wide average wage. Italicized figures in this case denote social assistance minima, while those in roman type are the minimum unemployment benefit figures. As minima are often arbitrarily set by governments, actual (as opposed to statutory) benefit minima and average wage data in the 1992–3 period have been used. Especially when the focus is on social assistance (which, unlike unemployment benefits, is either open-ended or renewable), the non-employment benefit floors appear to be lower in Bulgaria and Romania than in the other CEECs. The differences are even more marked if we bear in mind that the Bulgarian and the Romanian systems have a much flatter progression with household scale than in the other countries. For example, although in the Czech and Slovak republics the levels of social assistance for no-earner households with two dependent children reached about 100 per cent of the average wage in 1995, in Bulgaria it did not exceed 40 per cent. Moreover, one should factor in the lower coverage of social assistance in Bulgaria and Romania in comparison with countries like the Czech and Slovak republics.

Overall, among CEECs, Romania and Bulgaria are those with lower benefit minima and a closer relation of the benefit to previous earnings, or those involving less redistribution in favour of the low-income earners. The international differences are more striking when comparisons are

---

[33] In Poland, flat-rate benefits are fully adjusted to past inflation at quarterly frequencies.

made between, on the one hand, the Visegrad group and, on the other hand, Russia. Here, unemployment benefit minima coincide with the minimum wage, which under the hyperinflation of 1992 fell to about 10 per cent of the average wage and never regained the ground lost. Moreover, in Russia as in most of the former Soviet republics, there are no national standards for the provision of social assistance and there is a virtual absence of fiscal transfers across regions enabling the poorest oblasts to pay social assistance of the last resort. Nominal replacement rates for high-income earners may appear of the order of those provided in CEECs, but in real terms they are negligible for all groups. It is often claimed that in Russia and in most of the former Soviet republics there is virtually no unemployment benefits system in place, and it is difficult to disagree with this point of view.

Finally, the three columns on the right-hand side of Table 3.2 provide measures of the variance of the earnings distribution. As there were significant differences in initial conditions across countries[34]—for instance Hungary had a rather unequal pay distribution, while the former Czechoslovakia was the case at the opposite extreme in terms of earnings inequality—we have tabulated the *changes* in standard indicators of inequality (Gini coefficients and the decile ratio, the latter being the ratio of the top quintile to the bottom quintile of the earnings distribution). We have also provided information on the extent of low pay, defined as the percentage of workers earning less than two-thirds of the median wage. Acknowledging problems with cross-country comparisons of earning inequality measures,[35] the table shows that Russia by and large experienced the strongest increase in earning inequality. The asymmetry between Russia and the CEECs is even more marked when account is taken of the fact that Gini coefficients available for Russia refer to the distribution of overall income rather than to the distribution of *earnings* as in the other countries; and, typically, earnings are more dispersed than incomes, given the role played by cash-transfer mechanisms in reducing inequality.

Significant increases in earnings inequality and, above all, in the inci-

[34] These differences in initial conditions are well characterized in Atkinson and Micklewright (1992).

[35] Andorka *et al.* (1997) as well as Garner and Terrell (1998) suggest that data problems may have led observers to underestimate the extent of earnings inequality in Hungary and overestimate it in the Czech Republic. The overall ranking of countries in terms of inequality is, however, unchanged even after taking into account their 'corrected' Gini coefficients. These issues are further discussed in Chapter 4.

dence of low pay were recorded also in Bulgaria, Romania and the Czech Republic. Needless to say, these are all countries with relatively low benefit floors (at least after taking inflation into account) and a closer link between past earnings and the distribution of non-employment benefits. Hungary and Poland—the countries with flatter benefits and higher min-ima[36]—experienced a much less marked increase in earning inequality and in the extent of low pay.

All in all, consistently with the theoretical results discussed in the previous section, the countries with the largest dispersion in the structure of non-employment benefits have experienced the largest increases in the inequality of the earnings distribution. Although it is difficult to draw causal inferences from international comparisons involving such a few observations, and differences within the CEEC group are sometimes of second-order magnitude, the evidence does not contradict the view that the design of non-employment benefits plays an important role in affecting changes in the pay distribution.

According to the model characterized in Annex 3., the relationship between the distributions of benefits and earnings is to a large extent driven by self-selection; that is to say, under relatively high benefit floors the least educated and less productive workers are either subject to long-duration unemployment (and hence are underrepresented in the employment pool) or decide to withdraw from the labour force altogether (as is likely to happen, according to the model, especially in rural areas). These selection effects can be better assessed by econometric estimates of the earning functions, notably by including terms correcting for the probability of not being employed.

Table 3.3 shows estimates of Mincer-type wage equations in all countries for which individual earning data were available. In particular, two specifications of the wage equation are, whenever possible, offered: the first specification does *not* control for selectivity bias (that is, it does not include a term reflecting the probability that the individual is employed, and hence earning a wage), while the second includes a so-called Heckman correction term.[37]

---

[36] This is evident when comparing minima provided by the unemployment benefits: the Czech and Slovak systems have no unemployment benefit minima, while Hungary and Poland have one at about 35 per cent of the average wage.

[37] This second equation is specified as follows:
$$\ln(w_i) = \alpha + \beta_0 GENDER + \beta_1 AGE_i + \beta_2 AGE_i^2 + \gamma_1 EDU_i + \gamma_2 EDU_i^2 + \phi\lambda_i + \varepsilon_i$$
where the notation is as previously used in this chapter and λ is the selectivity term estimated by running a probit of the probability of being employed against the same set

The estimated earnings functions confirm the impression given by Table 3.2 concerning the greater wage dispersion present in Russia compared with Poland and Hungary. Gender wage differentials and wage premiums placed on those who are older and having a higher educational attainment are, other things being equal, larger in Russia than in Hungary and Poland. However, when self-selection is taken into account, the coefficients of the Polish earnings function appear much closer to those for Russia.[38] Moreover, the Heckman correction term is statistically significant in Poland, but not in Russia. It is also significant in the Czech and Slovak republics, for which LFS could only tabulate individual earnings information grouped in a discrete number of wage cells. While this data constraint can be addressed by estimating earnings functions with methods allowing for limited dependent variables (for example, order probit regressions) or by taking the mid-point within each wage cell,[39] it is not advisable to make comparisons of the Czech earnings function with those estimated in the other countries, which could also exploit the variation within groups.

Overall, the fact that some education groups are underrepresented among the ranks of the employed would seem to affect earnings dispersion only in the CEECs, while it does not seem to reduce earning differentials in Russia. This is also consistent with the implications of the model, which suggests that under low and earning-related unemployment benefits, selectivity bias should not be a major issue.

3.4.2 Where is Russian Unemployment?

I remember having attended meetings where Russian labour economists and Western scholars of statistics in formerly planned economies were desperately trying to show in various ways that Russian unemployment really did exist. The puzzling fact that was making them so anxious is shown in Fig. 3.2. In spite of its steep output falls, Russia has experienced since 1990 a much slower decline of employment (and growth of

of regressors plus a dummy capturing the area of residence. This amounts to weighting observations based on their likelihood of being in the sample. In so far as education and age are positively correlated with the probability of being employed, omission of the selectivity term is likely to bias the estimated wage premiums downwards.

[38] Unfortunately, in the case of Hungary, it was not possible to implement Heckman two-step procedures because we did not have data on wages and labour market status (allowing estimation of the probability of being employed and hence computation of the various inverse Mills ratios) from the same statistical source.

[39] I tried with both methods, and the results were broadly consistent. In both cases, the Heckman correction term turned out to be significant.

Table 3.3. Wage structures and self-selection: estimates of mincerian earning functions for private enterprises

Variable	Czech Republic[a] 1994 Q4		Poland 1994 Q4		Hungary 1995	Russia 1995	
Constant	1.01**	2.31**	7.90**	10.16**	8.90**	6.22**	5.62**
	(0.05)	(0.10)	(0.10)	(0.07)	(0.02)	(0.33)	(0.37)
Gender[b]	0.10**	0.23**	0.27**	0.28**	0.20**	0.30**	0.28**
	(0.00)	(0.00)	(0.01)	(0.01)	(0.00)	(0.35)	(0.04)
Age	0.02**	0.03**	0.01	0.05**	0.03**	0.04**	0.04**
	(0.00)	(0.00)	(0.01)	(0.00)	(0.00)	(0.01)	(0.01)
Age^2	−0.0002**	0.0003**	1.00E-05	8.00E-04**	0.00**	−4.00E-04**	−4.77E-04**
	(0.00)	(0.00)	(0.00)	(0.00)	(0.00)	(0.00)	(0.00)
Years education[c]	0.06**	0.02**	0.07**	0.10**	0.02**	0.06	0.07
	(0.01)	(0.01)	(0.01)	(0.01)	(0.00)	(0.05)	(0.05)
$Years\ education^2$	−0.002**	−0.001**	−5.00E-04	0.01**	0.00**	0.00	0.00
	(0.00)	(0.00)	(0.00)	(3.00E-04)	(0.00)	(0.00)	(0.00)
Heckman correction		−0.32**		−0.29**			0.017
		(0.00)		(0.01)			(0.04)
Adj. R^2	0.05		0.54		0.30	0.06	
Nr. obs	27646	37353	11385	36577	153382	2898	4542

[a]Wage data are reported according to 8 classes: average values among these cells were taken (similar results were obtained by running ordered probit regressions).
[b]Male = 1, Female = 0.

Notes: Standard errors in parentheses. One asterisk denotes significance at 95, two at 99 per cent.

Source: For the Czech Republic LFS Q4 1994; for Poland LFS Q4 1994; for Hungary National Labour Centre Wage Survey 1995; for Russia Longitudinal Monitoring Survey, 1995.

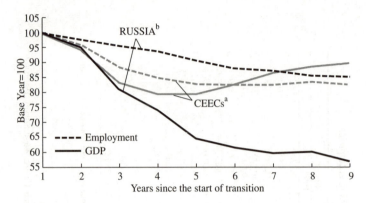

Figure 3.2. Employment and output adjustment: Central and Eastern European countries and Russia

[a] Unweighted average, 1989 = 100.

[b] 1990 = 100.

Source: EBRD, *Transition Report 1998*.

unemployment) than other transitional economies. While in the CEECs employment just lagged behind output adjustment (labour productivity declined in the early years of the transitional recessions and started to rise as soon as the recovery began—a behaviour broadly in line with cyclical movements of output and employment in OECD countries), in Russia the gap between employment and output has been steadily widening.

In order to explain the low responsiveness of employment and unemployment to output declines in Russia, a number of factors were mentioned in these meetings, relating mainly to measurement issues. In particular, first, the fact that administrative counts of the unemployed tend to underestimate the extent of labour slack when unemployment benefits are low and, second, the widespread use of unpaid leave for employees were pointed out as two factors capable of explaining the puzzle.

However, when LFS results—hence data unbiased by regulations and comparable across countries—became available, they replicated the gap between CEECs and Russian unemployment. Unpaid leave (or, worse, unpaid work, given the emergence of wage arrears in Russia) could not therefore be used to explain the puzzle. If one stays attached to one's job even if one does not get paid, there should be a reason for it. Often, the unemployed are without a job because they refuse to work for lower salaries and are not ready to consider the possibility of not being paid at all. The puzzling fact about wage arrears in Russia is that workers do not quit their jobs when they are not paid.

The model discussed in the previous section fits the 'Russian puzzle' quite well and may contribute to unfolding its secret. The model implies that a more dispersed earnings distribution, namely one where there are no floors to wage setting imposed by cash transfers to those without a job, is the one that maximizes employment throughout transition. Russia is clearly a case in point: there are virtually no benefit minima, and benefit relativities apply that replicate differences in earnings at 85 per cent. The model also contributes to a downplay of two common, and rather extreme, ways of evaluating labour-market adjustments in Russia. If you believe in this framework, Russia is neither a 'neo-classical dream'—*the* example of a flexible labour market (Layard and Richter, 1995)—nor a land where firing costs are high and prevent employment adjustment (Commander *et al.*, 1998), forcing enterprises to 'hoard' labour (Aukutsionek and Kapeliushnikov, 1996). More simply, due to the virtual absence of non-employment benefits, wages had to bear fully the weight of adjustment in Russia, while elsewhere it was mainly labour—that is, quantities rather than prices—that had to be adjusted.

The Russian way minimizes employment losses at the early stages of transition but keeps more workers, namely the unskilled, attached to the old jobs. Thus, it generates locking-in effects in unproductive—and, often, unpaid—employment. By this means, urban workers maintain a formal attachment to the state sector and meanwhile carry out informal activities, or they migrate to rural areas in order to survive on individual plots. Household survey data on Russia (from the Longitudinal Monitoring Survey[40]) well document the dimensions of informal employment and the locking-in effects that it generates. The data indicate a steady increase in the number of individuals combining employment in the old sector with informal activities and increasing proportions of the population living on individual plots. Thus, the Russian way has high efficiency costs: there is a high cost to maintaining many individuals in unproductive jobs, rather than prompting them to seek jobs in the new sector. The Russian way also generates non-employment in the long run, like the other adjustment strategy followed by the CEECs.

---

[40] The question being asked was 'Did you engage in the last 30 days in some additional kind of work for which you got pay?'. Among the guided answers were: 'I sewed someone's dress'; 'I gave someone a ride in a car'; 'I assisted someone with repairs to an apartment or a car'; 'I purchased and delivered food'; and 'I looked after a sick person'.

Significantly, in Russia there has been much less structural change than in the CEECs. Table 3.4 summarizes data on non-employment benefit floors, on the adjustment to output losses of employment versus wages, and on the extent of structural change in the Visegrad group, in the Balkanic group, and in Russia. Table 3.4 documents the two different adjustment patterns outlined above: indeed, Russia displays much less marked employment-to-output elasticities and larger real wage declines than the countries of Visegrad and the two Balkanic countries. Strikingly enough, the standard deviation of employment growth rates across sectors (as well as the other measure of structural change, the SR Index, described in Chapter 1) in Russia have been typically between one-half and two-thirds of the level observed in other transitional economies. This asymmetry in the speed of structural change is even more marked when account is taken of initial conditions: the employment structure of countries such as Hungary was much closer to market economies at comparable GDP per capita levels than those of the Balkanic group or of Russia (Jackman and Pauna, 1997). In other words, the other side of the coin of low unemployment has been low structural change.[41] Also, from an equity standpoint, maximizing employment may not be preferable to having less employment and more redistribution, particularly if the dynamic costs of keeping obsolete jobs in existence are large. Such equity issues will be more thoroughly discussed in Chapter 4.

In the same way that, in the presence of relatively high non-employment benefit floors, unemployment hit those with lower levels of education disproportionately, differences in the incidence of unemployment across countries with similar non-employment benefit structures may be the by-product of a different distribution of the population by educational attainment. As documented above, Hungary, Poland and the former Czechoslovakia are all characterized by rather compressed structures of non-employment benefits, involving a significant redistribution in favour of low wage earners. The Czech Republic had the lowest proportion of the labour force with primary or lower levels of education and higher enrolment rates in secondary education than any other country in the region, including its former partner, Slovakia. The above may offer an additional explanation for

---

[41] Not necessarily low worker turnover. There is indeed evidence in Russia of significant churning at the enterprise level (OECD, 1997a). Significantly, while in CEECs state enterprises froze hires, in Russia the large conglomerates of the pre-transition era continued to hire throughout the transition process. This is another indication of the attachment of workers to old jobs when no benefit floor is provided.

Table 3.4. Non-employment benefit minima and structural change

Country	Benefit minima (% average wage)	Employment–output elasticity[a]	Real wages decline[b]	Standard deviation employment growth	SR Index[c]
Visegrad group[d]	29	0.91	19	17	0.55
Balkanic group[e]	17	0.73	41	11	0.48
Russia	10	0.31	57	9	0.39

[a]Employment–output elasticity, meaning employment growth/output growth, during the 'transitional recession' (1990–3, except for Russia 1990–5 and Poland 1989–92).

[b]Percentage change in real wages over the same period, considered in the case of employment-to-output elasticity (except for Russia, 1990–5).

[c]Sectoral reallocation coefficient defined as follows: SR = 1− NET/(POS+NEG) where POS and NEG denote the sum of employment variations in expanding and declining sectors, respectively. See Chapter 1 and the list of abbreviations in this book for details.

[d]Czech Republic, Hungary, Poland and the Slovak Republic.

[e]Bulgaria and Romania.

Notes: Benefit minima include social assistance and refer to 1995 (see Table 3.2).

Source: The same as in Table 3.2 for non-employment benefits. OECD-CEET, Short-term Economic Indicators for primary data on employment (also by sector) and output. Vienna Institute for International Economic Studies (WIIW) for data on wages.

unemployment differentials between the two former twin federal states.

One factor that may instead have played some role in increasing differences in the incidence of unemployment (and, above all, its association with output declines) between, on the one hand, the four Visegrad countries, and, on the other, Romania and Russia are differentials in the concentration of population in rural areas. In Russia, more than 70 per cent of the population lives in rural areas compared with an average of about 40 per cent in the Visegrad group. In Romania the share of the population in rural areas is slightly above that of the Central European countries (46 per cent). More importantly perhaps, the privatization of agriculture did not lead to concentration of arable land as in other CEECs, but favoured the creation of relatively small plots (averaging about two hectares of land per owner). [42] According to the model spelled out in Annex 3, the same non-employment benefit system may generate less unemployment when a larger proportion of the population is located in rural areas, as unskilled non-employed individuals in rural areas are more likely to leave the labour force altogether and devote their time to household-based production rather than seeking jobs in the formal sector.

3.4.3 Regional Inequalities

A third implication of the model is that, under flat-rate non-employment benefits, urban areas will experience a concentration of unemployment—notably long-term unemployment—among the unskilled, while rural areas will display a more balanced incidence of unemployment across all education groups. This is because, according to the model, individuals with lower educational attainments are likely to leave the labour force altogether in rural areas. Put another way, while the distribution by education of non-employment rates should not be significantly different between the two kind of regions, we can expect rural areas to display a larger proportion of persons of working age and without a job who are not actively seeking employment.

Table 3.5 shows non-employment and long-term unemployment rates by educational attainment in urban and rural areas. The information comes from LFS sources, which allow better discrimination between unemployment and inactivity than administrative sources. For purposes of cross-country comparability (data on the size of the district of residence are available only for Bulgaria and Poland), urban areas are defined herein as the regions with a major urban centre.

---

[42] See Bobeva and Hristoskov, 1995.

Table 3.5. Educational attainment, non-employment and the urban/rural divide

Country	Non-employment rate			Long term unemployment rate		
	urban	rural	urban/rural differential	urban	rural	urban/rural differential
Bulgaria						
Total	42.5%	56.3%	−13.8%	6.1%	9.7%	−3.6%
of which						
primary education	68.9%	67.9%	1.0%	13.8%	13.1%	0.7%
secondary education	34.7%	36.6%	−1.9%	4.9%	6.4%	−1.4%
tertiary education	17.9%	28.2%	−10.2%	2.4%	5.1%	−2.7%
Coefficient of variation	0.26	0.21		0.06	0.04	
Czech Republic						
Total	73.5%	71.4%	2.1%	0.8%	1.1%	−0.3%
of which						
primary education	37.4%	35.3%	2.1%	1.8%	1.6%	0.1%
secondary education	18.3%	17.9%	0.5%	0.2%	0.6%	−0.3%
tertiary education	16.6%	19.8%	−3.2%	0.1%	0.3%	−0.2%
Coefficient of variation	0.48	0.39		1.35	0.87	
Hungary						
Total	41.6%	43.0%	−1.4%	4.1%	4.3%	−0.2%
of which						
primary education	50.1%	53.5%	−3.4%	5.8%	6.4%	−0.6%
secondary education	29.8%	34.1%	−4.2%	2.4%	3.1%	−0.7%
tertiary education	12.6%	13.7%	−1.1%	0.6%	0.9%	−0.3%
Coefficient of variation	0.61	0.59		0.90	0.80	
Poland						
Total	42.4%	40.4%	2.0%	4.5%	6.2%	−1.7%
of which						
primary education	51.9%	46.0%	5.9%	5.8%	7.2%	−1.3%
secondary education	36.5%	35.0%	1.6%	4.6%	6.0%	−1.5%
tertiary education	14.6%	16.8%	−2.2%	0.8%	1.9%	−1.1%
Coefficient of variation	0.55	0.45		0.70	0.54	
Slovak Republic						
Total	42.8%	43.0%	−0.1%	6.6%	7.5%	−0.9%
of which						
primary education	71.8%	73.7%	−1.9%	18.4%	18.3%	0.0%
secondary education	28.8%	27.7%	1.2%	6.3%	6.5%	−0.1%
tertiary education	34.1%	29.6%	4.5%	2.8%	3.5%	−0.7%
Coefficient of variation	0.52	0.60		0.89	0.83	

Notes: Urban area groups are the most densely populated urban centres, while rural areas are all the remaining regions.

Source: National Labour Force Surveys: Bulgaria, March 1996; Czech Republic, Q3/1996, Hungary, Q4/1996, Poland, Q4/1996 and Slovak Republic Q1/1996.

Three facts are noteworthy. First, with the exception of Bulgaria all countries display broadly similar non-employment rates in urban and rural areas. Second, long-term unemployment rates are always more pronounced in rural areas. Third, in rural areas differences across educational groupings in terms of the incidence of long-term unemployment are less marked than in urban areas. This is indicated not only by the coefficients of variation of the distribution of long-term unemployment, which are always smaller in rural than in urban areas, but also by the fact that long-term unemployment rates for the least educated are in most countries lower in rural than in urban areas, in spite of the fact that long-duration unemployment is more pronounced outside urban centres.

These findings are consistent with previous studies using administrative sources rather than the national LFSs. For instance, based on unemployment register data, Lehman *et al.*, (1998) found that unemployment—notably long-term unemployment—disproportionately hit the less educated in urban areas of Poland, while in rural areas the incidence of unemployment by educational attainment is much more balanced.[43]

Although household survey data are more accurate than administrative data in the measurement of long-term unemployment and in distinguishing unemployment from inactivity, information from unemployment registers has to be preferred to that from LFSs when the focus is on small areas, because these are unlikely to be satisfactorily represented by the (relatively small) Labour Force Survey samples. Measures of the regional dispersion of unemployment are, therefore, generally computed by using data from unemployment registers. It is on the basis of such data that Boeri and Scarpetta (1996) found a large (by Western European standards) regional dispersion of the incidence in the CEECs of registered unemployment—a measure likely to lie somewhere in between non-employment and unemployment. Significantly, this dispersion was found to be larger in the Czech Republic, Poland, Hungary and the Slovak Republic—all countries endowed, as we have seen, with non-employment benefits more strongly redistributing in favour of low-wage

[43] The explanation that Lehman *et al.* offer for this finding is that in rural areas there are too few vacancies and hence actually no screening by educational achievement going on, but the authors do not explain why there are so few vacancies in rural areas. My model does. When the reservation utility of individuals is flatter in educational attainment, there is a smaller group of education types targeted by employers.

earners than in Bulgaria.[44] Moreover, the coefficient of variation of regional unemployment rates in the Visegrad group is larger than in the Russian Federation,[45] in spite of the differences in the size of the countries and the extreme heterogeneity of the Russian regional structures. Since rural areas have a higher proportion of individuals with primary or lower levels of education than urban regions,[46] relatively high benefit floors (when account is taken of the fact that the cost of living in urban areas is generally at least one-third higher than in the countryside) may have been a major factor behind the build-up of regional labour-market imbalances. Although the profile of these imbalances was initially rather mixed, with relatively high unemployment rates registered not only in rural areas but also in some heavily industrialized regions (OECD, 1995b), more recently regional unemployment differentials have tended to conform closely with the urban–rural divide (Köllö, 1999).

Finally, the fact that non-employment among the least educated in rural areas mainly takes the form of inactivity (or involvement in a family-run business, where the distinction between home production and self-employment is blurred) may contribute towards explaining the low (and declining) mobility of the workforce in CEECs in response to widening regional unemployment differentials (Boeri and Scarpetta, 1996; Köllö, 1999), notably low out-migration from rural areas (Erbenova, 1995). Usually, the low interregional mobility of workers is attributed to the high costs of housing in urban areas. However, given the small size of many of these countries, workers can often move where vacancies are located without changing residence. Commuting flows, however, have not picked up after the emergence of large and increasing labour-market imbalances across regions. The coefficient of variation of regional unemployment rates is currently 0.40 in Poland and 0.41 in Hungary, from

[44] There are a number of problems with international comparisons of measures of regional unemployment dispersions, the most serious being the difference in the size of regions for which data are available in the various countries. Boeri and Scarpetta (1996) report nevertheless that analyses using alternative regional aggregates does not appear to change the ranking across Central and East European countries in terms of regional unemployment differentials.

[45] Kapeliushnikov (1999) reports coefficients of variation for the distribution of unemployment rates in Russia of the order of 0.24–0.36. In Boeri and Scarpetta (1996), coefficients of variation of regional unemployment rates in the CEECs ranged between 0.3 and 0.8.

[46] In the five CEECs displayed in Table 3.5, an average of about 55 per cent of the rural population of working age had in 1996 primary or lower educational attainments, compared with roughly 35 per cent in urban areas.

being about 0.35 in both countries in 1996. This is well above the regional dispersion typically observed in Western countries (Mauro *et al.*, 1999), with the exception of both Germany after the Eastern enlargement and Italy. The model presented in Annex 3. provides an interpretation of this phenomenon. In particular, it suggests that even rather small commuting costs (which also include any difference between the real value of unemployment benefits in rural and urban areas) can discourage low-skilled individuals from commuting in response to the concentration of vacancies in urban areas.[47]

Summarizing, we can see that high benefit floors tend to generate among the unskilled long-term unemployment in urban areas and non-employment in rural areas. These are the typical conditions making migration from high-unemployment (mainly rural) regions to low-unemployment (urban) regions less likely to occur. Those who could feed rural–urban migration flows—the most sizeable group of the rural population—prefer to remain in the countryside in order to combine (more generous) cash transfers with (relatively more efficient than elsewhere) home production. By moving to urban areas, they would run a high risk of falling into unemployment, and non-employment is a much more precarious condition for the unskilled in urban than in rural areas.[48]

Thus, it should not come as a surprise that regional labour-market imbalances persist, especially in those countries having in place flat-rate non-employment benefits, either explicitly by regulation, as in Poland, or *de facto* as in Hungary. Fig. 3.3 displays standardized ratios of registered unemployment to the labour force in all countries for which such data have been available along a sufficiently long-time span, and Table 3.6 gives the related rank correlation coefficients in tabular form. The horizontal axis in each case reports registered unemployment rates for 1991 while the vertical axis provides the same information for 1996 or 1997. Significantly, there is a cluster of points along the main diagonal, notably in Hungary and Poland, indicating that relative positions have been maintained over time. Also, the (Spearman) rank correlation coefficient reported in Table 3.6 is for some countries more than 0.9 (compared with 0.49 in the United States over the 1983–91 period). In the Czech and

---

[47] The costs of commuting are relatively large in CEECs due to a poor transportation network. Boeri, Burda and Köllö (1997) document very high costs of commuting in Hungary relative to the minimum wage from villages to urban centres.

[48] This is consistent with evidence from Spanish regions suggesting that the unskilled workers are the least mobile component of the population (Mauro and Spilimbergo, 1998).

Table 3.6. Correlation coefficients for standardized regional unemployment rates

Country	Years	Correlation coefficient	Spearman rank correlation coefficient
Czech Republic[a]	1991 and 1997	0.79	0.67
Hungary[b]	1991 and 1997	0.92	0.91
Poland[c]	1991 and 1997	0.91	0.89
Slovak Republic[d]	1991 and 1996	0.56	0.56

[a] 15 regions: Prague; Central Bohemia; Ceske Budejovice; South Bohemia; Pizen; West Bohemia; Usti nad Labem; North Bohemia; Hradec Kralove; East Bohemia; Brno, South Moravia; Ostrava; Karvina; North Moravia.

[b] 20 countries.

[c] 49 voivodeships.

[d] 15 regions: Bratislava; Trnava; Trnavsky; Trencin; Trenciansky; Nitra; Nitriansky; Zilina; Zilinsky; Banska Bistrica; Banskobistricky, Presov; Presovsky; Kosice; Kosicky.

Source: Ministries of Labour and Social Affairs in various Countries.

Slovak republics, the correlation is lower than in Poland and Hungary, which can be explained by the fact that the twin republics have non-employment benefits maintaining a closer link with previous earnings. Other explanations for the lower persistence of regional inequalities in the Czech and Slovak lands compared with Poland and Hungary have to do with the smaller size of the regional units in the former combined country.[49] Tighter procedures to clean up the registers implemented in the latter may also have excluded many inactive individuals from unemployment compensation rolls and hence also unemployment registers,[50] reducing the number of those wrongly counted as unemployed, especially in rural areas.

In addition to differences in skill endowments and in the value of non-employment for the unskilled, another relevant factor behind sizeable and persistent regional imbalances in the CEECs is the concentration in some regions of ethnic minorities characterized by significantly larger non-employment rates than the country's average, for instance the Roma and Sinti populations living in the most depressed regions of

[49] International comparability can be only partly improved by aggregating district-level observations for these two countries in the regions listed in Table 3.6.

[50] According to the OECD (1997b), the rank reversals observed in the Slovak Republic can be explained by flows to non-participation (e.g. discouraged workers) and by the 'cleaning' of unemployment registers from individuals not actively seeking jobs.

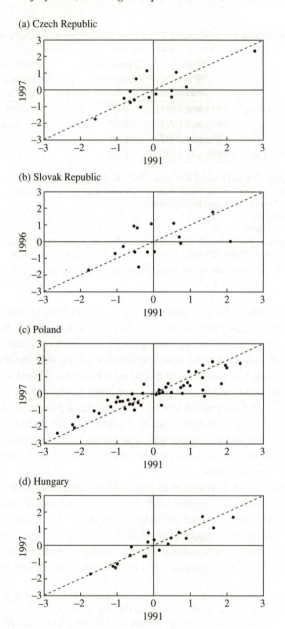

Figure 3.3. Persistence of regional labour-market imbalances (normalized unemployment rates)

Source: Ministries of Labour and Social Affairs in various countries.

Bulgaria, the Czech Republic, Hungary, Slovakia, and Slovenia.[51] What is often left unexplained is why these groups live in high unemployment regions rather than moving to urban areas where most job opportunities are concentrated—these are, after all, nomad groups, and hence are almost by definition more mobile than the rest of the population—and also why such groups display high non-employment rates to start with.

Two explanations are hinted at by the previous analysis of the legacies of the past. First, ethnic minorities are particularly penalized by the informational asymmetries characterizing economies undergoing rapid structural change. The fact of belonging to an ethnic minority may be interpreted, and used, by employers as a signal of a marginal attachment to the world of work. Ethnic minorities are viewed as concentrations of high-reservation utility types. I remember having heard a number of devastating stories and jokes (some of them told confidentially by a Minister of Labour and Social Affairs of a CEEC country—someone who was supposed to encourage social cohesion!) about the laziness of Romanies. This prejudice turned out to be a self-fulfilling prophecy. Given that they were facing particularly high risks of non-employment and were discriminated against in hiring policies and layoffs,[52] ethnic minorities tended to live where non-employment is more rewarding. For this very reason they also became less prone to move and to actively seek jobs. Needless to say, there is nothing genetic in this drive to inactivity.

3.5 Final Remarks on Earnings Distribution

Among the windows of opportunities opened by the transition to a market economy, one has been rather neglected by the literature on transition

[51] See Uldrichova (1994) and Kertesi (1994).

[52] Abraham and Vodopivec (1993) had the quite unique opportunity to work on longitudinal data on Slovenia, tracking individuals through labour-market status over time and providing reliable information on nationality that was unlikely to be seriously affected by self-selection (because it was defined in the context of pre-transition Population Censuses). They report significantly larger probabilities of dismissals for the non-Slovenians between 1989 and 1991, after controlling for individuals' characteristics. In particular, the flows from employment to non-employment are twice as large for the minority groups than for the Slovenians. Re-employment probabilities are also much lower for persons belonging to minorities. While, in 1989, outflows from unemployment to jobs as a proportion of the population of origin were broadly comparable to those of the Slovenians, in 1991 minorities were, by a factor of more than one-third, less likely to find a job than the Slovenians. See also ILO (1997) for evidence on discrimination against ethnic minorities in the CEECs.

economies. This is the possibility offered to governments to shape earnings distributions by adjusting the floors to non-employment benefits. Governments in the region could do much more in this respect than was thought possible at the outset.

Attention was concentrated at early stages of transition on aggregate wage dynamics rather than on the structure of earnings. The danger of wage-inflation spirals was often pointed out, and the scope for administrative intervention identified in fixing ceilings (rather than floors) to wage setting and enforcing them via tax-based income policies. Much less attention was devoted to the lower end of the wage distribution. However, owing to the weakness of bargaining institutions, the generosity and structure of cash transfers provided to those without employment had the potential significantly to affect wage distributions. This chapter has demonstrated that this actually happened. Low benefit floors and a closer correspondence between benefits and previous earnings resulted in more unequal wage distributions than in the countries with explicit or *de facto* flat-rate benefits established at relatively high 'social minima'.

These differences in wage distributions, notably in the incidence of low pay, can explain at least in part the large cross-country variation in labour-market adjustment and in unemployment rates. In particular, the virtual absence of non-employment benefits, and hence wage floors, in Russia can help to explain the very low build-up of unemployment in that country in the midst of particularly severe output losses: wages, rather than employment, bore most of the weight of adjustment to output falls. The CEECs, by contrast, display employment-to-output elasticities significantly larger than Russia due to the presence of 'safety nets' somewhat constraining wage declines at the lower end of the earnings distribution.

The effects of the structure of non-employment benefits on the wage distribution are also important in order to understand the widening regional labour-market imbalances in the CEECs and the lack of interregional worker flows. According to the extended model developed in this chapter, such disparities and the surprisingly low regional mobility of the workforce accompanying regional inequalities have to do with the fact that, in rural areas, higher education does not significantly increase the opportunity cost of employment, whilst it does do so in urban areas. This difference in the profile by education of labour supply, which is supported by estimates of the reservation utility function of Polish workers, implies that, in the presence of non-employment benefit floors, the less educated in urban areas are crowded out of employment and experience long-term unemployment, whilst in rural areas they become inactive in the job market and, instead, often get involved in home production or casual work on family plots.

Thus, non-employment benefits redistributing revenues in favour of low-wage earners generate more unemployment throughout the transition and more regional labour-market inequalities than unemployment benefits systems maintaining a very close link with previous earnings. However, in the absence of 'safety nets', job reallocation is slower for reasons that have nothing to do with the opposition of workers to restructuring, emphasized by the OST literature reviewed in Chapter 1. The 'Russian puzzle' can indeed be explained by the fact that, when virtually no benefit floor is provided, unskilled workers have everything to lose by moving to the new sector, and hence reallocation can only be accommodated via involuntary separations rather than job-to-job shifts. Under these conditions, underemployment is generated and is highly persistent, whereby individuals combine attachment to state sector jobs (unpaid at times, due to the widepread presence of wage arrears) with informal activities. If the unskilled become unemployed, low benefits will also push them to migrate to rural areas, where they can survive on individual plots. This is an additional source of persistence of underemployment in Russia, because low-paid (and unstable) jobs in the urban areas are unlikely to convince these people to come back.

It should be stressed that the focus of this chapter has been only on earnings (as opposed to income) distributions and that the approach has been positive. So far, whether high unemployment with fewer low-paid jobs was to be preferred at the early stages of transition to low unemployment and a large incidence of low pay has not been discussed. These issues belong to the fourth and last chapter of this book.

Annex 3
The Structure of Benefits and Reallocation

A3.1 Endogenizing Workers' Heterogeneity

In the model presented in Annex 2., the reservation utility of individuals and job destruction are exogenous. Here, I extend this model in two respects.

First, consistent with evidence on reservation wages of Polish workers as mentioned in Chapter 3, I allow the reservation utility u (unobservable by employers) to be positively correlated with some (observable) measure of individuals' skills, for example years of schooling. In particular, let s denote this signal, whose lower and upper bounds are $a(0 < a < 1/2)$ and $1 - a$ respectively. For any given s, u is uniformly distributed over the $[s - a, s + a]$ interval. We may think of s as years of schooling normalized by the average age of entry in the labour market, while a is a measure of the information provided by the education system as to the reservation utility of individuals. As a tends to zero, the reservation utility is no longer private information to individuals; conversely, when a tends to $\frac{1}{2}$, the signal is not informative. The reservation wage functions estimated in Chapter 3 suggest that the relationship between wage aspirations and years of schooling is flatter in rural than in urban areas. Hence, in the case of rural areas as in the basic model, a is just too large to convey any information, and consequently $E[u/s] = E[u] = \frac{1}{2}$, while in urban areas the conditional expectation is $E[u/s] = s$.

As a second extension, I allow the probability of job loss in the new sector to vary across workers; that is, I add a vertical source of heterogeneity to the horizontal dimension (varying reservation utilities) introduced so far. While s may not affect the instantaneous productivity of a match (because of the problems of education systems in formerly planned economies, discussed in Chapter 2), it should nevertheless increase the degree of fungibility of workers to change between jobs. There is evidence in OECD countries that education does indeed increase the duration of a match. In formerly planned economies, this relationship is milder (mainly because of the anomaly of vocational education) but partly still there—notably when the focus is on separations related to exogenous shocks hitting the value of a match (rather than to on-the-job search activities). Thus, I model the exogenous layoff rate as a function of the signal for skills s. In particular, we have $\lambda_n(s)$ where $\lambda'_n < 0$ and $\lambda_n(0) > \lambda$.

We are interested here only in assessing participation decisions and job finding probabilities for individuals with varying s, rather than in characterizing the evolution of unemployment and employment levels (which was done in Annex 2.). Hence, there is no need to impose *a priori* restrictions on the distribution of s across individuals, provided that the latter is non-degenerate.

All this seems to frame in a very parsimonious fashion the conditions where observables, such as the age, tenure or educational attainment of individuals, convey noisy signals as to the actual productivity of workers. Employers do not know the ability in home production (the reservation wage) of each applicant. However, they realize that more educated people are somewhat more adaptable to changes in their tasks brought about by alterations in product designs, technological change, etc., and hence that matches embodying a larger s are likely to last longer[53] than matches with a low value for s.

As there are signals as to the fungibility of workers, it is reasonable to assume that the labour market is segmented along s. This means that now employers choose not only the recruitment pool (as in Annex 2.), but also the type of vacancy to be offered. The two choices are, clearly, interdependent and related no longer simply to the size of the two pools but also to the (conditional) distribution of u given s.

We denote the value for an employer of a job involving workers of type s by $J(s)$. For any s-type, we will therefore have the usual free-

---

[53] Notice that here s only affects the duration of a match, not the likelihood that a match occurs. Having both effects would complicate algebra without adding insights to the model.

entry conditions:

$$\delta \frac{J(s)}{\theta_o(s)} \le c \qquad (A3.1)$$

and

$$\delta \phi \frac{J(s)}{\theta_u(s)} \le c \qquad (A3.2)$$

satisfied as equalities whenever $\theta_o(s) > 0$ and $\theta_u(s) > 0$, respectively. The value of a post filled with a type-s worker is then given by

$$J(s) = 1 + \rho - w(s)(1 + \tau) + \delta(1 - \lambda_n(s))\,J(s), \qquad (A3.3)$$

and the associated Nash bargaining rule is

$$W_n(s) - W_u(s) = \gamma[J(s) + W_n(s) - W_u(s)], \qquad (A3.4)$$

where $0 < \gamma < 1$ denotes, as usual, the bargaining power of workers. As is apparent from the above, we can continue to allow the threat point for the worker to be determined by the non-employment status, although there may be employed jobseekers in the 'old' sector. The justification for this assumption is, once again, that the old sector is bound to disappear.

Let us turn now to characterize the various asset-value conditions and come back later to wage determination.

The value added of the old sector jobs is independent of the skill of the workers. Consequently all workers are paid the same wage in the old sector. The asset value of being employed in the old sector for a type-s worker is then

$$W_o(s) = 1 + \delta\{\pi_o(s)W_n(s) + \lambda[1 - \pi_o(s)]W_u(s)$$
$$+ [1 - \pi_o(s) - \lambda(1 - \pi_o(s))]W_o(s)\}, \qquad (A3.5)$$

where $\pi_o(s)$ denotes the probability that a type-s worker in the old sector finds a job in the new sector.

Similarly, the value of being employed in the new sector is given by

$$W_n(s) = w_n(s) + \delta\{(1 - \lambda_n(s))W_n(s) + \lambda_n(s)W_u(s)\}. \qquad (A3.6)$$

Non-employment benefits (encompassing unemployment benefits, early retirement, liberal access to invalidity pensions, etc.) can be characterized either as a flat-rate benefit, b = const., or as a subsidy proportional to the wages in the new sector (in the old sector all workers are paid alike), where, $b = kw(s)$ where $0 < k < 1$. In both cases, the value of being non-employed is given by

$$W_u(s) = b + \max \{\delta[\pi_u(s)W_n(s) + (1 - \pi_u(s))W_u(s)], u + \delta W_u(s))\}.$$
(A3.7)

As in the basic model laid out in Annex 2., there will be a cutoff reservation utility at which those non-employed are indifferent between searching and non-searching. Such a cutoff reservation utility will vary depending on the skill-type of individuals, that is such that $\tilde{u} = \tilde{u}(s)$.

A3.2 Main Results

The properties and empirical implications of the model can be best characterized by a set of propositions. One should bear in mind that the model works as discussed in Annex 2. except that now market tightness varies by skill level. For simplicity we will ignore throughout (proportional) payroll taxes τ, because they do not add insights as to the relation between unemployment benefits and the structure of earnings while they somewhat complicate our proofs.

Proposition 1 When non-employment benefits are paid at a flat-rate, market tightness is monotonically increasing in s.

Proof. Under the new configuration of the model, the equation for the equilibrium transition path of θ_u (A2.15) can be rewritten as

$$-\frac{cq(\theta_u)}{\phi(\theta_u)\delta} + \frac{(1 - \gamma)}{\gamma} \left[\frac{w_n}{1 - \delta(1 - \lambda_n(s))} - \frac{b(1 - \delta)}{A(s)} \right] = 0 \quad (A3.8)$$

where $A(s) = [1 - \delta - (\delta - \delta^2)(1 - \lambda_n(s) - \pi_u(s))]$. By the implicit function theorem and using equations (A2.5) and (A2.16) we then obtain

$$\frac{\partial \theta_u*}{\partial s} = -\frac{\frac{(1-\gamma)}{\gamma} \left[\frac{-w_n \delta \lambda_n'}{(1-\delta(1-\lambda_n(s)))^2} + \frac{b(1-\delta)\frac{\partial A}{\partial s}}{A^2} \right]}{\frac{-\delta c(q'\phi + \phi' q)}{(\phi \delta)^2} - \frac{(1-\gamma)}{\gamma} \left[\frac{b(1-\delta)\frac{\partial A}{\partial \theta_u}}{A^2} \right]}. \quad (A3.9)$$

As can be readily shown, the numerator is positive because $\lambda_n' < 0$ by assumption, while the denominator is negative by concavity of q. It follows that $\frac{\partial \theta_u*}{\partial s} > 0$.

It should be stressed that the above result holds true for both urban and rural areas.

When benefits are earning-related, an additional term should be included on the right-hand side of equation (A3.9), namely $\frac{\partial b}{\partial s}$. It follows that market tightness will still be non-decreasing with the signal, but the effect of education on market tightness will tend to zero for $\left|\lambda'_n\right|$ relatively small with respect to k, the parameter capturing the generosity of (earning-related) benefits.

Proposition 2 When u is uncorrelated with s (in rural areas) and non-employment benefits are paid at a flat-rate, the cutoff reservation utility, $\tilde{u}$ is always increasing in s.

Proof. By Proposition 1 and (A2.11), we have that

$$\frac{\partial \tilde{u}_o}{\partial s} > 0.$$

Moreover, by (A2.4) we also obtain that

$$\frac{\partial \tilde{u}}{\partial s} = \delta \frac{\partial \theta_u}{\partial s} \left[(1 - \gamma) \frac{\partial b}{\partial s} + \gamma(1 + \rho) \left(1 + c \frac{\partial \theta_u}{\partial s} \right) - \frac{\partial u}{\partial s} \right].$$

In rural areas the last term within squared brackets is zero. When benefits are paid at a flat rate, the first term is also nil. This means that the relationship between $\tilde{u}$ and s will be determined by the sign of $\frac{\partial \theta_u}{\partial s}$. We can then use Proposition 1 to complete our proof.

In other words, non-participation decisions should be more frequent at the lower end of the spectrum of educational attainments in rural areas when unemployment benefits are flat. In urban areas, non-participation is likely to involve, also when b is fixed, more highly educated than lowly educated individuals, as stated in the following corollary.

Corollary 2.1 When the reservation utility is correlated with s (in urban areas), the cutoff reservation utility above which workers will quit the old sector into inactivity increases with s.

Proof. This follows from (A2.11). In fact, now we have that

$$
\frac{\partial \tilde{u}_0}{\partial s} = \frac{(1-\delta)\left[\frac{\partial \pi_0}{\partial s}(\delta W_n(1-\pi_0-\lambda(1-\pi_0))\right.}{(1-\pi_0-\lambda(1-\pi_0))^2}
$$
$$
+ \frac{(1+\delta\pi_0 W_n)(1-\lambda)] + \delta\pi_0\frac{\partial W_n}{\partial s}(1-\pi_0-\lambda(1-\pi_0))]}{(1-\pi_0-\lambda(1-\pi_0))^2}.
$$

$$(A3.10)$$

Now, the first term is non-negative by Proposition 1, while the second is always positive by (A3.6).

Given that the proportion of workers with high reservation utilities is also increasing with s, the above does not imply that flows from the old sector into inactivity are also increasing among high-s types. This will certainly happen when benefits are earning-related, as stated in the following corollary.

Corollary 2.2 When non-employment benefits are earning-related, and k is large relative to $|\lambda_n'|$, the proportion of old sector workers in urban areas who quit into inactivity increases with s.

Proof. It suffices to show that the derivative of the cutoff reservation utility with respect to s is less than unity. Under the posited values of the parameters and when benefits are earning-related, $\frac{\partial \pi_0}{\partial s}$ tends to zero. Moreover, the effect of s on unemployment benefits should be taken into account. It follows that (A3.10) now reads:

$$
\frac{\partial \tilde{u}_0}{\partial s} = \frac{\delta\pi_0\frac{\partial W_n}{\partial s}}{(1-\pi_0-\lambda(1-\pi_0))} - \frac{\partial b}{\partial s}, \qquad (A3.11)
$$

which tends to zero for large k and small $|\lambda_n'|$.

Proposition 3 When benefits are earning-related and offer low replacement rates, under values of the parameters in line with empirical evidence, low-s types prefer to stay in the old sector rather than move to the new sector.

Proof. We need to show that under these conditions there is some $s < \hat{s}$ such that

$$
1+\delta\left\{\lambda W_u(s)+(1-\lambda)W_0(s)\right\} > w_n+\delta\left\{\lambda_n(s)W_u+(1-\lambda_n(s))W_n(s)\right\};
$$

that is, it is better to stay in the old sector rather than moving to the new one.

By assumption, at least for $s = 0$, $\lambda_n > \lambda$; hence, all what we need to show is that $w_n < 1$. Now, using (A2.16) we have that

$$w_n = \frac{\gamma(1 + \rho)(1 + c\theta_u)}{1 - (1 - \gamma)k}$$

for low k the denominator tends to unity, while the numerator is less than unity under the parameter values used in the numerical simulations of the basic model.

Corollary 3.1 Under the conditions of Proposition 3, if vacancies are issued also for old sector jobs, low-s unemployed jobseekers will always look for jobs in the old sector rather than in the new sector.

Proof. This stems from Proposition 3.

Proposition 4 When there are (fixed) costs of commuting from rural to urban areas such that $m > \gamma(1 + \rho)$, the low-s types in rural areas will prefer to remain inactive rather than working in urban regions.

Proof. By the arbitrage condition in vacancy formation and the fact that in rural areas $E[u/s] = E[u] = 1/2$ while in urban areas $E[u/s] = s$, we have the result that employers will only issue vacancies for the unskilled (those with $s < 1/2$) in urban areas. Thus, low-s types residing in rural areas either commute to urban areas (incurring the cost m and their forgone reservation utility) or remain inactive. It is then straightforward to use the wage equation (A2.16) to complete the proof.

Notice that m also includes any difference between the real value of unemployment benefits in rural areas and in urban areas, which may be substantial in the presence of benefits not adjusted to rural/urban cost-of-living differences. Notice further that the parameter γ (which can be empirically approximated by the wage share) is rather small in transitional economies (of the order of 40 per cent compared with 60 to 70 per cent in OECD countries) and that transportation costs, due to poor public infrastructure, are quite substantial.

4
Returning to Europe

4.1 Introduction

In the previous chapters it has been shown that the design of non-employment benefits and the timing of their reforms have deeply shaped transition. Such policies have affected the scope and speed of job reallocation and the dynamics of inequalities, and differences in the design of transfers provided to non-employed individuals of working age can explain much of the large dispersion in labour-market outcomes both across countries and over time. The focus so far has been on the *effects* of policies, which were taken as given. It is now time to discuss the *determinants* of policy, and the reasons why those policies differed so widely across countries. Positive and normative considerations almost inevitably overlap when characterizing policies. Hence, statements will also be made as to the pros and cons of the different social-policy models described in the previous chapters and, above all, desirable reform strategies for the years to come. These are the tasks reserved for this chapter, which will address the remaining puzzles of the transition. In particular, two main sets of issues will be discussed.

First: why did countries all coming from a central-planning environment adopt such a different mix of social policy throughout transition? In particular, why do we have the two polarized groupings, of the former Soviet republics and the Visegrad group, with Romania and Bulgaria in between? Is it an issue of fiscal constraints allowing some countries to be more generous than others? Are these asymmetries the by-products of differences in preferences of households amongst the various countries under consideration? Or are there exogenous factors that have induced countries to embark upon different reform strategies?

Second: both of these two extreme models—the Russian and the Central European way—have major shortcomings, and these policy limitations could have been anticipated from the outset. There were a few things that it was clear from the beginning should have been done and were not done, and others that should *not* have been done but nevertheless were done. Thus the question arises as to why governments did not perform any better than they did. What are the reasons for their bad choice of policies?

My preferred explanation for the differences in the social-policy mix across countries has to do with the common aspiration of these countries to join the European Union and the fact that not all of them have the same chance of succeeding. The less credible the accession to the EU for citizens of the former Soviet bloc, the weaker the role of the European Union in imposing a social-policy model to be followed by the other countries. Thus, the European Union was a strong attractor for the Visegrad group, while it exerted a lower conditionality on countries such as Romania and Bulgaria, and even less so on the former Soviet republics.

Other explanations for the differences in policies—for example asymmetries in household preferences, or in the opportunity sets of governments (namely more or less stringent budgetary constraints)—are less convincing. A legacy of the Marxist ideology was a strong aversion to inequality, and such an ideology had deeper roots in Russia than elsewhere. If the degree of inequality allowed under the previous regime was an indication of differences in preferences over the distribution of income, the rank reversals observed in inequality indexes across the countries in transition suggest that heterogeneous preferences can, at best, tell us only part of the story. Finally, budgetary constraints at the outset were no less stringent in Poland than in Russia, and Romania had a much more favourable external position than the Visegrad group. While constraints to the financing of social policies became increasingly important in the course of transition, differences in the initial fiscal position cannot explain why the countries in the region took different routes in setting policies to accompany restructuring and job reallocation.

The conditionality of the European Union can contribute to explaining why non-employment benefits were more generous in the Visegrad countries than in the former Soviet republics, but it has nothing to do with the gross mistakes made in social-policy design in these countries. Some features of non-employment benefits in transitional economies were—and in part still are—quite astonishing, and a few examples follow.

It is difficult to understand the rationale behind the introduction of open-ended unemployment benefits in Poland in 1990. There seemed also to be little justification for making school-leavers eligible for unemployment benefits, as done in most countries in the region: rather than offering (generally token) subsidies to first-time jobseekers, the latter should have been encouraged to continue their studies and assisted in their search for a job, promoting a better circulation of information on vacancies being opened in various segments (e.g. regions) of the labour markets. In many OECD countries job losers are offered stronger protection than job leavers, while in the CEECs those voluntarily quitting a job were often offered the same transfers as those who had been laid off. If mobility across jobs ought to be encouraged, then job leavers could have been entitled to unemployment compensation only after some waiting period, and at a reduced rate, in order to discourage free-riding.

The links between unemployment benefits and the safety nets could also have been better designed. In Bulgaria, for quite a long time the unemployed were subject to a very complex set of rules allowing people potentially to draw unemployment benefits for six months, then general social assistance for another six months, social assistance targeted to the long-term unemployed (more generous than general social assistance) for the next six months, and finally go back to general social assistance. Thus, benefits were not decreasing with unemployment duration, as required in order to reduce disincentives to job search. In Romania and Slovakia, there was no mechanism built into the system preventing replacement rates for unemployed couples without children from increasing with unemployment duration, with obvious negative consequences on incentives to job search. While these inconsistencies between unemployment insurance and (means-tested) social assistance are sometimes present also in OECD countries, due to segmented decision-making and legacies of the past, it was possible to avoid such mistakes in countries starting from scratch.

Finally, stricter rules should have been adopted when deciding upon eligibility to benefits (for instance, not allowing an accumulation of severance and benefits) and work tests could have been introduced from the very beginning of transition. This would have induced new employers to look at unemployment registers as a suitable recruitment pool. In a nutshell, the main concern of governments should not have been the reduction of unemployment via wide-ranging labour-supply-reducing policies but the containment of non-employment and, above all, of the fiscal costs associated with it.

Returning to Europe

Why didn't they do it, then? Certainly, it is easy to be wise after the event, and policy makers were undergoing a particularly steep learning process. Yet the experience of the partial reforms of the 1980s, and of countries, such as Spain and Portugal, that had recently seen an end to dictatorships and had strongly reduced the size of the public sector in order to return to Europe, was there to provide important lessons as to mistakes not to be repeated. Interestingly, there were very few economists coming from Spain and Portugal involved in the debate at the early stages of transition. Had they been asked to provide policy advice, they would certainly have suggested being very careful in setting non-employment benefits. This was, after all, one of the main lessons coming from the comparison of the experience of low-unemployment Portugal and high-unemployment Spain.

There are, in my view, three main reasons why such mistakes were made. The first has to do with pressures coming from managers of state enterprises for 'soft' measures to cope with redundancies, in other words measures to buy out workers of their firms. The second reason is related to the desire of policy makers to conceal the growth of unemployment and maintain political support from former state sector workers. The third reason relates to pressures coming from inside the bureaucracies to maintain a high degree of institutional complexity.

This chapter will first look at explanations for the cross-country differences in social-policy stance (section 4.2). Next, section 4.3 will consider explanations for wrong economic policies in the transition countries. Section 4.4 will discuss whether and how the EU enlargement process can contribute to improve matters in Eastern Europe; in particular, given the strong conditionality exerted by the European Union in the accession process, the consistency will be assessed of the requirements of the so-called *Acquis communautaire* with ongoing (and badly needed) social-policy reforms in the countries under consideration. Particular attention will be given in section 4.4 to the effects of policies on the size of the informal sector in these countries. Finally, section 4.5 will summarize the main lessons that can be drawn from this book as to the optimal design of non-employment benefits and, more broadly, social-welfare systems in economies undergoing radical transformations in the structure of employment and output.

4.2 Understanding the International Differences in Social-Policy Models

It may be worth recalling the main ingredients of the two extreme models of transition whose effects on labour-market adjustment, income inequality and labour force participation were discussed in Chapter 3. On the one hand, we have the Central European route—notably the transition of the four countries of Visegrad—with a relatively large social-policy expenditure, and significant redistribution occurring via non-employment benefits. On the other hand, we have the Russian way, with low social policy expenditure, virtually no unemployment benefit system, and a minimum role of the State in reducing income inequalities and promoting social cohesion. The most striking sign of the absenteeism of public authorities in Russia from the provision of poverty relief is the fact that the authorities allowed a huge stock of wage arrears to build up in the budgetary sphere.

There are three possible explanations for this fundamental asymmetry between Russia and the Visegrad countries: first, differences in the degree of inequality aversion; second, differences in the degree of economic development and access to international capital markets, making it more difficult for Russia to sustain large social-policy outlays; and, third, the more or less strict conditionality and appeal of the EU social-policy model in relation to the transition countries. These three explanations are discussed below.

4.2.1 Initial Conditions

Contrary to common wisdom, not all formerly planned economies entered the 1990s with a low degree of inequality. As documented by Atkinson and Micklewright (1992), at the beginning of the 1990s there were wide differences in the degree of income inequality across the group of CEECs and between these and the former Soviet republics. The latter were generally characterized by a greater degree of inequality—even the least unequal of the Soviet republics displayed larger Gini coefficients than any of the CEECs. Given that all these countries had in common a tariff wage system and full-employment conditions, and hence their income distribution was largely predetermined by governments,[1] it is likely that such differences reflected, at least to some extent,

---

[1] Atkinson and Micklewright (1992) also show that the cross-sectional dispersion in *earnings* inequality was very strictly and positively correlated with the variance across

the weight attached to equality and social cohesion by these societies. By the same token, one may be tempted to explain the two different routes to transition characterized in Chapter 3 as the by-product of different degrees of inequality aversion, notably stronger preferences for equality in Europe than in the other formerly planned economies. In particular, cultural and religious factors—for instance, the strength of the Catholic Church in countries like Poland—are often attributed a key role in maintaining relatively equal societies in Europe. Three factors are, however, at odds with this explanation for the diverging transition patterns in Europe and the former Soviet republics.

First, the appearance of greater inequalities in Russia than in Europe was mainly an outcome of the 1980s, rather than an enduring asymmetry and consolidated tradition of the Soviet Empire.[2] Moreover, increasing inequality in Russia in the 1980s was hidden by the Communist ideology and not revealed to public opinion even under *glasnost.* As perceptions rather than reality are what ultimately matter for individuals, it is difficult to believe that inequality was more accepted there than in the European segment of the CMEA. More likely, increasing inequality was not even perceived by many citizens of the former Soviet Union, let alone their possibility of influencing the extent of the redistribution operated by their governments.

Second, even if we take the Gini coefficients prevailing before the fall of the Berlin Wall as an indication of societal concerns over income distribution, we will find that these are only mildly correlated with the degree of income inequality prevailing ten years later. Fig. 4.1. plots the Gini coefficients computed over the distribution of household incomes in 1987–8 and 1993–5 for all transition countries in which such data are available.[3] We know from Chapter 3 that *earnings* inequality has been on the rise; hence the fact that in Fig. 4.1 all countries, except the Slovak Republic, lie above the bisecting line through the origin (indicating that

---

countries in the degree of *income* inequality. In other words, the least (the most) unequal countries were also those with the least (the most) unequal earning distributions.

[2] The data reported in Atkinson and Micklewright (1992) as well as in McAuley (1979) and Ofer and Vinokur (1980) points to greater inequality in Hungary than in the former USSR in the 1970s and at the beginning of the 1980s.

[3] Needless to say, cross-country comparisons with Gini coefficients are problematic. Atkinson and Micklewright (1992) are, once more, a compulsory reference for measurement problems in the various countries. Importantly, asymmetries across countries in the coverage and accuracy of income distribution statistics tend to persist over time. Hence, it is likely that they do not significantly affect the rankings of the Gini coefficients displayed in Fig. 4.1.

income inequality has increased almost everywhere) does not come as a surprise. However, there are significant differences in degree, as countries like the Kyrgiz Republic, Russia and Ukraine have experienced a much larger rise of inequality than the CEECs.

In order to assess whether initial conditions play an important role in explaining the wide variation displayed in the rise of inequality, results are also shown (in the panel within Fig. 4.1) that are obtained by regressing the 1993–5 against the 1987–8 Gini coefficients. These results suggest that initial conditions account for less than one-fifth of the international variation in the post-transition income inequality. Furthermore, the initial ranking of countries in terms of income inequality has been quite significantly altered throughout the transition period: the Spearman rank correlation coefficient is 0.57, which is low if one takes into account that we are comparing inequality indexes only a few years apart.[4]

Thus, inherited institutional and cultural differences affecting the degree of inequality aversion in the various countries can only partly explain diverging patterns in the distribution of income since the start of transition. According to this reading, such differences cannot explain why inequalities in Russia are currently so large. Were Russia to have preserved the same distance with respect to Central and Eastern Europe in terms of income concentration, it would currently be characterized by significantly lower Gini coefficients.[5]

4.2.2 Feasibility Constraints

Another explanation for the different paths followed by Russia and the CEECs has to do with the opportunity sets of governments, namely with the fiscal sustainability of redistribution. There are significant differences across countries in the capacity to collect social security contributions earmarked for the various cash-transfer programmes and, more broadly, large asymmetries in revenue collection. Total tax revenues in 1997 reached about 35 per cent of GDP in the CEECs and half of

[4]The simple correlation coefficient is 0.47, also significant at a 95% confidence level.

[5]Importantly, international differences in static (cross-sectional) income inequality between CEECs on the one hand and Russia on the other are only partly associated with asymmetries in the extent of income mobility (or dynamic inequality). While Galasi (1998) reports quite significant income mobility in Hungary, especially at early stages of transition, Commander *et al.* (1997) also point to relatively high escape probabilities from poverty in Russia. Data issues (for instance the longitudinal sample that can be built out of the Russian data is not representative of Russia), nevertheless make cross-country comparisons in income mobility somewhat questionable.

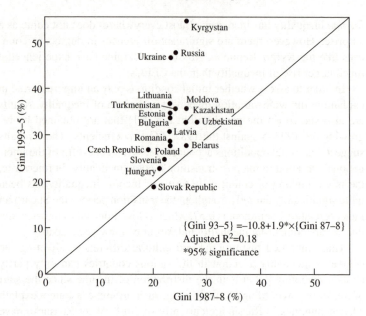

Figure 4.1. The role of initial conditions in the dynamics of income inequality

Notes: The Spearman rank correlation coefficient between Gini 1987–8 and Gini 1993–5 is 0.57, which is significant at a 95% confidence level.

Source: UNDP (1996); Milanovic (1997).

this level (roughly 18 per cent of GDP) in the CIS. Needless to say, redistribution is costly. Policies involving distribution within generations (for example the large battery of non-employment benefits provided in the West) amount in the European Union to about 15 per cent of GDP. Redistribution across generations takes roughly another 15 per cent.

Based on household budget survey data from the Luxembourg Income Studies over a panel of OECD countries, Kenworthy (1998) estimated that a 1 per cent increase in government transfers (state benefits for sickness, old age, family allowances, social assistance and unfunded employee-welfare benefits paid by the general government) can reduce relative poverty rates by approximately one-fifth of a percentage point. It should be stressed that Kenworthy's estimates refer to countries having a long-standing experience in administering social policies, and hence that presumably have achieved greater effectiveness in the running of such programmes than the weak (and corrupt) state administrations of the transitional economies. In countries such as Russia, about 30 per cent of the individuals had in 1993 incomes below 40 per cent of the median income (the measure of relative poverty used by Kenworthy). According to Milanovic's 1997 estimates, the elimination of absolute poverty in Russia would have required in 1993–4 (supposedly perfectly targeted) transfers of the order of US$6 billion per year, equivalent to, approximately 3.5 per cent of Russia's GDP. Needless to say, this is far more than the resources allocated to anti-poverty measures in Russia: expenditure in social assistance throughout the transition never exceeded 0.4 per cent of that country's GDP.

Overall, it would seem that CIS countries are not currently in a position to sustain large-scale social programmes as would be required to reduce income inequality, at least bringing the distances in inequality in comparison with the CEECs back to the levels prevailing at the beginning of the 1990s. However, the different scope of redistribution in the CEECs and Russia can be only partly attributed to legacies of the past, namely asymmetries in revenue collection inherited from the previous regime. Three points need to be made in this connection.

First, current differences in revenue collection between CEECs and the CIS are to a large extent the result of developments since the beginning of the 1990s. While tax revenues as a percentage of GDP have declined throughout the region, the fall has been much steeper in Russia and the other CIS countries than in the CEECs.[6] Significantly, the fall in revenues has only marginally involved social security contributions, which are the main source of social-policy financing. Payroll taxes were generally earmarked to the various extra-budgetary funds created at the outset of transition; this reduced the scope for governments to use social security contributions for other purposes. For instance, the Russian National Employment Service (in charge of unemployment benefit payments and active policies) operated with a comfortable surplus for several years. Hence, more generous unemployment benefits could have been paid in Russia at least up to 1995 without requiring new levies—or even simply improvements in revenue collection.

Second, the strong decline in revenue collection in the CIS is largely a by-product of the delays with which tax structures in these countries were adjusted to market conditions, rather than being a legacy of the past. In other words, it has to do also with the choice set of governments rather

[6]Total tax revenues in the CEECs declined by about 4.5 percentage points between 1989 and 1997, compared with 8.5 per cent in the CIS (EBRD, 1998).

than being an external, exogenous, constraint. In particular, Russia and the CIS would seem to have been much less successful than the CEECs in shifting the tax structure away from corporate taxes towards personal income and indirect taxation. While in the CEECs the decline in total tax revenues is almost entirely associated with the decline in corporate tax revenues (income and expenditure taxes have been kept broadly at the same levels, relative to GDP, as at the beginning of the 1990s), in the CIS it is indeed income and expenditure taxes that have fallen the most compared with the pre-transition phase (EBRD, 1998).

Third, redistribution is not only a matter of *quantity*, but also of *quality* of spending. Table 4.1 provides information on the structure of social spending and its contribution to changes in the Gini coefficients in various transition countries. Two facts stand out. First, CIS countries devote less resources to cash transfers than other transitional economies (as shown by column (D)), with social spending averaging about 9 per cent of national GDP compared with 20–30 per cent in the other two groups of countries). Second (and more importantly for our line of reasoning) CIS countries spend a much larger proportion of social expenditure in pensions (column (B)) rather than in paying non-employment benefits (unemployment benefits, social assistance, early retirement and disabilities, column (A)). The average ratio between the two expenditure items (column (C)) is indeed in the CIS countries of the order of 8 per cent, which is between one-half and one-third of the ratios observed in the other two groups of countries.

Given this dominant orientation of social spending towards the older generations in the CIS, social spending in countries such as Russia would seem to contribute to *increasing* rather than reducing inequality. This is shown by the last two columns on the right-hand side of Table 4.1, which displays the contribution of social policies to changes in the Gini coefficient, as estimated by Milanovic (1999) on the basis of microeconomic, household budget survey data.[7] Social policies contribute to increase inequality also in some OECD countries, notably Germany and Italy, where the bulk of social expenditures is concentrated on pensions. How-

---

[7] The overall change in the Gini coefficient, ΔG, was decomposed into the contribution of the three main income sources (wages (w), non-wage private incomes (n), pensions (p), and non-employment benefits (ne)) as follows:

$$\Delta G, = w_w \Delta C_w + w_n \Delta C_n + w_p \Delta C_p + w_{ne} \Delta C_{ne},$$

where w is the share of the income source in total income and C is the corresponding concentration coefficient.

ever, in Russia social transfers increase inequalities, not only because of the overwhelming weight of pension outlays in total cash transfers but also due to the fact that non-employment benefits themselves are poorly targeted. As shown in Chapter 3, unemployment benefits for instance do not have a progressive structure. While in the CEECs cash transfers other than pensions tend to reduce inequality or at least are neutral with respect to income distribution, in Russia such policies would seem to have contributed to a 2.3 percentage point increase of the Gini (last column on the right-hand side of Table 4.1).

Thus, the very many governments ruling over the Russian federation in the 1990s have not only spent less in social policies than in the CEECs but have also allocated a much larger fraction of social expenditure to pensions rather than to individuals of working age experiencing spells of non-employment. Moreover, this low-level outlay (in absolute and relative terms) targeting the non-employed were not structured in such a way as to redistribute in favour of low-wage earners. All this has significantly reduced the scope of redistribution. Especially under conditions of rapid structural change and massive income declines, the bulk of redistribution tends to fall on unemployment benefits and targeted social programmes. Further, unemployment benefits in the CEECs also played the role of minimum wages in the emerging private sector and earning differentials were a major factor behind the rise of Gini coefficients in all formerly planned economies.

Overall, greater difficulties in raising taxes than in the CEECs may have forced Russia to allocate a lower share of GDP to social transfers, but problems on the revenue-collection side were to a large extent a result of policy failures rather than a legacy of the past. Furthermore, revenue constraints did not prevent Russia and the other CIS countries from altering the composition of social spending in such a way as to make cash transfers an anti-poverty device rather than a system for increasing the concentration of incomes.[8]

---

[8] Political constraints may contribute to explaining the predominant role given to pensions in social spending in this country. It is generally easier to postpone the introduction of income support schemes for those of working age losing their job and/or incomes in the course of transition than to cut existing entitlements. However, nothing prevented the Russian authorities from making pensions themselves more redistributive, that is by paying them at a flat rate and fully spending the tax revenues earmarked to the Employment Fund in order to grant more generous unemployment benefits.

Table 4.1. Social policy models, redistribution and European Union accession

Countries	Social policy expenditure as a percentage of GDP[a] (1991-5)				The role of social policies in redistribution		
	(A) NE benefits[b]	(B) Old-age pensions[c]	(C) = (A)/(B)	(D)Total	ΔGini[d]	Contribution of social transfers to ΔGini[e]	of which non-pensions
Group 1							
Czech Republic	3.6%	11.0%	32.7%	25.5%	8.0	0.9	0.4
Estonia	1.1%	6.6%	16.6%	26.0%	12.0	—	—
Hungary	2.4%	11.5%	20.9%	32.3%	2.2	1.2	-0.2
Poland	5.0%	15.8%	31.8%	29.5%	10.6	3.3	-0.1
Slovenia	2.7%	9.8%	27.5%	29.5%	2.6	-0.5	-0.4
Unweighted average	*3.0%*	*10.9%*	*25.9%*	*28.6%*	*7.1*	*1.2*	*-0.1*
Group 2							
Bulgaria	1.6%	9.4%	17.2%	14.1%	10.0	0.9	0.4
Latvia	0.5%	9.5%	5.3%	26.5%	10.0	-1.5	0.5
Lithuania	1.1%	6.6%	16.7%	19.3%	14.0	—	—
Romania	1.9%	6.9%	27.5%	16.5%	6.0	—	—
Slovak Republic	2.7%	9.1%	29.6%	26.0%	-1.0	—	—
Unweighted average	*1.6%*	*8.3%*	*19.2%*	*20.5%*	*7.8*	*-0.3*	*0.5*

CIS countries

Belarus	0.6%	5.8%	10.3%	8.3%	7.0	—	2.3
Russia	0.6%	5.5%	10.9%	8.5%	29.9	6.0	—
Ukraine	0.3%	7.7%	3.3%	9.8%	24.0	—	—
Unweighted average	*0.5%*	*6.3%*	*8.2%*	*8.9%*	*20.3*	*6.0*	*2.3*

[a] Dates: Czech Republic 1991/95, Hungary 1991/94, Poland 1990/1994, Slovenia 1990/95, Bulgaria 1991/95, Romania 1990/94, Slovak Republic 1990/95.

[b] Non-employment (NE) benefits include unemployment benefits, social assistance, early retirement, disability pensions and sickness benefits.

[c] Average-period data.

[d] Czech Republic 1987–8/1993–5, Estonia 1987–8/1993–5, Hungary 1987/1993, Poland 1987/1995, Slovenia 1987/1995, Bulgaria 1989/1995, Latvia 1989/1996, Lithuania 1987–8/1993–5, Romania 1989/1993–5, Slovak Republic 1987–8/1993–5, Belarus 1987–8/1993–5, Russia 1989/1996 and Ukraine 1987–8/1993–5.

[e] Contribution of social policy to changes in the Gini coefficient between the pre-transition phase and 1995–6. See the text and Milanovic (1999) for details on the decomposition method.

Notes: Groups 1, 2 and 3 refer to the likely rounds of accession to the European Union.
'—' = not available

Source: Boeri and Edwards (1998) for data on NE benefits in CEECs; Milanovic (1999) for data on income inequality; WB Technical Paper 339 (1996) for data on pension expenditure; Unicef, Regional Monitoring Report, n.4 1997, for data on total social expenditure.

4.2.3 The 'Fatal Attraction' of the European Union

Of the three explanations provided at the beginning of this chapter for the different design of social policies in Russia and the CEECs in the midst of transition, we are left with that related to the return to Europe. The very fact of having a chance one day to enter the European Union would seem to have led public authorities in the Visegrad group to adopt a reform strategy allowing for significant redistribution and relatively compressed earnings structures. The transition was, in other words, viewed—at least West of the Urals—as a long-term process of economic integration requiring some sort of institutional harmonization. Needless to say, one of the key distinguishing features of Europe in comparison with the other models available around the world is the fact that about one-third of value added is allocated to social policies, compared with 16 per cent in North America and 14 per cent in Japan. Wage structures are also more compressed in Europe than elsewhere in the West.

The conditionality of the 'European model' was stronger for the countries that had a chance to enter the European Union. Significantly, the countries targeted for the first round of EU accession are those that have spent more in social policies, notably more on non-employment benefits, throughout the transition (see Table 4.1).

Was such a conditionality a good thing or a bad thing, and, above all, will it be good or bad in the years to come? Before addressing such issues, we need to spend some time trying to understand policy making in the East because it significantly affects the way in which EU conditionality will shape the future course of events in the candidates for accession.

4.3 The Reasons for Bad Policies

While it is possible to explain why social policies were so widely diversified across countries, it is more difficult to understand why in Eastern Europe they were so poorly designed. There were not only the usual inconsistencies present in the West between various policy instruments but also measures that were manifestly inadequate. Broadly speaking, there were too many schemes in place providing too few cash transfers to too many people. Typical is the case of the plethora of family benefits. Some of these schemes had higher administrative costs than the total amount of the transfers involved.

There was also little justification for providing—as was the case in most countries—token unemployment benefits to school-leavers, some-times even without any waiting period. The conditionality of the Eu-ropean Union was certainly not a factor in this case, because school-leavers and first-time jobseekers are rarely offered unemployment ben-efits in the West. EU conditionality could also not explain why the Polish unemployment benefits system was introduced as an open-ended scheme, allowing individuals, in principle, to draw benefits for the rest of their life. Finally, the shift from one type of non-employment benefit to another (for example, from unemployment benefits to social assistance) in many cases involved replacement rates increasing over time, a design feature that clearly does not encourage job searching.[9] Although these problems are present in some OECD countries, economies in transition had to build these schemes from scratch and hence were in a better position than countries with long-standing entitlements in place to avoid such inconsistencies across policy instruments.

The easiest explanation possible for these weaknesses is that bad policies were the result of bad politicians, or the natural by-product of a political class inadequate for market conditions. However, it is difficult to find this simple explanation entirely convincing. One of the things that most struck me during my initial missions to Central and Eastern Europe in 1990–1 was the fact that I met ministers of more or less my own age. I was used to the irremovable and aged ministers of the Italian post-war governments and it took me a while to decide whether it was me who was getting older or whether I was confronted by a newer and younger political class. I finally opted for this second explanation— certainly more reassuring than the first one!

There is no doubt there *was* a new political class emerging in CEECs and many new young faces around. It was composed, for the most part, of well-educated people (certainly more educated than many ministers in the West) who had had some exposure to Western-type economics. Some of the most credited makers of economic policy in the early years of transition—for instance Balcerowicz and Klaus—had even been trained in the United States. Thus, policy mistakes cannot be entirely attributed to the confusion of politicians, who might be using the wrong economic models and obtaining bad policy advice. Even though learning about the consequences of policies was a fundamental component of the transfor-

---

[9]See Boeri and Edwards (1998) and the papers on individual nations in the special issue of *Empirical Economics* (nos 1/2, 1998) on 'Long-term Unemployment and Social Assistance'.

mation, policy makers were equipped to make a good (if not the best) use of available information, and some events, such as the drive to non-employment, were largely predictable. It is true that there were many bad Western advisors coming for one-day visits and dispensing policy recommendations; but policy makers were, for the most part, reasoning with their heads and capable of discerning bad from good advice. There was also a big enough selection of Western economists to allow them to choose between good and bad advisors.

Why, then, were such mistakes made? I have come up with three tentative explanations, set out below.

4.3.1 The Power of Managers

There are several models of political economy dealing with the setting of unemployment benefits. They describe this choice as one involving a conflict between those who have a stable job and those who do not have one (Wright, 1986; Saint-Paul, 1993 and 1996). Those with a tenured job prefer to protect themselves with firing restrictions (generally involving severance payments increasing with tenure in the firm) rather than with generous unemployment benefits. Those outside the firm are instead in favour of high unemployment benefits. As long as the employed people are the majority, the resulting equilibrium is typically one involving low unemployment benefits and strong protection against dismissals.

In transitional economies there were at the outset very few insiders, because those with the longest tenures were working in firms likely to undergo major restructuring and the new jobs were, for the most part, offering short tenures (like most jobs in the expanding retail trade) and low employment security (as discussed in Chapter 3, the new sector was to a large extent not unionized). Employees in state firms could have gone for stricter employment protection, but there was no stronger legal employment protection than that provided by the Labour Codes of the old regime,[10] which generally banned altogether dismissals of any kind. The issue is that employment protection rules were simply not credible under the revolutionary circumstances of the early 1990s and the tightening of state firms' budget constraints. Neither legal restrictions to dismissals nor high severance payments could have prevented dismissals

---

[10]Almost all CEECs have by now completed the process of revision of their Labour Codes, and those involved in the first round of accessions to the European Union have in place employment protection legislation in line with that of continental Europe (see section 4.5 below).

from occurring simply because it was the survival of most firms that was at stake. The fear of being dismissed was widespread. Thus, there were virtually no strong opponents to a rise in unemployment benefits.

Yet, there were at the outset also a few people without a job, virtually no experience of (open) unemployment, an ideology strongly stigmatizing unemployment, and no entitlements to unemployment benefits inherited from the previous system. Hence, although the opposition to relatively high benefits may not have been too strong, the support for high unemployment benefits was likewise rather weak. Who pushed, then, for generous non-employment benefits? There are reasons to believe that it was mainly the managers of state firms.

Putting in place non-employment benefits means, after all, relieving managers from their social responsibilities. Generous unemployment benefits give managers more flexibility in adjusting labour, a greater likelihood of gaining support for restructuring plans involving reductions in the workforce, and lower levels of compensation to pay to those forced to leave the firm. It should be remembered that the strongest opponents to cuts in unemployment benefits in the West are often not the unions but the employers' associations. Actually, employers and unions often collude in the case of redundancies in order to extract more generous transfers from the state. This may actually explain the difficult start of some of the new unions, which were often supporting the new reforming governments, and the survival of the old unions, which were instead fiercely opposing the radical steps being taken at the beginning of the 1990s in most countries in the region.

No unemployment benefits system introduced at the outset of transition was experience-rated; that is, none involved higher contributions for firms actually making use of these instruments while dealing with redundancies. Non-employment benefits were also, to a large extent, funded via general revenues, because payroll taxation often did not provide sufficient resources to pay the subsidies. Special funds collecting employers' contributions and paying unemployment benefits out of them were generally created only two to three years down the road of transition. Thus, in some cases, there was not even a nominal link between payroll taxation and the payment of unemployment benefits contributing to partly internalize the fiscal costs of job loss for firms or, at least, making managers aware of the implications for the public finances of staff reductions.

The important role played by managers of state enterprises in the setting of non-employment benefits is consistent with the timing of reforms documented in Chapter 2. A sequence of initially high and subsequently low benefits was optimal from their standpoint, for it gave the initial boost to employment reductions and, later on, prevented payroll taxes from exploding in order to finance non-employment benefits for a large pool of jobseekers.[11]

The ideal scheme for managers would actually have been one providing a lump-sum transfer (possibly funded via general government revenues rather than taxes on the payroll) to workers voluntarily accepting to leave a firm without creating long-lasting entitlements to non-employment benefits. A similar scheme was implemented in the case of Romanian miners in 1997 and was indeed strongly supported by the managers of mines.[12] The scheme was rather generous in so far as it involved from 6 to 12 months of tax-exempt monthly wages plus an additional 3 months of severance pay for those living in high-unemployment regions and/or so-called 'one-company towns' (urban centres where the

---

[11] The objective of managers can be defined as the minimization of the loss function $L[(1 + \tau_0(b))e_0(b)]$ where τ_0, as usual, denotes payroll taxes collected from firms in the old sector, e_0 is employment in each (state) enterprise, and b stands for unemployment benefit. Supposing that firms are overmanned, we have that $L' > 0$; that is, losses can only be reduced by decreasing employment in the firm (and/or payroll taxes). In line with the model presented in Annex 2., it is assumed that e_0' is negative, so that higher unemployment benefits stimulate reductions in the workforce (for instance by inducing a larger number of quits). The derivative of the loss function with respect to non-employment benefits b gives us the impact on the objective function of managers of a marginal increase in the generosity of subsidies provided to those leaving the firm:

$$\frac{\partial L}{\partial b} = L'\left[e_0\frac{\partial \tau_0}{\partial b} + (1 + \tau_0)\frac{\partial e_0}{\partial b}\right].$$

That is, on the one hand higher benefits reduce losses by negatively affecting employment in the firm (first term within the brackets), but, on the other hand, they may need to be financed by raising payroll taxes (second term within the brackets). Using (2.11) and (A2.24), we then have

$$\frac{\partial L}{\partial b} = L'\left\{e_0\frac{N}{E_0} - [\mu(\tilde{u}_0 + db) - \mu(\tilde{u}_0)](1 + \tau_0)\right\},$$

where $\mu(\tilde{u}_0)$ is, as usual, a measure of unemployed with reservation utility lower or equal than $\tilde{u}_0$, and N and E_0 are, respectively, non-employment and total employment in the old sector. The above expression is decreasing for small N, meaning a small share of the population out of work, as it was at the outset of transition. However, as the effect of benefits on quits from state enterprises (the second term within the square brackets in the first expression in this footnote) vanishes over time and N increases, the loss function begins to increase with larger b.

[12] See The World Bank (1998) for a detailed description of the package and for a summary of the results of a survey among the beneficiaries of this scheme.

mines were actually the only employment provider). Take-up rates were larger than expected: about 50 per cent of the miners, mostly youngsters and skilled workers, decided to take the money and quit. As a result of such departures, labour productivity increased significantly in the mines and the remaining workforce displayed stronger discipline, notably a significant decline of absenteeism.[13]

Although profitable for the managers of the mines, such a package failed in its primary attempt to stimulate outward migration from the mining regions and the start-up of new activities on the part of those leaving the mines. Thus, rather than reducing the need for further cash transfers to former miners in the future, the scheme just paved the way for continued requests for subsidies and assistance. The argument for providing the redundancy pay in one instalment was indeed to finance mobility costs or the initial investment associated with the opening-up of a new activity on the part of those made redundant. However, a very small fraction of the redundant miners (the so-called *disponibilizzati*) actually changed residence, and about 90 per cent of those who left the region immediately after receiving the lump sum came back to the mining regions within less than a year. Moreover, start-ups were very infrequent,[14] and a significant fraction of the severance payment was spent in daily consumption or in the purchase of household appliances. It soon became apparent that conditions had *not* been created to avoid those made redundant from continuing to draw social transfers, such as unemployment benefits or social assistance of the last resort. By January 1999, Romanian miners were once again marching to Bucharest to demand the reopening of mines, new subsidies, and/or pay rises.

Overall, strong pressures—perhaps the strongest pressures—to put relatively generous redundancy schemes and unemployment benefits in place at the outset of transition came mainly from the managers of the state firms. Especially at the early stages of transition, before the large privatization waves, managers exerted strong influence on political decisions. Managerial compensation is a good indication of the power

---

[13]To give an example, the coalmine in Lupeni after the quit of about 50 per cent of its employees, registered a decline of only 10 per cent in its daily extraction of coal. Absenteeism declined significantly: before the redundancies between 80 and 100 miners were absent daily, while afterwards there were an average of around 3 cases a day. See The World Bank (1998), p. 12.

[14]This is certainly not only the result of the poor design of severance pay for miners but also of adverse local demand conditions. Based on regional data on new small businesses and plant start-ups in Hungary, Köllö (1999) convincingly shows that the key factor behind the growth of self-employment in that country has been proximity to urban areas.

of managers of state enterprises: surveys carried out in Bulgaria (Jones and Kato, 1998) suggests that, other things being equal, chief executive officers (CEOs) of state enterprises could enjoy in the first five years of transition a 60 per cent premium over the pay of their counterparts in private or so-called 'commercialized' firms (a definition of units in the process of being privatized). Another indication of the power of managers was their capacity to maintain their position throughout the political changes and radical transformations occurring at the beginning of the 1990s. Djankov and Pohl (1997) report that 19 out of 21 large Slovak firms surveyed in 1996 had the same top management as at the beginning of the 1990s.

While asking for transfers enabling managers to buy out workers, these managers were often not aware of the fact that politicians would interpret their request in a way that was to make it more difficult to cut non-employment benefits later on. Managers were aware of the opportunity offered by non-employment benefits to externalize to society at large the costs of redundancies, but not of the political constraints that would have made it so difficult later on to cut entitlements to open-ended benefits.

4.3.2 Political Concerns

Long-lasting, rather than short-lived, entitlements, like most of the schemes introduced at the outset of transition, rather than being conceived as temporary, were aimed at achieving permanent reductions in the labour supply. Thus, to be fair, politicians gave a very personal interpretation to the requests of managers of state enterprises for transfers to the unemployed. They put those leaving state firms into relatively generous and open-ended cash-transfer systems, and they did not do it out of unfamiliarity with the rules of democracy. Quite the opposite. Vaclas Klaus was long considered one of the smartest transition-country politicians around.[15] He introduced one of the most generous early-retirement schemes (without actuarial reductions of pensions, and allowing beneficiaries to combine pensions *and* work) used at the beginning of the 1990s in the CEECs, and widely used child-care benefits as a way to achieve labour-supply reductions.

---

[15] To put it in the words of Andrei Shleifer: 'Unless these countries are lucky enough to get very good politicians from the start—as the Czech Republic was with Vaclav Klaus— their transition is going to be slow' (Shleifer, 1996, p. 21).

Why did politicians create such long-lasting entitlements to cash transfers? Wasn't it a way of tying their own hands?

Public opinion polls carried out at the outset of transition suggest that there was a majority of the population ready to accept a period of social hardship as a personal tribute to the transformation of the system. There was a minority not ready to trade current costs with future benefits, and this minority was, needless to say, mainly composed of elderly people. They could only see the wrong side of the coin because they would, in any event, hardly enjoy the benefits of the transition to a market economy.

It is one thing to state that one is ready to make sacrifices, and another to actually accept them. The previous system had not exposed the population at large to open unemployment. Persons of working age were used to job security, to earning a salary no matter what their or their firm's productivity performance. Open unemployment was an unknown phenomenon, and one to be particularly concerned about. In Western countries the level of unemployment does not seem to significantly affect political preferences. Right-wing governments survived steep rises in unemployment as Europe went through the job crises of the 1970s and the 1980s without major political turmoil. In transition countries, the situation was significantly different—or at least politicians expected it to be different: unemployment was deemed by them to be a very important factor (if not *the* most important factor) affecting political preferences. And they were right. Unemployment turned out to be a very important determinant of political preferences, with major shifts in voting taking place—and generally in favour of left-wing parties—in the countries and years with the highest levels of unemployment.[16]

Why was there such a strong aversion to open unemployment in these countries? Wasn't it enough to pay unemployment benefits in order to win political resistance to restructuring? Under the previous system, jobs were offered as a sort of benefit in kind. They were a means of maintaining consensus. Also in the West, posts in overmanned state enterprises are frequently used as a device to maintain political control over important segments of the electorate and, when staff reductions become unavoidable, workers leaving state firms are often offered better treatment, in terms of access to early-retirement schemes and severance

---

[16]Based on regional data on unemployment and seats assigned to the various parties in the context of (proportional) elections, Fidrmuc (1999) finds a highly significant and strong effect of unemployment on political support for left-wing parties in CEECs, both cross-sectionally and over time.

payments, than workers made redundant in the private sector. It is true that unions are often stronger than elsewhere in some state monopolies (for example the railway sector), but one of the reasons for the power of trade unions in these sectors is precisely the preferential treatment offered to workers in state firms. In formerly planned economies it was no longer possible to preserve artificial full-employment conditions and managers of *state* enterprises were pressing for staff cuts. Hence, politicians had to find a substitute for jobs as a control device for political preferences. Such a substitute was found in long-lasting entitlements to cash transfers provided to those leaving the firm.

These three factors—the need to compensate the elderly for experiencing only the dark side of transition, the role played by unemployment in affecting voters' preferences, and the use of non-employment benefits as a mechanism for controlling the electorate—played an important role in affecting the way in which politicians interpreted the requests coming from the managers of state enterprises. Rather than providing unemployment insurance, which was inevitably bound to have a limited duration, they created open-ended entitlements either via poorly designed unemployment benefits (for example the Polish open-ended unemployment benefits of the early 1990s), or via bridging schemes to retirement, or liberal access to disability pensions. Reduction in the actual age of retirement were also encouraged by allowing farmers to draw pension benefits or other cash transfers after having transferred land ownership to their children.[17]

In summary, although managers asked for (short-term) lump-sum payments to those leaving a firm, politicians offered pensions. It was not a viable strategy in the long run, and indeed it soon turned out not to be fiscally sustainable or to be sustainable only via significant reductions in the real value of cash transfers. It is important to notice, in any event, that when the fiscal unsustainability of these policies became apparent, the first reaction of politicians in most countries was not to cut eligibility to pensions, but mainly to reduce the benefits by letting inflation erode the real value of cash transfers. Public authorities in these countries have always displayed a strong propensity to maintain entitlements spreading available resources too thinly. Throughout transition there were too many beneficiaries of transfers that were too small. Some nominal benefits were close to nil in real terms, and they were still in place. This

---

[17] According to Leven (1998), pension benefits count for about one-quarter of revenues for the small plots still predominant in Polish agriculture.

leads us to the third explanation for the bad policies—and a reason that has to do with the behaviour of bureaucracies.

4.3.3 Self-Perpetuating Bureaucracies

I was once told by a senior civil servant—someone who had spent his entire working life in a public administration—that there are two situations in which administrations enjoy more discretionary powers in the enforcement of the rule of law. The first case is when laws are rather vague and contain many gaps, so that legislative vacuums have to be filled by the bureaucracies. The second case paradoxically occurs at the other end of the spectrum, when the regulatory framework is too heavy and there are too many laws and norms to be respected, too many entitlements in place, lots of exemptions, and ad hoc provisions.

All centrally planned economies entered the 1990s with a very heavy regulatory framework and large bureaucracies. Under the old regime, after all, virtually all aspects of working life had been regulated, and the price of each commodity had been set by law. I have a book taken from the Ukrainian Ministry of Finance, fixing in detail the price of each lamb cut, which was the result (I was told by a particularly proud official of the Ministry) of lengthy negotiations with farmers and unions. There was also a large battery of cash transfers provided to the workers and their families to be administered. The case of family allowances was particularly striking in this respect: in the former Soviet Union there were more than 60 kind of subsidies that families with children could draw.

With the transition to a market economy, many of these norms became redundant. However, rather than abolishing the old norms and introducing new ones encompassing a broad range of provisions, the new legislative bodies adopted an incremental approach, where they tended simply to add new norms to those previously existing. As a result, the legislative framework became even more complex than at the outset, with a jungle of (often overlapping) provisions, some of which were mutually inconsistent.[18]

---

[18] Significant, in this respect, is the opinion of the managers of large multinational enterprises who have exposure to a variety of national regulations. According to a report of the European Roundtable of Industrialists (gathering the top 45 European industrialists), 'in a number of CEECs there are too many regulations, some of which are enforced in an inconsistent fashion' (ERT, 1999).

This institutional complexity was a way to maintain bureaucracies, so as to give them a role to play in creating specific knowledge about single aspects of the legislative framework. Nobody could dare having a full picture of the legal provisions even within rather well-defined regulatory areas. The case of Russia is enlightening in this respect. There were until 1997 four ministries in charge of social protection and labour policies. I had to visit them repeatedly in an attempt to get updates for OECD policy review work. Such meetings were frustrating; we could hear up to ten different descriptions of the same set of norms, with officials of the various ministries contradicting each other and treating the others as manifestly incompetent. At first, we thought that it was due to a lack of cooperation or of communication between the various bodies; so we started organizing meetings where representatives of the various ministries and agencies were all sitting around the same table, and it seemed to us that it was perhaps one of the most useful services we were offering at that time to the Russian government. We soon realized, however, that it was not just a problem of communication. The various bodies were trying to justify their existence; it was a fight for their *raison d'être*—something we could do little about and, above all, did not *want* to do anything about. In our policy reviews, we were always arguing for a simplification of the administration and a reduction in the number of ministries, but by so doing we were threatening their jobs.[19]

An indication of the self-perpetuating role played by bureaucracies comes from the dynamics of employment in the public administrations of these countries. Fig. 4.2. shows strikingly divergent patterns of employment in the public administration (central government plus local administrations, dotted line) and in the business sector (continuous line) in the CEECs. While employment in the business sector was declining by 10 to 20 percentage points during the five years under scrutiny, the ranks of public administrations were getting larger and larger. The asymmetry between the two series would be even more marked if it were possible to disentangle employment in public administration from defence in all countries, as military personnel have been reducing in

---

[19]Holmes and Sunstein (1999) have collected some figures on the budgetary 'costs of private rights', defined as the resources required to have in place an administration enforcing the legal rights of citizens. Interestingly enough, the social security and social assistance administrations would seem to be more expensive than any other administration for enforcing rights, except the military. This suggests that overregulation in the social-policy field may have indeed significantly inflated the rank of cival servants in the CEECs.

numbers everywhere.[20]   At the end of 1996 the employment share of
public administration in the CEECs was almost 4 per cent, from about
2.5 per cent in 1990. It is worth remembering that one of the legacies
of the previous regime was considered by many as being an overmanned
public administration and that the reduction of the public intermedia-
tion of resources was expected to involve significant reductions in the
number of civil servants. Neither can these trends be explained by the
break up of nations which occurred in the transitional arena. It is true
that some of the countries had to develop from scratch administrations
dealing with functions which were previously assigned to a federal state.
However, the aggregate data displayed in Fig. 4.2. represent *weighted*
averages, only mildly affected by the behaviour of the small national en-
tities emerging from the split of former Federal states. Indeed the trends
in Fig. 4.2. are mainly associated with the dynamics of employment in
the public administrations of Bulgaria, Hungary, Poland, and Romania.

Institutional complexity was not only a way to maintain large bureaucracies but also a recipe for corruption. Even in the Czech Republic, a
country that had inherited from the past a rather efficient, Prussian-style
state administration, corruption among civil servants is perceived by the
general population as remaining pervasive. According to a survey carried
out in 1998, only 12 per cent of the population believes that ministerial
offices are not corrupt.[21] Significantly, the survey reveals that the share
of acts of corruption witnessed by respondents in the state administration
increased over time and, indeed, public administration is unanimously
deemed as the most corrupt sector of the economy.

Country scores on corruption in the public sector produced by Transparency International (1998) on the basis of at least three surveys in
each country also point to high levels of corruption among civil servants
throughout the transition countries. Russia 'leads' the group, and former
Soviet republics like the Ukraine generally appear to have higher levels

[20]International sectoral classifications (comparable across countries); merge employment in public adminisration with defence. Expenditure on the latter has declined in many
countries, which is often pointed out as one of the causes of transitional recession (Boone
et al., 1998). Data (available only for a few years and countries) isolating employment in
local and central public administrations display an upward trend even more marked than in
Fig. 4.2. For example, according to the data collected within the OECD's Sigma project,
in the Czech Republic the increase was of the order of 50 per cent between 1990 and 1993,
in Slovenia the number of civil servants increased by 30 per cent between 1994 and 1998,
and in Latvia the increase in civil servants was 16 per cent between 1995 and 1997.

[21] See Bohata (1998).

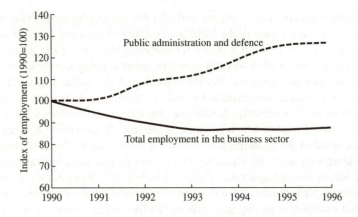

Figure 4.2. Evolution of employment in public administration

Notes: 'Public administration' is defined to cover administration, defence and compulsory social security; education, health and social works are excluded. The figures represented on the graphs refer to the weighted averages of employment in Bulgaria, Czech Republic, Hungary, Poland, Romania, Slovak Republic and Slovenia.

Source: WIIW, Countries in Transition 1998.

of corruption than CEECs.[22] Yet, *all* former Communist countries reveal comparatively high levels of corruption, which suggest that corruption among civil servants, rather than being related to country-specific institutional features, limits of the political class or even transient characteristics, is a systemic characteristic of formerly planned economies. The conclusions from a survey of private-sector businesses carried out by the World Bank (Brunetti *et al.*, 1999) are not dissimilar: they point to corruption among civil servants as one of the major obstacles to doing business in the former Communist regions. Our explanation is that corruption is closely related to the complexity of the legal framework. These bureaucracies were (and still are) trying to capitalize on the specific knowledge they had of the regulatory framework and their discretionary power in deciding upon exemptions. Corruption results from the *power* of bureaucracies.

It is sometimes argued that some degree of corruption may be func-

[22] The high frequency of corrupt practices among civil servants in the region is confirmed also by surveys carried out by the Economist Intelligence Unit and the DRI McGraw Hill Global Risk Service (see EBRD, 1998, for a summary of the results of such surveys). Interestingly, the rankings of countries in terms of corrupt practices provided by Transparency International are confirmed by these sources.

tional to reforms at the outset of transition (Basu and Li, 1998). Reforms imply the dismantling of the inessential parts of bureaucracies, and corruption may play the role of a one-time compensation to bureaucrats who are asked in practice to destroy their own livelihood. If corruption can be traded with a commitment of bureaucrats to support the reform of the public administration and reveal their superior knowledge of its inefficiencies, then it may be actually a device to foster market-oriented reforms. However, this use of corruption presumes the existence of a government remaining in power (and expected to remain in power) for a sufficiently long time to reduce corruption in the future (so as to be credible in its commitment). Needless to say, the stability of governments was something very much lacking in the young democracies of the former Soviet bloc, where corruption played (and still plays) the role of a devil rather than of a temporary device to win the cooperation of bureaucracies in the reform process. Corruption is a key factor playing against the development of competitive markets: a recent study by McKinsey (1999) suggests that privileged access to government procurement for incumbents, and more broadly systemic discrimination against new entrants, has been a key factor against the burgeoning of a genuinely new private sector in Russia.

The persistence of high levels of corruption throughout the transition process set in motion a vicious circle. On the one hand, large bureaucracies had to be maintained within tight budgetary constraints and, hence, wages to civil servants had to be kept at very low levels and sometimes, as in Russia, they were even paid with significant delays. Low wages are notoriously a factor inviting corruption in so far as they reduce the opportunity costs of being caught and of losing one's job. On the other hand, in order to reduce corruption, supervisory bodies had to be strengthened, but this resulted in a further increase in the size of bureaucracies. Overall, it was a typical case where—without changing the rules, without reducing the specific knowledge of regulations and discretion of public administrations in enforcing them, and hence ultimately the number of civil servants—stiffening supervision could do little about corruption or could even have perverse effects on bribery.[23]

---

[23]Carrillo (1995) has developed a model in which increased supervision has perverse effects on bribery. In his model, this is due to the fact that supervisors are themselves carrying out a cost–benefit analysis of accepting bribes and that they have no career promotion incentives. In the case of transitional economies, the perverse effects of supervision on corruption may simply come from the fact that increasing monitoring efforts squeezes the wage bill to be shared among civil servants.

4.4 EU Conditionality and the Informal Sector

As argued in the previous sections, the so-called return-to-Europe syndrome opened a divide in the arena of transitional economies. On the one hand, there are those countries—mainly the Central European economies—that adopted at the very start of transition a wide range of transfers to non-employed individuals of working age, mimicking non-employment benefits existing in Western Europe. On the other hand, we have the former Soviet republic governments allowing redistribution policies to decline as a share of GDP and concentrating social-policy outlays almost exclusively on pensioners. Which of the two models worked best? Surprisingly enough the answer is unambiguous. Whatever the normative criterion, the Visegrad model ranks above the Russian one.

Central European non-employment benefits were poorly designed and heavily interfering with wage determination. Better-designed benefits could have avoided a dramatic fall in employment rates without reducing the pace of job reallocation. We have provided several explanations for these design failures and argued that they placed a heavy fiscal burden on the active population, which is harmful for economic growth and, even more so, for employment growth. Yet no unemployment benefits at all would have been an even worse option. The Russian experience suggests that this would have delayed the process of worker reallocation from obsolete to expanding industries and firms, in turn delaying—if not altogether preventing—the economic recovery following the transitional recession. No benefits is worse than *some* benefits when the goal is to maximize value added, even when those benefits are rather poorly designed.

The Visegrad model ranks above the Russian one also when the normative criterion is social welfare, particularly if equity considerations are important. It is true that transition without benefits generates less non-employment, notably less long-term non-employment and particularly at early stages of transition, but this non-employment is a condition much harder to cope with. In the CEECs, non-employment was larger, but mainly consisted of individuals with a high reservation utility. In Russia, the non-employed derive less satisfaction in the use of time out of (formal) employment and, on the top of that, receive negligible benefits. Moreover earnings–income differentials are larger among employed individuals.

Finally take social cohesion as a goal. In the Visegrad countries, the non-employed are mainly inactive. Under this heading, a highly heterogeneous population is assembled, for example those persons devoting time outside work to child-rearing, individuals surviving out of family networks and/or casual work, and those living on cash transfers provided by social policies. What matters is that, in the light of the prevailing labour-market conditions, these individuals prefer not to be seeking jobs in the new sector; that is, these persons are in equilibrium. In Russia, the non-employed individuals are not in equilibrium and the employed persons are often seeking better jobs.

Thus, so far the 'attractor' of the EU welfare systems has done some damage, but also prevented the worst from occurring. Will the return-to-Europe syndrome continue to be less harmful than beneficial to these countries, now that—after being at the outset implicit and rather mild— EU conditionality is getting stronger and stronger and the EU accession card is being played as a way to impose the adoption of standards and regulations over a wide range of policy areas? Very much depends on whether the conditions imposed on accession are deemed realistic by the international community and by the population at large of the countries under consideration. It will also depend on whether the conditions imposed by the European Union itself, through its *Acquis communautaire*, are interpreted literally or adapted to the specific conditions of the acceding countries, so that the entry process becomes an opportunity to reform some of the least desirable features of Western Europe, notably the inconsistencies of its own welfare systems.

4.4.1 Credibility Effects

It is common to read in Western newspapers alarming and imaginative stories about many firms—if not altogether entire industries—relocating to the Eastern part of Europe in order to benefit from cheaper labour. It is also a common threat made by Western industrialists when negotiating with unions: if you do not reduce your wage claims, we will move to the East. But what is actually surprising is that foreign direct investment (FDI) in many of the CEECs has been rather marginal to date. Only Hungary, and more recently Poland, experienced large FDI inflows from the very beginning of transition and cumulated over time a significant stock of foreign capital (reaching in Hungary almost 35 per cent of GDP in 1996). All the other countries in the region have been struggling—often in vain—to attract more foreign investors.

Why has the level of FDI been so low in countries that are likely in due course to enter the European Union? The historical experience of other accession episodes—for example the Southern enlargement of the EU—suggests that low-wage countries entering a common market benefit from a large increase in FDI inflows. In Spain and Portugal, FDI inflows increased from about half a percentage point to 2.5–3.0 per cent of GDP in the space of two years on their accession before returning, by the mid-1990s, to pre-accession levels.[24]

The small scale of FDIs oriented to the CEECs can be explained by the lack of credibility of these economies. FDIs involve large sunk costs, and hence irreversible commitments on the part of investors. Moreover, low wages in these countries are often associated with low labour productivity: as unit labour costs are what ultimately matters for profit maximizers, investors need to be convinced that the recipient countries are on an irreversible path to a rather rapid convergence with the productivity levels prevailing in the West. Thus, the need to be reassured that these countries will actually join the EU (credibility) is essential for FDIs.

Credibility is also essential for portfolio investment and domestic investors, and hence for the financing of the public debt accumulated over the transition period (and largely associated with social security outlays) at rates that do not displace productive investment. Significantly, spreads over US Treasuries or German Bunds on Eurobond issues have been in 1998 six times larger in Slovakia than in Poland, in spite of the better external position of the former and of comparable fiscal deficits in the two countries. Poland belongs to the group of countries that are included in the first round of EU accessions, while Slovakia in 1998 was not.

Finally, credibility is important for domestic institutions and law enforcement. Western countries have much better records of law enforcement than the CEECs. According to a survey carried out by the World Bank, governments of formerly planned economies are not credible, rarely stick to the rules, and are likely to enforce new regulations retroactively, reneging on previous commitments.[25] EU accession may,

[24] In Greece the rise of FDI was much more contained because of greater political instability and of the restrictions imposed in this country on capital movements after accession (Alogoskoufis, 1995).

[25] See Brunetti *et al.*, 1999. More than 60 per cent of the private entrepreneurs interviewed declared that CEECs governments are unpredictable (a bit more than 30 per cent in developing countries, DCs), more than 50 per cent that they rarely (or never!) stick to announced policies (30 per cent in DCs), and more than 45 per cent that regulations can be changed retroactively (roughly 25 per cent in DCs).

in this context, play the role of a powerful disciplining device. If citizens believe that accession is going to be forthcoming, they will be more prone to comply with the law. Law abidance by a large fraction of the population in turn makes it less costly to repress illegal behaviour. In other words, credible accession allows the rule of law to be better enforced because it lends more credibility to the penalties given to those breaking the law and reduces the costs of the repression apparatus.[26]

The issue is that the Eastern enlargement process is proceeding at a much slower pace than envisaged at the time when the bilateral association agreements were signed. There are increasing indications that a tendency to delay the overall accession process and be very tight in checking that the *Acquis communautaire* is not only legally binding but is also actually enforced by new entrants is prevailing in Brussels. Under such conditions, EU accession—even on the part of those countries previously in the so-called 'Group 1' (Czech Republic, Estonia, Hungary, Poland and Slovenia)—may lose credibility, thereby reducing the beneficial role played by prospective entry on law enforcement. In other words, there is a high risk that a vicious circle is set in motion whereby strong conditionality on the part of the EU, rather than increasing law compliance, ends up feeding the informal sector. Requests for tight enforcement of the *Acquis* make accession less credible and hence jeopardize efforts made by governments in the region to enforce the rule of law.

Strong repression of illegal behaviour may be a substitute for the credibility of EU accession, but repression is costly and poor law enforcement typically goes hand in hand with weak tax collection[27] and the presence of a large informal sector. Increasing tax rates in order to pay for larger and better-equipped inspectorate functions[28] may, in this context, have perverse effects, by increasing the size of the informal sector.

Unfortunately, there is hardly any evidence on the determinants of the decisions of firms to hide their activities, enabling one to assess the links between taxation and the size of the informal sector. Aggregate data reported graphically in Fig. 4.3. (and the multivariate regression whose results are summarized in the box) hint at a positive correla-

---

[26]The role of EU accession in law enforcement in CEECs is discussed in Roland and Verdier (1999).

[27]Improvements in tax collection are also impeded by the role played by barter transactions, not only in the CIS but also in EU candidate countries such as Romania.

[28]Neither is foreign borrowing a viable alternative in this context, as reducing the public and external debts are often additional requirements imposed on the road to accession.

tion between the share of the hidden economy in GDP and compulsory social-security contributions, when control is made for the size of the private sector (a broad measure of progress made in the road to a market economy).[29] Although the line of causation may also go the other way round (that is, a large informal sector forces governments to raise compulsory contributions), mandatory social-security contributions have not significantly picked up in the countries on the road to EU accession, while all estimates of the size of the informal sector display a marked upward trend. This may suggest that high taxation on labour,[30] coupled with inefficiencies in the state sector, indeed plays an important role in the spread of the unofficial economy.

Poor tax collection administration and, more broadly, poor enforcement of the rule of law are necessary conditions for the development of the informal sector. Microeconomic evidence drawn from surveys of employers in these countries suggests that many firms underreport their sales in order to pay lower bribes (Johnson *et al.*, 1999)—something that suggests that bribes are proportional to sale volumes and that tighter law enforcement may actually reduce the size of the informal sector.

Thus, it is quite likely that strategies aimed at reducing the size of the informal sector in transitional economies will have to combine stricter enforcement of the rule of law with declining or, at least, non-increasing tax rates on the formal sector. This can only be achieved by rationalizing the public administration, reducing corruption within the state machinery, and streamlining regulations in order to ease the supervision of law compliance. The European Union can support this effort by financially and technically assisting accession candidates in their efforts to reform their public administrations and conditioning entry on progress made on that front. This is much different from the literal notion of the harmonization with EU rules (a notion based more on the legislative side and on parliamentary approval of new laws, rather than on actual enforcement), which prevailed in most CEECs' answers to the EC (1995) White Paper and which is still surfacing in ongoing rounds of

[29]I used both the estimates of the informal sector provided by Lacko (1999), which are based on the household electricity consumption approach, and the 'expert guesses' offered by Johnson *et al.* (1997), obtaining thereby comparable results. The two rankings of countries are highly correlated.

[30]Lacko (1999) reports a strong positive correlation between capital taxation and the size of the informal sector. This correlation is likely to capture delays in the transition. Marginal tax rates on capital are higher in the CIS countries that failed to reform their tax systems, and hence were not able to shift taxation away from corporate taxes towards personal income and indirect taxation.

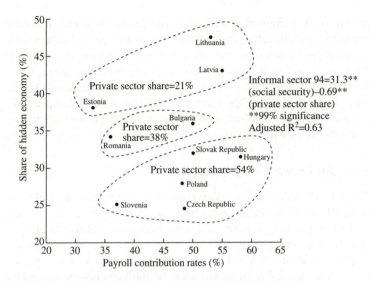

Figure 4.3. Payroll contribution rates vs share of hidden economy (1994)

Notes: Payroll Contribution Rates are defined as Social Security and Health contributions. For Latvia and Lithuania, Effective Marginal Tax Rates. The share of hidden ecomomy as a percentage of GDP is derived via the Household Electricity approach.

negotiations over accession.[31] This approach does not take into account the fact that enforcement of the EU conditionality will remain in the hands of the CEECs' public administrations. Thus, it will in any event be difficult for the European Union to monitor the implementation of the legislation of the *Acquis*, and too strong a conditionality may increase the incentives of governments in the CEECs to exploit these monitoring problems.

Overall, there is a trade-off between the credibility of accession and the conditionality of the European Union. In order to smooth this trade-off and so make it less stringent, conditionality should target the streamlining of regulations and law enforcement, more than the regulations *per se*. However, the postponement of accession, especially if not accom-

---

[31] I had the opportunity to discuss with officials of Labour Ministries of several accession countries the answers being provided to the social part of the EC (1995) White Paper questionnaire. My impression was that very little, if any, attention was devoted to enforcement issues. Put another way, compliance with the *Acquis* was considered as a matter for jurists (and legal departments of Ministries) more than as a challenge for public administrations.

panied by the definition of a credible agenda for entry, may make the enforcement of the rule of law and the unavoidable reforms of public administrations in these countries more difficult, increasing the costs over the benefits of the return to Europe. Focusing on enforcement, therefore, should not imply imposing conditions on these countries that are unrealistic in the light of the current state of their public administration. It means proposing realistic agendas for reform of the state machinery, coupled with technical assistance towards institutional reform.

4.4.2 The Eastward–looking *Acquis*

The difficult challenge facing the countries in the region is therefore how to rapidly meet the requirements of *Acquis communautaire* in practice, rather than just in legal terms, and at the same time continue the process of economic convergence. The task is complicated by the fact that the *Acquis* should be described as 'Eastward-looking' in so far as the list of requirements and legal provisions to be fulfilled goes far beyond the conditions imposed in earlier accessions and, unlike these previous enlargement episodes, emphasis is placed not only on legal harmonization but also on the actual implementation of norms.[32] Particularly stringent criteria are, moreover, defined in terms of environmental standards as well as health and safety at work, public health, and labour law and working conditions, which sometimes go beyond those actually enforced in some of the current EU member states.[33] Country memoranda prepared by the European Union to monitor progress made by the candidates towards meeting the EU requirements often involve issues such as the degree of centralization of collective bargaining—a matter that is *not* regulated in many EU countries.

Thus, it is hard to view this 'Eastward-looking' *Acquis* as merely an expression of solidarity among workers in an enlarged European Union and a genuine attempt to enshrine this idea in a common doctrine. A more cynical, but also more convincing, rationale for the tight conditions placed on entry is that they aim mainly at levelling the playing

[32] Significantly, the 1995 Madrid European Council particularly emphasized the need for accession countries to 'adapt their administrative structures so as to guarantee the harmonious implementation of community policy after membership'. Moreover, reviews of 'progress towards accession' devote particular attention to reforms of state administration, the expansion of the judicial capacity, inspectorate functions of the various ministries and, more broadly, 'the reinforcement of the rule of law'.

[33] Typical is the case of the provisions of the Social Charter and the Social Protocol, which were for many years not endorsed by the UK administration.

field by preventing 'wage and social dumping'.[34] There are, after all, distributional dimensions of the accession which cannot be overlooked, especially in the light of the fact that this is the first accession episode involving countries with significantly lower GDP per capita levels than current EU members. Accession can hardly make *everybody* better off, although it is very likely to increase aggregate welfare. The distributional impact and associated social tensions arising with some of the accession scenarios help to explain the presence of strong pressures from current EU member states to reduce the competitiveness of the newcomers in the internal market as well as reduce the attractiveness for FDIs of the European low labour-cost countries.[35]

Whatever the explanation for the tight conditions imposed on accession, the challenge ahead for these countries is how to comply with these conditions without losing the necessary flexibility required to further the ongoing structural transformation. Delaying accession unilaterally while waiting to complete the transition process does not seem to be a viable option for these countries because, as argued above, expectations of a smooth and irreversible accession path are essential to make progress towards more effective law enforcement and this, in turn, is a strong condition on entry placed by current EU members. In other words, the difficult challenge ahead is how to cope with Western European regulations without introducing the same rigidities in quantity adjustment that these norms generally imply.

4.4.3 Labour Supply and the Informal Sector

Surprisingly enough, the literature on the informal sector is mostly focused on incentives for employers to underreport sales or wages, while it devotes little if any attention to incentives coming from the supply side. However, the decision not to hide or underreport economic activities should be backed by the workers. Otherwise it is bound to fail even when account is taken of the inefficiency and corruption of state administrations in these countries.

Contrary to popular wisdom, properly designed non-employment

[34]This is actually stated explicitly in the EC (1995) White Paper: 'An uneven approach in national legislation concerning workers' rights or health and safety in the workplace could result in unequal costs for economic operators and threaten to distort competition ... At the same time, certain social legislation is not aimed *exclusively* [our emphasis] at achieving a level playing field' (see EC, 1995, pp.18–9).

[35]See von Hagen (1996) for a discussion of the political economy of accession.

benefits can be labour-supply-enhancing. Notably, they can induce those outside the labour market to take up jobs in the formal sector. The key design feature enabling cash transfers to jobless people to play such a role is that non-employment benefits should be truly *un*employment benefits, that is, cash transfers provided only to those who are actively searching rather than to all inactive, able-bodied individuals.

Extensions of the reallocation model proposed in the previous chapters can show these incentive effects associated with unemployment benefit provision. In the annex to this chapter (Annex 4.), the informal sector is modelled as tax evasion or, more precisely, as avoidance of the payment of compulsory social security contributions. We consider, for simplicity's sake (and in some countries this assumption is actually very realistic) a case where detection technologies are so primitive that the probability of being caught by the tax authorities while working in the informal sector is negligible. In this context, the decision to pay or not to pay social security contributions falls entirely on the workers as they bear entirely the consequences of this choice. If they do (not) contribute, they get as take-home pay their net (gross) wage. However, in the case of job loss, they do (not) receive unemployment benefits. Clearly the choice between the two strategies will depend on the probability of dismissal and on the replacement of previous earnings provided by unemployment benefits. Thus, low dismissal probabilities increase the incentives not to declare jobs.

As shown by the model, there is a trade-off between the generosity of the system and the size of the informal sector. If benefits are low and earning-related (the Russian way), workers have no incentives to pay social security contributions because the duration of any job search in case of job loss is expected to be short and benefits offer a negligible fraction of previous earnings. Moreover, the virtual absence of benefit floors (and hence wage floors in the new sector) makes low-skilled individuals reluctant to move to the new sector. This means that jobs in the new sector are relatively stable because of composition effects, where new jobs involve a relatively large proportion of skilled (and therefore more fungible) workers. The presence of benefit floors may, as discussed in Chapter 3, foster workers' reallocation, increase the incidence of unemployment and the share of employees contributing to unemployment insurance. However, if benefits are flat, they will continue to encourage tax evasion at the top end of the wage distribution in so far as highly-skilled workers perceive the contributions as transfers to the low-skilled workers who are subject to more frequent unemployment episodes.

All in all, in order to maximize compliance with social security contributions, unemployment benefits should have minima and be earning-related above such benefit floors at least up to a given wage–educational-attainment level. Beyond this level, the probability of job loss and the duration of unemployment are so low that no unemployment insurance scheme without regressive features (something that is unlikely to be politically feasible, at least judging from the progressive nature of unemployment benefits in OECD countries) can be palatable to job holders. On this latter group of workers, particularly if they are a minority of the employees in the new sector, detection efforts should be concentrated.

Other design features of unemployment benefits that can play an important role in inducing larger compliance to compulsory insurance against the risk of job loss have to do with the access to unemployment benefits. If eligibility criteria require that workers have a relatively long contribution/work record, then evasion from payment of social security contributions may be encouraged for those with low educational attainments because the expected tenure in the new sector may appear too short to be sufficient to gain access to unemployment compensation. In general, eligibility criteria linking the maximum duration of benefits to the length of the contribution period without requiring significant minimum employment records should be preferred on the ground that jobs in the new sector offer relatively short tenures.

The World Bank has collected data on the number of contributors to the social security system in various CEECs (World Bank, 1996). Although workers and employers may still underreport wages in order to reduce the amount of the contributions, the number of contributors over the eligible population (the population of working age) offers a good measure of compliance, which can also be obtained for various countries and time periods in order to gain the degrees of freedom in econometric estimates. Table 4.2 reports the results obtained by regressing the share of persons in working age contributing to compulsory social security (unemployment insurance and pensions) against unemployment benefit coverage rates (the share of unemployment benefit claimants in registered unemployment), the average replacement rates offered in the course of the first year of unemployment to those who were earning twice the average wage relative to those earning two-thirds of it (a summary measure of the extent to which benefits are earning related), as well a transition-time trend, that is a variable counting of the years since the start of transition in the various countries (1989 for Poland, 1990 for Hungary, and 1991 for Bulgaria and the Czech and Slovak

Table 4.2. Shares of contributors, risk of unemployment and unemployment benefit coverage rates (regression results)

Dependent variable	Method	Earnings Relation[a]	Coverage[b]	Years since beginning of transition[c]	Private[d]	Adj.R^2	Number of Observations
Contributors/working age population	linear regression	0.18** (2.37)	0.44** (2.90)	0.002 (0.05)	−0.05 (0.18)	0.67	25
Contributors/working age population	probit regression	0.09** (2.09)	2.46** (2.47)	0.010 (0.04)	−0.54 (0.29)	0.59	25

[a] Average of the (gross) nominal replacements rates (inclusive of social assurance for one-person households) offered in the course of the first year of unemployment to those who were earning twice the average wage relative to those earning two-thirds of it. Measure obtained by applying a benefit indexation mechanism to actual inflation rates 1992–3.

[b] Share of the unemployed covered by unemployment insurance.

[c] Country-specific time trend taking value 0 in 1989 for Poland, 1990 for Hungary, and 1991 for the Czech and Slovak republics and Bulgaria.

[d] Share of private sector in value added.

Notes: Absolute value t-statistics in parentheses. One asterisk denotes significance at 90%, two asterisks at 95% confidence levels.

Source: OECD-Labour Market Database, World Bank: SCT Database.

republics) and, finally, the share of the private sector in GDP, capturing actual progress made in the economic transformation. Given the limited number of observations available, we certainly cannot claim robustness for these results. Unemployment benefit coverage rates and the extent by which benefits preserve wage relativities in the previous jobs would seem positively to affect the probability to contribute, both when a linear regression model and a grouped-logit specification of the regression are used. Overall, these results do not discourage further research on supply-side determinants of decisions to hide economic activities, and they suggest that features of unemployment benefit systems, like its coverage, are likely to play a relevant role in encouraging compliance with statutory contribution rates.

4.5 Still Time to Change . . .

The above suggests that the large size of the informal sector in these countries is also due to failures in the build-up of social welfare systems coping with market conditions. Throughout this book inferences have been made concerning various design features of non-employment benefits and their effect on reallocation and income distribution. It is now time to summarize the main results achieved in this analysis, and to act with freedom (or bravery, if you wish) to try to state these results as policy advices, not only for the formerly planned economies dealt with in this book but also for hypothetical countries that still have to embark upon major structural change episodes similar to those experienced by the CEECs.

Given that non-employment benefits are interlinked with other features of the social welfare system, they cannot be discussed in isolation. Thus, in this section I will first concentrate on unemployment benefits and then devote some attention to other institutional features of social welfare systems.

4.5.1 Improving the Design of Non-Employment Benefits: Seven Principles

Unemployment benefit systems introduced at the outset of transition were supposed to play the twin and crucial roles of providing a safety net while at the same time not discouraging the reallocation of workers involved in the systemic transformation. They actually turned out to play a third role as well, not less important than the other two: they provided floors to wage setting, so that they were *de facto*, nationwide minimum wages. At the same time, other cash transfers, such as pensions and various kind of invalidities, played the role of unemployment benefits, where, they offered income support to workers abandoning the state sector.

The considerations developed in this book suggest that better-designed unemployment benefits for middle-income countries undergoing major structural transformations should satisfy seven basic principles.

The *first principle* is that different policy instruments should be used to achieve different objectives. In particular, it is preferable to have an unemployment insurance scheme tailored to job losers (as job search can also be effectively carried out on the job), allowing them to search efficiently and not discouraging outsiders from accepting jobs offering low employment security, with an income-support scheme of the last resort for those who fall at the margins of transition and statutory minimum wages, coping with asymmetries in the coverage of collective bargaining institutions between the old and the new sector, and providing sufficient incentives for the unskilled to leave state firms. The fact of starting with one instrument rather than three does not give many degrees of freedom to policy makers in the design of unemployment benefit systems, because it forces governments to put in place transfers of relatively long duration (the social-assistance function) and to offer rather generous replacement rates (the minimum-wage function).

The *second principle* is that the unemployment insurance function does not require overgenerous benefits. Unemployment insurance schemes—schemes aimed only at providing *temporary* income support to unemployed jobseekers—offering high replacement rates for a long period for any one individual ultimately turn out to play against the workers' interests because their effect on the instantaneous welfare of the unemployed is offset by the increased duration of unemployment. Redistribution to non-employed individuals with no marketable skills any longer may possibly be achieved with other policy instruments. A common justification provided for generous benefits even on these accounts is that unemployment benefits may provide (partial) insurance against exogenous and temporary adverse events. In particular, unemployment benefits can raise the utility of the unemployed if they are relatively generous during downturns, when the duration of unemployment is longer, independently of the search efforts of the unemployed.[36]

Yet, this justification does not hold in the case of economies undergoing systemic transformations because the speed and scope, and hence the success itself, of the transformation is affected by the incentives put in place to move from one sector to another as well as by the general equilibrium effects of the cash transfers, namely the fiscal externalities associated with unemployment benefit payments. Put another way, there is no guarantee that the 'transitional recession' will end, and the likelihood that a halt is put to the initial adverse shock is not independent of the design of unemployment benefits. The fact of not being generous does not mean that benefits should cover only specific categories of job losers, such as those with relatively long employment records; the considerations made above about the role of unemployment benefits in affecting the size of the informal sector suggest, on the contrary, that coverage should be broad for those having previous work experience.

One of the reasons why non-employment benefits were set in some countries at rather generous terms at the outset of transition, where they were explicitly or *de facto* open-ended, is that they were used to compensate the 'total losers', namely people who were deemed—mainly because of their age and skills—not to be in a position to enjoy the benefits of the systemic transformation to occur. Bridging schemes to retirement were conceived as a compensation for those who, having lived for long under Communism, had spent almost their entire working life in the wrong occupation and were too old to upgrade their skills. This rationale for offering 'exit contracts' implicitly assumes that it is possible to identify in advance the 'total losers' without having to collect information that can be altered at will by individuals, and hence without adverse incentive effects. Needless to say, this is quite a strong assumption, particularly under the conditions of formerly planned economies in which there were no market signals to draw upon when evaluating the marketability of individuals' skills. Had it been truly possible to target the total losers in advance, it would have been preferable not to condition the offer of early retirement schemes to the registration at labour offices. Separating those retiring from work from the actual jobseekers would have, at least, increased the incentives of employers in the new sector to use registered unemployment as a recruitment pool for their workers.

---

[36]The case for 'cyclically adjusted unemployment benefits' is advocated by Coles (1996).

The forgoing leads us to the *third principle*: if it is at all possible to identify in advance and without adverse incentive effects the 'total losers' of transition, then they should be offered income support schemes that do not require as an eligibility condition the registration at labour offices as unemployed. Mixing the registered unemployment-pool individuals, with skills that are no longer marketable, together with jobseekers who have instead the potential to succeed in the new environment induces employers in the new sector to choose a different recruitment pool for their workers. The model developed in Chapter 2 to cope with the puzzles of transition has very much this implication: if the unemployment pool is perceived as a cluster of individuals with a weak attachment to the labour market, then recruitment strategies of employers will target workers in the old sector. In this way, a vicious circle is set in motion, whereby employers look for workers elsewhere and the unemployed themselves get discouraged from job searching, yielding the low participation repeatedly characterized in this book.

The issue is that informational asymmetries are relevant at all levels and that even the managers of state enterprises are often not in a position to identify those with non-marketable skills.[37] When this is the case, the only way to give less noisy signals to employers as to the quality of those registered at labour offices is to rely on incentives that make potential applicants actively seeking and induce those who do not seek jobs to select themselves into an alternative cash-transfer mechanism. For this reason, it is essential—and this is the *fourth principle*—to have in operation a social-assistance scheme from the very beginning of the transition, which should be administered *separately* from unemployment insurance. These schemes were instead generally created a few years down the road of transition, mainly as a reaction to the fact that, after the reforms of 1992, many unemployed were falling out of unemployment compensation rolls.

Social assistance was also mixed with unemployment benefits either by introducing this income support scheme as a (flat-rate) extension of unemployment benefits or by linking the provision of social assistance

---

[37] A Moravian CEO of a state enterprise once told me that, at the outset of transition, he had called his best workers together and invited them to leave the enterprise: 'We have redundancies and you are in a better position than others to find another job'. It does not come as a surprise that several attempts failed, at least to my knowledge, to privatize that firm and make it financially viable. This example, however, is indicative of the fact that some managers were convinced about being able to separate market winners from market losers.

to able-bodied individuals to their registration at labour offices. Social assistance ought not to have been a basic income scheme that provides all individuals, independently of their residence with the same level of benefits; it is argued below that benefits should have been differentiated between urban and rural areas in order to take into account of differentials in the cost of living and of the coping strategies allowed for by subsistence agriculture. An additional reason for running social-assistance schemes at the local level (which clearly does not mean that their financing should also be fully localized) is that it is possible to set allowances taking into account the opportunities offered in various communities to provide part of the benefits in kind.

The *fifth principle* is that it is essential to enforce work tests on those having reached relatively long unemployment durations. Strict enforcement of work tests is essential for two reasons. In the first place, it provides reassurance to employers that the time they devote to interviewing people referred to them by labour offices is not wasted. Second, work tests push those who are not interested in finding a 'suitable' job, or who deem that they will never find one and hence are not making efforts to retrain and improve the marketability of their skills, to leave the register for a less generous income-support scheme such as social assistance. As discussed in Chapter 2, one of the reasons behind the Czech unemployment miracle has been the enforcement of strict work tests on unemployment benefit claimants.

The *sixth principle* is that unemployment benefit levels in rural areas should be lower than in urban areas. They should be adjusted in order at least to take into account of differences in the cost-of- living between the two types of regions, in some cases well above 30 per cent. This would also deal with the differences in the profile by education of wage claims of individuals (characterized in Chapter 3), which—in the presence of relatively generous benefits—tend to discourage job search among the unskilled in rural areas. Adjustments of unemployment benefits and social assistance on the basis of differences in living costs are also important in order to foster regional labour mobility, which is badly needed to reduce wide and persistent regional differentials in non-employment rates.

Finally, the *seventh principle* is that job leavers should not be entitled to unemployment compensation, or only after some waiting period.[38]

---

[38]This principle can be enforced provided that quits do not represent hidden layoffs. Realistic employment-protection regulations (see section 4.5.2) not imposing too heavy

Under the conditions of transitional economies, job search can be effectively carried out even while maintaining a job in the old sector and
hence people should be discouraged from quitting a job before they
have found a suitable alternative. By the same token, there seems to
be little justification for providing unemployment benefits to school-
leavers: rather than providing subsidies to first-time jobseekers, these
should be encouraged to further their studies or assisted in their search
for a job, for instance by promoting a better circulation of information
on vacancies being opened in various segments of the labour market and
regions.

Summarizing, we can state that unemployment benefits during transition should have been of fixed duration, and administered separately
from bridging schemes to retirement or other labour-supply-reducing
policies. This means also that specialized instruments should have been
used to deal with poverty. Adjustments to the level of benefits should
have been made in order to take into account any differences in the
cost of living between rural and urban areas. Eligibility should have
been confined to persons with previous work experience, and benefits
provided from the very beginning of the unemployment spell to job
losers only.

4.5.2 Interactions with Active Policies

This book argues also in favour of a different timing of reforms of unemployment benefits than that experienced by CEECs. In particular, it
suggests that it was important not to have generous non-employment
benefits at the early stages of transition, as the risk was high to induce
large flows into inactivity and fill registered unemployment pools with
individuals not actively seeking jobs. An additional reason for increasing
the generosity of the system only later in the process is that generous
schemes can be operated efficiently only when accompanied by an offer of active labour-market policy instruments (ALMPs), and it takes
time to develop an appropriate infrastructure to run such active schemes.
Especially under the conditions of transitional economies, where job
opportunities for the unemployed are sometimes so scarce as not to allow
any test of the willingness of unemployment benefit recipients to take up
the job offers that they receive, work tests for individuals who have been

administrative and procedural obligations (on top of severance pay) onto employers can
reduce incentives to hide layoffs or use hybrid separation clauses such as the separation
'by mutual agreement' in the labour codes inherited from the previous regime.

unemployed for more than one year can only be made by offering to them slots in ALMPs. If an individual does not take up an offer, she/he is struck out of the unemployment compensation rolls.

The interaction between active and passive policy instruments is conducive not only to a more efficient use of unemployment benefits but also to a more effective use of ALMPs themselves. Significantly, the best results in the implementation of active programmes (at least judging from data on aggregate outflows from unemployment to jobs) have been achieved in countries such as the Czech Republic, which has made the extension of the duration of unemployment benefits conditional upon participation in some active programme (Boeri and Burda, 1996; Boeri, 1998). The experience of Western countries suggests, however, that participants in training or public work schemes should not be automatically reinstated in unemployment compensation rolls at the end of the programme, in order to avoid the unemployed getting trapped into entitlement 'circles' (Calmfors, 1994).

The rationale for implementing active policies in economies undergoing major structural change is mainly in remedying the informational asymmetries of the market mechanism and in complementing the insurance function of unemployment benefits.[39] The best insurance against the loss of a job is ultimately provided by measures increasing the chance of finding a new job, and ALMPs are supposed just to foster re-employment probabilities of the unemployed individuals. Active policies were part of the policy package introduced in the CEECs at the outset of transitions. Expenditure in active schemes has been in some countries—notably the Czech Republic—relatively large at early stages of transition. Yet, the commitment to active policies has been significantly scaled down in recent years in the course of fiscal consolidation efforts. While individuals acquire a right to unemployment benefits, access to ALMPs is not based on entitlements and it is quite natural that they are crowded out by expenditure on passive policies. Moreover, the downscaling of these programmes may be attributed to the fact that they tend to be given a rather low priority by governments.

---

[39]Other rationales for ALMPs in transition countries are discussed in Boeri (1998). They include the need to support the startup of new activities, remedying to a lack of entrepreneurship in these countries, the presence of a skills mismatch (assuming that it is possible to clearly identify the skills requirements in a new sector and to retrain the workforce), and the attempt to offset the effects of unemployment duration on skills depreciation and, more broadly, on the 'marketability' of the unemployed.

Yet, the material provided in this book and in the applied literature on labour-market policies does not lend support to a large-scale
implementation of active labour-market policies in economies undergoing structural change, and the evidence produced so far on the effects of ALMPs in transitional economies is mixed. There are no clear-
cut conclusions that can be drawn from macroeconomic impact assessments carried out so far,[40] nor as well as from the mounting volume
of microeconomic evaluation literature.[41]   Some programmes appear
to work in some countries and be wasteful in others; moreover, when
ALMPs do not work, they not only are associated with a misuse of
public resources (for instance the dead-weight costs documented in some
studies, whereby the unemployed participating in a scheme would have
found a job in any event), but may also crowd out regular employment
by substituting employees with unemployed people involved in the active programmes (the so-called 'substitution effects' associated with the
implementation of active programmes).   Hence, it is fair to say that
ALMPs are still an area of experimentation, where learning processes
as to the effects of policies have still a long way to go. For governments
facing tight budgetary constraints, it may be unwise to overinvest in these
schemes.

Better circulation of information on employment opportunities,
or formal or ad hoc schemes promoting the regional mobility of
workers, have an important role to play in the countries preparing for
EU accession, and the countries of the European Union themselves have
a vested interest in supporting these efforts so as to encourage more
interregional mobility of persons of working age. It is estimated that,
in the candidate countries, nomadic populations living in rural areas
characterized by chronic and acute shortages of jobs total as many as
five million individuals. If current EU members wish to avoid large
migration flows from the candidate countries, they ought to encourage
policies that reduce both labour-market imbalances and discrimination
against ethnic minorities in the CEECs. Fortunately, given the small
size of most of the candidate countries, significant interregional
mobility can be achieved within daily commuting, but there is a
gap within the transportation infrastructures to be filled in order to

---

[40] See, for instance, Boeri and Burda (1996) and Boeri (1998) for estimates of matching
functions augmented for active policies in transitional economies.

[41] See the essays contained in the Symposium issue of the *Journal of Comparative
Economics*, 27, 1999.

expand the scope of commuting and reduce its costs.[42]

Overall, ALMPs in economies undergoing major redeployment of labour can best be implemented by exploiting the mutually advantageous interactions between active and passive policies. Active programmes should be used mainly as a device to enhance the effectiveness of the unemployment benefit systems, and their primary objective should be to improve the circulation of information on job opportunities and reduce informational asymmetries between unemployed and employed jobseekers.

4.5.3 The Trade-off Between Unemployment Insurance and Employment Protection

Unemployment benefits and employment protection are often perceived as substitutes, and there is indeed some evidence that countries with generous unemployment benefits have rather liberal employment-protection legislation in place and vice versa (Buti *et al.*, 1998). This suggests that governments of transitional countries can actually choose where to locate along this trade-off. The analysis in this book and the arguments on ALMPs made above, however, indicate that employment protection is a highly imperfect substitute for unemployment insurance in economies undergoing major structural change. When massive redeployment of labour is required, major losses can be expected by trading unemployment benefits with employment protection, because the latter slows down the job-reallocation process and, on the top of that, it is unlikely in any event to be effective in granting protection to workers in the old sector.

According to indicators produced by the OECD (1999) of the degree of employment protection, Hungary is the only country of the Visegrad group having rather strict legislation protecting workers against the risk of dismissals (Fig. 4.4). However, the relatively high value of the Hungarian overall indicator of employment protection reflects mainly the role played by legal restrictions on the use of *temporary* employment, rather than overstrict norms concerning the dismissal of workers under *permanent* contracts. The experience of OECD countries suggests that it is politically feasible to remove restrictions on temporary employment even in highly unionized countries. Actually, in the countries where insiders are most powerful and strongly oppose reductions of employ-

---

[42]Based on results from a survey on commuting costs from 3,000 Hungarian villages, Boeri *et al.* (1997) show that commuting costs from rural areas are as high as the minimum wage at a distance of 25 km from home (see Fig. 2.3 of that work. p. 21).

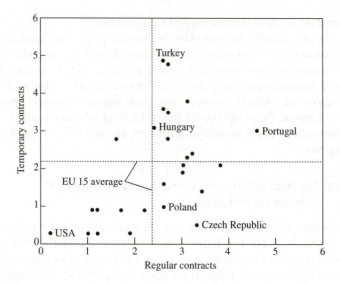

Figure 4.4. Strictness of employment protection (OECD[a])
Notes: Higher values of the index denote stricter employment protection.
Source: OECD (1999).

ment protection, the expansion of temporary employment can be used as a sort of Trojan horse in winning support to reforms of the legislation on permanent contracts because they create a large group of workers whose interests are vested by having easier access to permanent contracts (Saint-Paul, 1996). Thus, labour-market flexibility does not seem to be—at least at present—a major issue in the CEECs and the CIS countries, and this impression is confirmed by surveys of employers attributing relatively high 'grades' to labour legislation in these countries.[43]

An additional reason for not introducing strict employment-protection regulations into transitional economies is that artificially

[43] According to the International Institute for Management Development (IMD) survey of about 4,000 business executives worldwide (IMD, 1998), labour market regulations in Eastern Europe and Russia have scores ranging from a low 5.2 in Poland to a high 7.2 in Hungary, compared with 6.9 in the United States and 2.3 in Italy. The Economist Intelligence Unit (EIU, 1999) survey of managers of multinational corporations ranks Eastern European labour-market restrictions broadly at the same level as the European Union and above Italy. Significantly CIS countries are graded on these grounds well above Western Europe.

low dismissal probabilities tend to favour avoidance from paying social security contributions (see the model in Annex 4.). After all, Southern European countries, such Italy and Greece, that combine strict employment protection with unemployment benefits offering a very low coverage of the non-employed population are characterized by a large degree of 'informalization'. Hence, EU member states pushing the acceding countries to introduce strict employment-protection rules that are present in many Western European countries should be aware of the fact that a likely consequence of this condition is an increase in the size of the informal sector.

4.5.4 Wage Floors and Bargaining Institutions

The minimum wage function played by non-employment benefits in the CEECs is a by-product of the asymmetries in union coverage between the old and the new sector. The effort made at the outset to build tripartite structures operating at the national level in most CEECs was also an attempt to level the playing field. By having negotiations over wages and inflation targets carried out at the national level, governments aimed also at forcing unions to internalize the costs of collective bargaining.

In addition to playing a relativity marginal role in wage setting (the failure of most tax-based income-policy experiments is discussed in Chapter 3), these tripartite structures have not significantly shaped the evolution of bargaining institutions in the countries under consideration, which are still mainly organized at the branch level and continue to cover, for the most part, former state enterprises. So far, employers in the new private sector have enjoyed a high degree of flexibility and significant scope for downward wage adjustment. These conditions are likely to change, particularly now that Western European unions, and the European Union itself, are pressing their Eastern European counterparts to play a more active role, not least because of a fear of social dumping. And real wages are indeed in recent years on the rise in all CEECs, notably those included in the first round of EU accessions. Thus, the likely scenario for the years to come is one of a gradual widening of the coverage of branch-level bargaining. Governments in the region are often supporting this tendency by granting extensions of industry-level agreements.[44]

---

[44]To give an example: in the Slovak Republic, industry-level agreements are binding only for employers represented in collective agreements. However, extensions are almost

The experience of Eastern Germany suggests that branch-level bargaining binding uniformly across the board on the basis of institutional arrangements exported from the West to the East exacerbates regional unemployment differentials and requires large compensating transfers across regions.[45] If these transfers cannot be granted, for example because of problems in revenue collection or political opposition in the low-unemployment regions, collective bargaining institutions are put under strain. The radical reduction of transfers (in terms of labour-market subsidies) to the new German Länders has led to dramatic falls in membership to unions and employers associations, fading coverage rates of collective bargaining, and growing self-help through decentralized agreements violating industry-wide arrangements (Schnabel, 1999). If the collective bargaining system does not succeed in reigning in this development, its legitimacy may be severely weakened, leading to wildcat decentralization and a fundamental change of the bargaining landscape.

There is a strong case for decentralized bargaining structures in countries undergoing major changes in the structure of employment. Imposing the same wage rates uniformly across the board in the presence of sizeable differences in labour productivity within the same industry (because of the co-existence of new and old firms) and across regions (because FDIs tend to be concentrated in urban areas) is bound to increase labour-market imbalances. Centralized wage setting tends to go hand-in-hand with compensating transfers to low productivity regions, which are generally financed via taxes on labour. Moreover, empirical evidence suggests that intermediate or hybrid bargaining institutions, that is neither centralized nor decentralized at the plant level, may be the worst placed in terms of containment of wage inflation and of labour-market flexibility.[46]

Decentralized, plant-level bargaining does not rule out wage floors and—in cases where wage inflation spirals are actually at work—wage ceilings agreed upon at the national level. The tendency prevailing in most EU countries is indeed one towards the adoption of multi-level

---

always automatically granted when requested by the workers, so that the coverage of collective agreements is estimated to be of the order of 70–80 per cent.

[45] Not much different was the experience of Southern Italy after the removal of the so-called *gabbie salariali* (wage rates differentiated by macroeconomic regions) in the 1960s.

[46] See OECD (1997c) for a review of the theoretical and empirical literature on the relation between centralization (and coordination) in wage setting and labour market performance.

bargaining structures, accompanying national agreements with collective bargaining at the level of the firm or plant. While wage ceilings were largely ineffective throughout the transition (Chapter 3), they may play an important role in the EU accession process because of the strong pressures for wage convergence that are likely to emerge in this context.[47]

The case for minimum wages was made in Chapter 3: given wage compression prevailing in the old sector, it plays an important role in encouraging shifts of unskilled workers from low-productivity to high-productivity jobs. Adopting a statutory minimum wage would also allow for more degrees of freedom in the setting of unemployment benefits. If a minimum wage is in place at levels that can actually condition wage setting in the new sector, then unemployment benefit minima may be set only slightly above social assistance just in order to avoid individuals getting access to more generous benefits by staying out of work longer. There is a problem of enforcement of minimum wages, but given the ongoing reorganization of unions, this is currently much less of an issue than a few years ago.

4.5.5 Pensions and the Scope for Redistribution

In addition to efficiency considerations, there may be strong equity reasons for having statutory minimum wages in place. Unemployment benefits in the CEECs have to play a very important anti-poverty function. When unemployment benefits are to a large extent earning-related (and in order to stimulate interregional mobility it is important to link benefits to wages[48]), the task of avoiding an explosion of earning inequalities tends to fall on minimum wages, while the redistribution in favour of low-income earners is assigned to other cash-transfer mechanisms. One of these, generally the most important, is pensions. Especially under conditions where unemployment benefits are earning-related and confined to insurance functions, there are strong reasons for assigning to public pensions an important redistributive role.

[47] Slovenia is a case in point. Because of its increasing economic integration with Austria, it experienced the fastest growth of real wages of the region in the second half of the 1990s. At present, Slovenian wages are roughly two-and-a-half times those observed in the Czech Republic, Hungary and Poland.

[48] As discussed in Chapter 3, earning-related benefits serve the purpose of avoiding a large drive to non-employment in rural areas. In order to reduce the persistence of labour-market imbalances, which almost inevitably arise in economies undergoing major structural change, it is important to increase the opportunity cost of staying in rural areas.

As in Mediterranean European countries, pensions in the CEECs absorb a significant share[49] of social policy expenditure and are often improperly used as non-employment benefits. Statutory retirement ages are lower than in Western Europe, and actual retirement ages can be up to seven years below the official age of retirement. Although attempts have been made in these countries to build up private pensions, most CEECs have essentially single-tiered, pay-as-you-go systems. In Hungary, to give an example, four years after a legal framework for private pensions had been put in place, the funds had accumulated assets worth only about 1 per cent of GDP. In the Czech Republic, two years after the introduction of the Supplementary Pension Insurance System, 44 private funds had been established, but with a very low endowment value. The difficulties met in the take-off of private pensions stem mainly from the large social security contributions documented in Fig. 4.3, which displace savings that would otherwise feed into private pension accounts.

On the one hand, high social security contributions do not leave room for the development of multi-tiered systems. On the other hand, compulsory contributions to public pension systems tend to be perceived as taxes financing the pensions of those who are retiring before reaching the official retirement age rather than as deferred savings.[50] A survey carried out in Poland in 1997 on households' attitudes towards reforms of the pension system is indicative of widespread aspirations to improve the actuarial fairness of the system and to establish a stronger link between lifetime contributions and old-age pensions.[51]

In addition to making room for private pension schemes, savings on public pensions are essential to allow for the other components of the

[49] As shown by comparing the second and fourth column of Table 4.1, in countries such as Poland and Bulgaria this share exceeds 50 per cent.

[50] Another significant similarity between Mediterranean countries and the CEECs is the presence of a sizeable informal sector and of significant underreporting of wages for tax-avoidance purposes. Although making causal inferences based on cross-country correlations is notoriously risky, it is nonetheless quite revealing: pensions improperly used as non-employment benefits (or as 'social wages' in Esping-Andersen (1990) terminology) command a large hidden sector throughout Europe.

[51] I refer to the representative survey of Polish citizens carried out in April 1997, whose results are summarized in the governmental document illustrating the Polish pension reforms (*Security Through Diversity*, published in June 1997). In the survey, a question was asked about the fair pensions for two hypothetical persons of the same age, one of the two retiring (marginally) earlier than the other. Only a bit less than 20 per cent of the respondents was in favour of attributing to the individual 'roughly the same pensions', compared with about 75 per cent in favour of giving 'higher pensions to persons who worked longer (or paid higher contributions)'.

social welfare system to be in place. Non-employment benefits offering a broad coverage of job losers and with replacement rates of the order of 50 per cent in the first year of unemployment can cost up to 2–2.5 of GDP in countries experiencing double-digit unemployment rates. Social assistance is generally less costly, but under rapid structural change and a weak tax administration (both of which are obstacles to means testing) one cannot rule out large outlays for income-support schemes of the last resort. If these schemes should be in place—and this book argues very much in this direction—then possibly savings on other components of social security should be made.

Someone has to pay the bill for cuts in public pensions outlays. There was a window of opportunity at the outset of the Eastern European economic transformation, which was not exploited by governments in the region. It was provided by the possibility of using such 'periods of extraordinary politics' (in the words of Leszek Balcerowicz, the first Prime Minister of the new Poland) to renege on commitments made under the previous regime. The faith in the virtues of the market mechanism also gave much leverage to governments in proposing 'low contributions–low pensions' deals to high-wage earners, as there was a widespread perception that returns from savings could have been significantly higher than those offered by public pensions. Thus, pension reforms should have been put right at the top of the agenda for transition countries.

It is still possible to change, but it is much more difficult. Ongoing pension reforms in these countries aim at re-establishing a link between contributions and benefits by introducing 'notionally defined contribution' schemes, whereby pension amounts are calculated at the age of retirement based on lifetime contributions (generally indexed to the growth rate of the economy) and are allocated to annuities on the basis of residual life expectancy. Reforms also allow for the development of a second and third tier of private pensions.

The design of pension reforms varies from country to country depending not only on internal factors but also on the influence exerted by some (apprentice-sorcerer) Western model. The design of a reformed public pension system—the first supporting pillar under the mixed pension systems to prevail after the reforms—is deeply affected by public choices concerning the scope of income distribution. In general, countries where the rise of inequality has been contained by significant non-employment benefits are moving towards attributing a small role to public pensions in redistribution. The case of Hungary is quite revealing in this respect: the original Hungarian pension reform scheme conceived the role of public pensions as eminently redistributive, in line with the British Beveridgian tradition. However, the law finally passed by the Parliament in July 1997 phased out the progressivity of the system, leaving the task of redistributing in favour of the poor retirees to fall entirely on means-tested social assistance (Palacios and Rocha, 1997), which in practice plays the role of a fourth pensions pillar (in addition to public pensions, occupational pensions and individual accounts). The Polish public pensions pillar to prevail after the ongoing reform is also a defined contribution system, and hence it does not involve significant redistribution within generations. Conversely, ongoing reforms in the Baltic countries allow for more redistribution to be carried out directly by public pensions, because the government underwrites a minimum level of pensions. This is the case for the Estonian, Latvian and Lithuanian pension reforms. Also, in Russia, while the initial pension reform proposals were quite radical in the phasing-in of a fully funded system, the tendency more recently would seem to be towards designing the new public pension system in such a way as to maintain in it a significant redistributive component.

As in the tradition of pension reforms in the West, all the new pension regimes are being introduced while grandfathering in long-lasting entitlements. The success of reforms and their contribution to reducing the informal sector will crucially depend on how fast the transition from the old to the new pension system occurs. Given that the transition inevitably hurts someone, speeding up the process involves finding proper ways to compensate the losers, while the development of second and third pillars to a multi-tiered scheme requires a reduction of statutory contributions to the public system. Put another way, faster transition involves significant, although transitory, public pension deficits.

While improvements in work incentives and the reduction of the informal sector call for refinements of social-welfare systems (rather than simply stronger labour inspectorates and tax collection administrations, as envisaged in the EU accession rounds), reforms can hardly be fast when countries face very tight fiscal constraints. This sort of consideration should perhaps occupy a more prominent role in ongoing negotiations about the timing and characteristics of accession by Eastern European nations to the European Union.

4.6 Final Remarks

In conclusion, the return-to-Europe syndrome has been beneficial so far, but may soon become an obstacle to successful transformation. Given the very tight conditions being imposed by EU member states on others on the road to accession, the only way that transitional economies can make it into the European Union is by putting in place more effective non-employment benefits or, more broadly, a better social-welfare system than that of many countries of Western Europe. A key ingredient of this system is the presence of a stronger link between contributions and transfers. This is indispensable in order to improve the trade-off between the provision of unemployment insurance—which is essential to foster the reallocation of workers—and size of the informal sector. It is encouraging to notice that ongoing reforms of the unemployment benefits systems in many CEECs are going precisely in that direction. Moreover, reforms of pension systems being undertaken in some countries are also oriented towards strengthening the association between contributions and benefits.

Linking benefits to contributions means that social policies should play little, if any, role in income distribution. Does such a Bismarckian notion of the welfare state fit well into the social values prevailing in formerly planned economies? Although the CEECs started their transition with relatively low income inequality (for they were not used to large income differences), they managed to cope with a large increase in the dispersion of earnings generally without serious breaks in social cohesion. Yet, there is a threshold beyond which the rise of inequalities is a source of social tensions and weakens democracies and institutions, as revealed by the case of many CIS countries, including Russia. Moreover, international experience suggests that the trend towards increasing income inequality may be harmful to growth. Thus, ways to redistribute should also be found that possibly do not discourage labour-force participation decisions.

Some of these devices have been discussed in this book. For instance, it has been argued that there is a strong justification for providing income support to those older workers with obsolete skills who will never be able to enjoy the full benefits of transition. It has also been argued that it is better to provide this assistance explicitly, not mixing up those not participating in the labour market with unemployment benefit recipients so as not to inflate the ranks of the unemployed with individuals who are not looking for jobs. Other ways to redistribute without negatively affecting work incentives can also be found—for example, by accompanying means-tested social assistance with a system of disregarding certain earnings for low-income earners now that wage dispersion has increased in most of these countries—along the directions discussed in the present debate on 'active social security'. Finally, it is possible to redistribute within the generation of retirees, by allowing, in a mixed pension system, the public pensions pillar to be more progressive than envisaged under some of the reforms being discussed, if not already passed, in the CEECs.

In essence, the only way for these countries to succeed in returning to Europe is not to imitate any of the existing welfare states of the West but be on the frontier of institutional transformation in this field. This is a difficult task, no doubt, but not one that is impossible for countries that have already proved themselves capable of achieving radical transformations over a short—a very short indeed—period of time.

Annex 4
Unemployment Benefits and the Informal Sector

The purpose of this annex is to spell out the model used in Chapter 4 to discuss the role played by non-employment benefits and, more broadly, labour supply, in affecting the size of the informal sector. We shall assume here for simplicity, that the probability of detection is zero. This does not involve a loss of generality, while it allows us to model the choice on whether to work formally or informally as a decision made only by the worker. In the case of a positive detection probability, the employer will also be involved in this decision; however, provided that the penalty is equally shared between the employer and the worker, the decision would still be neutral with respect to the sharing rule governing wage determination.

When a match is formed in the new sector (bearing in mind that in the old sector all jobs are 'formal' because they were registered before the start of transition), the worker decides whether or not to pay the tax. If she/he does, then she/he bears entirely the tax burden (the sharing rule divides the *gross* as opposed to the *net* surplus) but is entitled to unemployment benefits in case of job loss. If she/he does *not* pay the tax, then she/he gets the gross wage as take-home pay but is not covered by unemployment insurance. Thus, in our simple setup the employer is indifferent as to whether or not being in the formal or in the informal sector. This is convenient as we are interested in labour *supply* determinants of the decisions not to report jobs and wages, and greatly simplifies notation.

The decision rule followed by the worker can be obtained by taking the difference in the (asset) value of a job for a worker with (W_n^b) and without (W_n) the unemployment tax–insurance. Clearly the worker will prefer to be in the formal sector if:

$$W_n^b - W_n > 0 \qquad\qquad (A4.1)$$

or, using the asset value conditions spelled out in Annex 3.,

$$\delta \lambda_n (W_u^b - W_u) > w_n \tau_n, \qquad\qquad (A4.2)$$

where W_u^b and W_u denote, respectively, the asset value of unemployment for an insured and for a non-insured worker (and we have dropped the skill signal, s, in order to simplify notation). The value of declaring and not declaring job wages can be set out as

$$W_u^b = b + \delta [\pi_u W_n + (1 - \pi_u) W_u^b] \qquad\qquad (A4.3)$$

and

$$W_u = \delta [\pi_u W_n + (1 - \pi_u) W_u], \qquad\qquad (A4.4)$$

because the job-finding probability is the same for insured and uninsured workers (and the value of the job is the same for both kind of workers to start with). Thus we can rewrite (A4.1) as follows:

$$\delta \lambda_n b > w_n \tau_n [1 - \delta(1 - \pi_u)], \qquad\qquad (A4.5)$$

which makes it apparent that the higher the non-employment benefits and the dismissal probability λ_n, the stronger the incentives to contribute to the (unemployment) insurance scheme. Conversely, the higher the tax rate and the larger the probability of being re-employed in the case of job loss, the stronger the propensity of the workers to stay in the informal sector.

We can then substitute into (A4.5) the tax rate clearing the budget (assuming, for simplicity, that unemployment benefits are entirely financed out of the wage bill in the new sector[52]), to obtain

$$\delta \lambda_n(s) > \frac{N^b}{W_n} [1 - \delta(1 - \pi_u(s))], \qquad\qquad (A4.6)$$

where $W_n = \int w_n(s) E^b(s) \, dF(s)$ is the wage bill in the (formal) new sector. The above shows that unemployment benefits affect the decision

---

[52] This is an easily altered assumption. Adding a non-zero tax rate for the old sector would only complicate the notation without adding insights to the model.

on whether or not to belong to the formal sector only indirectly, that is via their effect on the number of unemployment benefit recipients, formal job holders in the new sector, and labour-market transitions. In particular, the larger the pool of benefit recipients in relation to the number of contributors (two stocks taken as given by each individual[53]) and the more stagnant the unemployment pool, the more likely it is that the workers will choose to be in the informal sector. Both non-employment and the job-finding probability are endogenous in this model. Hence, the relevant question is: how does b affect the employment rate and the relevant labour-market flows influencing the decision to hide wages, that is flows from employment to unemployment and vice versa? We know, by Annex 2., that higher levels of the unemployment benefits are associated with lower employment rates throughout the transition. Hence, this would suggest that higher levels of b increase the informal sector. However, we also know by Annex 3., that b also affects the skills composition of employment in the new sector. In particular, it was proved therein that when b is earning-related and offers low replacement rates, it discourages those with lower observable skills indicators (for instance, lower educational attainments) to move from the old to the new sector. This selection effect implies that jobs in the new sector are more stable (λ_n is lower), and re-employment prospects in the event of job loss look rather bright for employees in the new sector. Thus, individuals employed in the new sector may feel less need for an unemployment insurance.

All in all, this extension of the basic model laid out in Annex 2. suggests that the share of the workers deciding to contribute to social security (deciding to be in the formal sector) should, other things being equal, be increasing with the probability of job loss and the coverage of unemployment benefits. We should also expect to have two extreme cases in which the informal sector is high, namely when b does not provide a floor to wage setting—that is, it is earning-related and offers a low replacement rate—and when b is flat and set at relatively high levels.

---

[53] This amounts to assuming that tax rates are those clearing the previous period's budget or, alternatively, that each individual is of measure zero.

References

Abraham, K., and Vodopivec, M. (1993). 'Slovenia: A Study of Labor Market Transition'. Mimeo. Washington, D.C.: The World Bank.

Agell, J., and Lommerud, K. E. (1992). 'Union Egalitarianism as Income Insurance', *Economica*, 59: 195–310.

Aghion, P., and Blanchard, O. (1994). 'On the Speed of Transition in Central Europe', *NBER Macroeconomics Annual*: 283–320.

—— (1996). 'On Privatisation Methods in Eastern Europe and Their Implications', Mimeo. MIT and EBRD.

Akerlof, G. (1982). 'Labor Contracts as a Partial Gift Exchange', *Quarterly Journal of Economics*, 97: 543–569.

Alogoskoufis, G. (1995). 'The Two Faces of Janus: Institutions, Policy Regimes and Macroeconomic Performance in Greece', *Economic Policy*, 20: 147–192.

Andorka, R., Ferge, Z., and Toth, I. G. (1997). 'Is Hungary Really the Least Unequal? A Discussion of Data on Income Inequalities and Poverty in Central and Central East European Countries', *Russian and East European Finance and Trade*, 33 (6): 67–94.

Atkeson, A., and Kehoe, P. (1997). 'Industry Evolution and Transition', NBER Working Paper no. 6002.

Atkinson, A., and Micklewright, J. (1992). *Economic Transformation in Eastern Europe and the Distribution of Income*. Cambridge: Cambridge University Press.

Aturupane, C., Djankov, S., and Hoeckman, B. (1997). 'Determinants of Intra-Industry Trade Between East and West Europe'. London: CEPR Discussion Paper no. 1721.

Aukutsionek, S., and Kapeliushnikov, R. (1996). 'Labour Hoarding in Russian Industry', *The Russian Economic Barometer*, 5 (2).

Bai, C., and Wang, Y. (1998). 'Bureaucratic Control and the Soft Budget Constraint'. *Journal of Comparative Economics*, 26 (1): 41–61.

Basu, S., Estrin, S., and Svejnar, J. (1997). 'Employment and Wage Behavior of Enterprises in Transitional Economies'. The William

Davidson Institute Working Papers Series, no. 114. Ann Arbor: University of Michigan.

Basu, S., and Li, D. L. (1998). 'Corruption in Transition'. The William Davidson Institute Working Papers Series, no. 161. Ann Arbor: University of Michigan.

Beleva, I., Jackman, R., and Nenova, M. (1995). 'The Labour Market in Bulgaria', in S. Commander and F. Coricelli (eds.), *Unemployment, Restructuring and the Labour Market in Eastern Europe and Russia.* Washington, DC: The World Bank.

Bilsen, V., and Konings, J. (1997). 'Job Creation, Job Destruction and Growth of Newly Established, Privatized and State-Owned Enterprises in Transitional Economies: Survey Evidence from Bulgaria, Hungary and Romania', *Journal of Comparative Economics*, 26: 429–445.

Blanchard, O. (1997). *The Economics of Post-Communist Transition*, Oxford: Oxford University Press.

—— and Diamond, P. A. (1992). 'The Flows Approach to Labor Markets', *American Economic Review*, 82 (2), May: 354–359.

—— and Kremer, M. (1997). 'Disorganization' *Quarterly Journal of Economics*, 111: 1091–1126.

Bobeva, D., and Hristoskov, Y. (1995). 'Unemployment in Agricultural Areas: An Overview of Central and Eastern Europe and a Case Study of a Bulgarian Region', in OECD, *The Regional Dimension of Unemployment in Transition Countries.* Paris: Organisation for Economic Co-operation and Development.

Boeri, T. (1994). 'Transitional Unemployment', *Economics of Transition*, 2: 1–25.

—— (1996). 'Unemployment Outflows and the Scope of Labour Market Policies in Central and Eastern Europe', in T. Boeri, H. Lehmann, and A. Wörgötter (eds.), *Lessons from the Experience of Transition Countries with Labour Market Policies*, Paris: Organisation for Economic Co-operation and Development.

—— (1997a). 'Labour Market Reforms in Transition Economies', *Oxford Review of Economic Policy*, 2: 126–140.

—— (1997b). 'Learning from Transition Economies: Assessing Labor Market Policies across Central and Eastern Europe', *Journal of Comparative Economics*, 25: 366–384.

—— (1998). 'Labor Market Flows in the Midst of Structural Change' in S. Commander (ed.), *Enterprise Restructuring and Unemployment in Models of Transition.* Washington, DC: EDI, Development Studies,

143–167.

—— (1999). 'Enforcement of Employment Security Regulations, On-the-Job Search and Unemployment Duration', *European Economic Review*, 43: 65–89.

—— and Bruno, R. (1997). 'A Short Note on the Characteristics of Labour Turnover in Central and Eastern Europe', in OECD, *Labour Market Dynamics in the Russian Federation*, Paris: Organisation for Economic Co-operation and Development.

—— and Burda, M. (1996). 'Active Labour Market Policies, Job Matching and the Czech Miracle', *European Economic Review*, 40: 805–817.

—— and Edwards, S. (1998). 'Long-term Unemployment and Short-term Unemployment Benefits', *Empirical Economics*, 23: 31–54.

—— and Flinn, C. (1999). 'Returns to Mobility in the Transition to a Market Economy', *Journal of Comparative Economics*, 27: 4–32.

—— and Keese, M. (1992). 'Labour Markets and the Transition in Central and Eastern Europe', *OECD Economic Studies*, 18: 133–163.

—— and Pulay, G. (1998). 'Labor Market Policy Reform and the Fiscal Constraint' in L. Bokros and J. J. Dethier (eds.), *Public Finance Reform During the Transition*. Washington, DC: The World Bank, 317–335.

—— and Scarpetta, S. (1996). 'Regional Mismatch and the Transition to a Market Economy', *Labour Economics*, 3: 233–254.

—— and Steiner, V. (1998). '"Wait Unemployment" in Economies in Transition: The Case of Poland'. *Konjunkturpolitik*, 3: 287–311.

—— and Burda, M., and Köllö, J. (1997). *Mediating the Transition: Labour Markets in Central and Eastern Europe*, London: Centre for Economic Policy Research, Economic Policy Initiative Report, no. 4.

Bofinger, P. (1994). 'Macroeconomic Transformation in Eastern Europe, the Role of Monetary Policy' in H. Herr, S. Tober, and A. Westphal, *Macroeconomic Problems of Transformation*. Edward Elgar Publication.

Bohata, M. (1998). 'Czech Republic: Macroeconomic Situation of the Czechoslovak Economy at the End of the 1980s', *Eastern European Economics*, 36 (4): 75–87.

Boone, P., Gomulka, S., and Layard, R. (eds.) (1998). *Emerging from Communism*, Cambridge, Mass: MIT Press.

Booth, A. (1995). *The Economics of the Trade Union*. Cambridge: Cambridge University Press.

Brenton, P., and Gros, D. (1997). 'Trade Reorientation and Recovery in

Transition Economies', *Oxford Review of Economic Policy*, 2: 65–76.

Brunetti, A., Kisunko, G., and Weder, B. (1999). 'How Businesses See Government'. *IFC Discussion Paper* no. 33.

Burawoy, M., and Krotov, P. (1993). 'The Soviet Transition from Socialism to Capitalism: Workers Control and Economic Bargaining in the Wood Industry', in S. Clarke et al., *What about the Workers? Workers and the Transition to Capitalism in Russia*, London and New York: New Left Books, Verso, 56–90.

Burda, M. (1993). 'Unemployment, Labor Markets and Structural Change in Eastern Europe', *Economic Policy*, 16: 101–37.

—— and Lubyova, M. (1995). 'The Impact of Active Labor Market Policies A Closer Look at the Czech and Slovak Republics', in D. Newbery (ed.), *Tax and Benefit Reform in Central and Eastern Europe*, London: Centre for Economic Policy Research, 173–205.

Buti, M., Pench, L. R., and Sestito, P. (1998). 'European Unemployment: Contending Theories and Institutional Complexities'. Economic and Financial Reports, BEI/EIB, Report 98/01.

Caballero, R., and Hammour, R. (1995). 'On the Ills of Adjustment', *Massachussets Institute of Technology Working Papers*, no. 9521.

Calmfors, L. (1994). 'Active Labour Market-Policies and Unemployment: A Framework for the Analysis of Crucial Design Features'. OECD, *Economic Studies*, 22. Paris: Organization for Economic Cooperation and Development.

Carrillo, J. D. (1995). 'Corruption in Hierarchies', mimeo. Universitéde Toulouse.

Castanheira, M. and Roland, G. (1998). 'The Optimal Speed of Transition: A General Equilibrium Analysis', mimeo, IGIER/ECARE.

Cazes and Scarpetta (1998). 'Labour Market Transitions and Unemployment Duration: Evidence from Bulgarian and Polish Micro-Data', *Economics of Transition*, 6(1): 113–144.

Chadha, B., and Coricelli, F. (1994). 'Fiscal Constraints and the Speed of Transition', London: CEPR Discussion Paper no. 993.

———— and Krajnyak, K. (1993). 'Economic Restructuring, Unemployment, and Growth in a Transition Economy', *IMF Staff Papers*, 40 (4): 744–780.

Chernyshev, I. (1997). *Statistics for Emerging Labour Markets in Transition Economies*. Geneva: ILO Studies Series.

Coles, M. (1996). 'Designing a Cheaper and More Effective Unemployment Benefit System'. London: CEPR Discussion Paper no. 1532.

Commander, S., and Yemtsov, R. (1995). 'Russian Unemployment: Its

Magnitude, Characteristics and Regional Dimension', in OECD, *The Regional Dimension of Unemployment in Transition Countries*. Paris: Organisation for Economic Co-operation and Development.

———— and McHale, J. (1995). 'Russia', in S. Commander and F. Corricelli (eds.), *Unemployment, Restructuring, and the Labour Market in Eastern Europe and Russia*. Washington, DC: The World Bank.

Commander, S., and Klugman, J. (1977). *Poverty in Russia: Public Policy and Private Responses*. Washington, DC: The World Bank.

—— and Lee, U., and Tolstopiatenko, A. (1998). 'Social Benefits and the Russian Industrial Firm', in S. Commander, Q. Fan, and M. Schafer, (eds.), *Enterprise Restructuring and Economic Policy in Russia*. Washington, DC: The World Bank.

Coricelli, F. (1996). 'Fiscal Constraints, Reform Strategies, and the Speed of Transition: the Case of Central-Eastern Europe'. London: CEPR Working Paper no. 1339.

Dewatripont, M., and Roland, G. (1992). 'Economic Reform and Dynamic Political Constraints', *Review of Economic Studies*, 59: 703–730.

———— (1996). 'Transition as a Process of Large Scale Institutional Change', *Economics of Transition*, 4 (1): 1–30.

Djankov, S., and Pohl, G. (1997). 'Restructuring of Large Firms in Slovakia', The William Davidson Institute Working Paper Series no. 73, Ann Arbor: University of Michigan.

Dolado, J., and Jimeno, J. (1999). 'EU Enlargements: Lessons from Mediterranean Accessions'. Mimeo.

EBRD (European Bank for Reconstruction and Development) (1995). *Transition Report 1995*, Annex 11.1, London: EBRD.

—— (1998). *Transition Report 1998*, London: EBRD.

EC (European Commission) (1995). *Preparation of the Associated Countries of Central and Eastern Europe for Integration into the Internal Market of the Union*, White Paper. Brussels: European Commission, 3 May, COM(95) 163, final 2 vols.

EC–ILO (European Commission and International Labour Office) (1995). *Reforming Wage Policy in Central and Eastern Europe*. Geneva: EC–ILO.

EIU (Economist Intelligence Unit) (1999). *Business Environment Rankings*, 1st Quarter 1999.

Erbenova, M. (1995). 'Regional Unemployment Differentials and Labour Mobility: A Case-Study of the Czech Republic', in OECD,

The Regional Dimension of Unemployment in Transition Countries. Paris: Organisation for Economic Co-operation and Development.

—— and Sorm, V., and Terrell, K. (1998). 'Work Incentive and Other Effects of Social Assistance and Unemployment Benefit Policy in the Czech Republic'. *Empirical Economics*: 87–120.

ERT (European Round Table of Industrialists) (1999). 'The East–West Win–Win Business Experience'. Brussels: ERT.

Esping-Andersen, G. (1990). *The Three Worlds of Welfare Capitalism*. Cambridge: Polity Press.

Estrin, S., (1998). 'Privatization and Restructuring in Central and Eastern Europe', in P. Boone, S. Gomulka, and R. Layard (eds.), *Emerging from Communism. Lessons from Russia, China and Eastern Europe*. Cambridge: MIT Press.

—— and Svejnar, J. (1998). 'The Effects of Output, Ownership, and Legal Form on Employment and Wages in Central European Firms', in S. Commander (ed.), *Enterprise Restructuring and Unemployment in Models of Transition*. Washington, DC: The World Bank.

EUROSTAT (1996). *Enterprises in Central and Eastern Europe*. Luxembourg.

Farber, H. S. (1978). 'Individual Preferences and Union Wage Determination: The Case of the United Mine Workers', *Journal of Political Economy*, 86: 932–942.

Fay, J. A., and Medoff, J. L. (1985). 'Labor and Output over the Business Cycle', *American Economic Review*, 75 (September): 638–655.

Feenstra, R., Yang, M., and Hamilton, G. (1997). 'Business Groups and Trade in East Asia: Part 2, Product Variety', NBER Working Paper no. 5887.

Fidrmuc, J. (1999). *The Political Economy of Reforms in Central and Eastern Europe*. Center Dissertation Series, Tilburg University.

Filer, R., and Hanousek, J. (1999). 'Output Changes and Inflationary Bias in Transition', mimeo. Prague: CERGE-EI.

Fitzpatrick, S. (1979). *Education and Social Mobility in the Soviet Union, 1921–1934*. Cambridge: Cambridge University Press.

Flanagan, R. J. (1993). 'Were Communists Good Human Capitalists? The Case of the Czech Republic', mimeo. Stanford University.

Freeman, R. (1994). 'What Direction for Labour Market Institutions in Eastern and Central Europe?', in O. Blanchard, K. A. Froot, and J. D. Sachs (eds.), *The Transition in Eastern Europe*. Chicago and London: University of Chicago Press, vol. 2.

Frydman, R., and Rapaczynski, R. (1994). *Privatisation in Eastern*

Europe: Is the State Withering Away?. Budapest, London and New York: Central European University Press.

Galasi, P. (1998). 'Income Inequality and Mobility in Hungary, 1992–6'. Innocenti Occasional Papers no. 64.

Garner, T., and Terrell, K. (1998). 'A Gini Decomposition Analysis of Inequality in the Czech and Slovak Republics during the Transition'. London: CEPR Discussion Paper no. 1897.

Gavin, M. (1993). *Unemployment and the Economics of Gradualist Policy Reform*. New York: Columbia University.

Gomulka, S. (1991). 'The Causes of Recession Following Stabilisation', *Comparative Economic Studies*, 33 (2): 71-89.

Grosfeld, I., and Nivet, J. (1997). 'Wage and Investment Behaviour in Transition: Evidence from a Polish Panel Data Set'. London: CEPR Discussion Paper no. 1726.

von Hagen, J. (1996). 'The Political Economy of Eastern Enlargement of the EU', in CEPR, *Coming to Terms with Accession*. London: Centre for Economic Policy Research, Forum Report of the Economic Policy Initiative, no. 2.

—— (1997). 'East Germany', in P. Desai (ed.), *Going Global: Transition from Plan to Market in the World Economy*. Cambridge: MIT Press, 173-207.

Ham, J., Svejnar, J., and Terrell, K. (1998). 'Unemployment and the Social Safety Net During Transitions to a Market Economy: Evidence from the Czech and Slovak Republics'. *American Economic Review*, 88 (5):1117-1142.

Hare, P. (1994). 'Social Protection and its Implications for Enterprise Restructuring', paper presented at CEPR/IAS Conference on Social Protection and the Enterprise in Transitional Economies, Vienna, 25–26 March 1994.

Hibbs, D., and Locking, H. (1995). 'Wage Compression, Wage Drift and Wage Inflation in Sweden', mimeo.

Holmes, S., and Sunstein, C. (1999). *The Cost of Rights*. New York: W. W. Worton and Co.

Ickes, B., and Ryterman, R. (1993). 'From Enterprise to Firm: Notes for a Theory of the Enterprise in Transition'. Pennsylvania State: Department of Economics Working Paper.

ILO (1998). *See* Vaughan-Withead (1998).

ILO-CEET (International Labour Office Central and Eastern European Team) (1997). *Ethnic Minorities in Central and Eastern Europe*. Budapest: ILO-CEET Working Paper no. 19.

IMD (International Institute for Management Development) (1998). *The World Competitiveness Yearbook*. IMD.

Jackman, R., and Pauna, C. (1997). 'Labour Market Policy and the Reallocation of Labour Across Sectors', in S. Zecchini (ed.), *Lessons from the Economic Transition*. Norwell, Mass.: Kluwer Academic Publishers.

Johnson, S., Kaufmann, D., and Schleifer, A. (1997). 'Politics and Entrepreneurship in Transition Economies'. The William Davidson Institute Working Papers Series; no. 57. Ann Arbor: University of Michigan.

Johnson, S., McMillan, J., and Woodruff, C. (1999). 'Why do Firms Hide? Bribes and Unofficial Activity After Communism'. London: CEPR Discussion Paper no. 2105.

Jones, D., and Kato, T. (1993). 'The Nature and Determinants of Labor Market Transitions in Former Socialist Economies: Evidence from Bulgaria'. Hamilton College: Department of Economics Working Papers.

—— —— (1998). 'Chief Executive Compensation during Transition: Further Evidence from Bulgaria'. The William Davidson Institute Working Papers Series, no. 146. Ann Arbor: University of Michigan.

Kapeliushnikov, R. (1999). 'On the composition of Russian Unemployment', *The Russian Economic Barometer*, no. 2.

Kaufmann, D., and Kaliberda, A. (1995). 'Integrating the Unofficial Economy Into the Dynamics of Post-Socialist Economies: a Framework of Analysis and Evidence', mimeo. The World Bank.

Kenworthy, L. (1998). 'Do Social Welfare Policies Reduce Poverty? A Cross-National Assessment', LIS working paper no. 188.

Kertesi, H. (1994). 'The Labour Market Situation of the Gypsy Minority in Hungary', mimeo. Budapest.

—— and Köllö, J. (1997). 'Wage Inequalities in Hungary: 1986–96'. Budapest: Institute of Economics, Hungarian Academy of Sciences.

Köllö, J. (1993). 'Unemployment and Unemployment Related Expenditures'. Budapest: Blue Ribbon Commission.

—— (1997). 'Transformation Before the Transition: Employment and Wage Setting in Hungarian Firms: 1986–89'. Budapest: Institute of Economics.

—— (1999). 'Regional Inequalities in Central and Eastern Europe: Implications for the Eastern Enlargement of the EU', mimeo. Budapest.

Konings, J., and Walsh, P. (1998). 'Disorganisation in the Transition Process: Firm Level Evidence from Ukraine'. LICOS Discussion

Papers no. 71.

—— —— (1999). 'Employment Dynamics of Newly Established and Traditional Firms: A Comparison of Russia and the Ukraine'. LICOS Discussion Papers no. 81.

Konings, J., Lehmann, H., and Schaffer, M. (1996). 'Job Creation and Job Destruction in a Transition Economy: Ownership, Firm Size and Gross Job Flows in Polish Manufacturing: 1988–91'. *Labour Economics*: 299–317.

Kornai, J. (1979). 'Resource-Constrained Versus Demand-Constrained Systems'. *Econometrica*, 47 (4): 801–819.

—— (1980). *Economics of Shortage*. Amsterdam: New Holland.

—— (1990). *The Road to a Free Economy. Shifting from a Socialist System: the Example of Hungary*. New York and London: Norton.

—— (1994). 'Transformational Recession: The Main Causes'. *Journal of Comparative Economics*. 19 (1): 39–63.

—— (1998). 'Legal Obligation, Non-Compliance and Soft Budget Constraint', in P. Newman (ed.), *The New Palgrave Dictionary of Economics and the Law*. London: MacMillan, 533–39.

Kotzeva, M., Mircheva, D., and Woergoetter, A. (1996). 'Evaluation of Active and Passive Labour Market Policy in Bulgaria', in OECD, *Lessons from Labour Market Policies in the Transition Countries*. Paris: Organisation for Economic Co-operation and Development.

Kyloh, R. (ed.) (1995). *Tripartism on Trial*. Geneva: International Labour Office Central and Eastern European Team.

Lacko, M. (1999). 'Hidden Economy: an Unknown Quantity? Comparative Analysis of Hidden Economies in Transition Countries in 1989–95', Johannes Kepler Universität Linz Working Papers no. 9905.

Layard, R., and Richter, A. (1994). 'Russian Unemployment'. Paper presented at the IIASA Conference, Luxembourg, June.

—— —— (1995). 'How Much Unemployment Is Needed for Restructuring? The Russian Experience'. *Economics of Transition*, 3 (1): 39–58.

Lehmann, H., and Walsh, P. (1997). 'Structural Adjustment and Regional Long-Term Unemployment in Poland'. Mimeo. Dublin: Trinity College Department of Economics.

Leven, B. (1998). 'Changes in Poland's Transfer Payments in the 1990s: The Fate of Pensioners'. The William Davidson Institute Working Papers Series no. 148. Ann Arbor: University of Michigan.

Li, W. (1994). 'Essays on the Economics of Transition: Why Is the 'Big Bang' Implosive in Output and Explosive in Prices. While Controlled

References   229

Market Reform Isn't?'. University of Michigan, Ph.D Dissertation
Thesis.
Lilien, D. (1982). 'Sectoral Shifts and Cyclical Unemployment'. *Journal
of Political Economy*, 90 (4): 777–793.
Lizal, L., Singer, M., and Svejnar, J. (1997). 'Enterprise Breakups and
Performance during the Transition'. London: CEPR Working Paper
no. 1757.
Lubyova, M., and van Ours, J. (1997). 'Unemployment Dynamics and
the Restructuring of the Slovak Unemployment Benefit System'. *European Economic Review*, 41: 925–34.
Maskin, E. (1999). 'Recent Theoretical Work on the Soft Budget Constraint'. *American Economic Review*, 89 (2), May.
—— and Xu, C. (1999). 'Soft Budget Constraint Theories: From
Centralization to the Market'. Paper presented at The Fifth Nobel
Symposium in Economics, Stockholm, Sweden.
Mauro, P., and Spilimbergo, A. (1998). 'How do the Skilled and the
Unskilled Respond to Regional Shocks? The Case of Spain'. IMF
Working Papers no. 77.
—— —— and Prasad, E. (1999). 'Perspectives on Regional Unemployment in Europe'. IMF Occasional Papers no. 177.
McAuley, A. (1979). *Economic Welfare in the Soviet Union*. Madison:
University of Winsconsin Press.
—— (1991). 'The Economic Transition in Eastern Europe: Employment, Income Distribution and the Social Security Net', *Oxford Review of Economic Policy*, 7 (4): 93–105.
McKinsey (1999). *Unlocking Economic Growth in Russia*. Moscow:
McKinsey Global Institute.
Micklewright, J., and Nagy, G. (1994). 'Flows to and from Insured
Unemployment in Hungary'. Florence: European University Institute
Working Papers, 94/41.
—— —— (1996). 'Labor Market Policy and the Unemployed in Hungary'. *European Economic Review*, 40: 819–828.
Milanovic, B. (1997). 'A Simple way to Calculate the Gini Coefficient
and some Implications'. *Economics Letters*, 56(1): 45–59.
Milanovic, B. (1999). 'Explaining Inequality during the Transition'.
Economics of Transition, 7 (2).
Milgrom, P., and Roberts, J. (1990). 'Rationalizability, Learning and
Equilibrium in Games with Strategic Complementarities', *Econometrica*, 6: 1255–1277.
Munich, D., Svejnar, J., and Terrell, K. (1999). 'Worker-Firm Matching

and Unemployment in the Transition to a Market Economy: (Why) Are the Czechs More Successful than Others?'. Prague: CERGE-EI Working Papers, no. 141.

OECD (Organisation for Economic Co-operation and Development) (1987). *Employment Outlook*, Chapter Five. Paris: OECD.

—— (1991). *The Transition to a Market Economy*. Paris: OECD.

—— (1993a). *Employment and Unemployment in Economies in Transition*. Paris: OECD.

—— (1993b). *Employment Outlook*. Paris: OECD.

—— (1994a). *The OECD Jobs Study*. Paris: OECD.

—— (1994b). *Unemployment in the Transition Countries: Transient or Persistent?*. Paris: OECD.

—— (1995a). *Review of the Labour Market in the Czech Republic*. Paris: OECD.

—— (1995b). *The Regional Dimension of Unemployment in Transition Countries*. Paris: OECD.

—— (1996a). *Reviews of National Policies for Education: Czech Republic*. Paris: OECD.

—— (1996b). *Employment Outlook*, Chapter Five. Paris: OECD.

—— (1997a). *Labour Market Dynamics in the Russian Federation*. Paris: OECD.

—— (1997b). *Labour Market and Social Policies in the Slovak Republic*. Paris: OECD.

—— (1997c). *Employment Outlook*. Paris: OECD.

—— (1998). *Employment Outlook*. Paris: OECD.

—— (1999). *Employment Outlook*. Paris: OECD.

—— (various issues). *Short-Term Economic Indicators. Transition Economies*. Paris: OECD.

Ofer, G., and Vinokur, A. (1980). 'The Distribution of Income of the Urban Population in the Soviet Union'. Mimeograph.

Ofer, G., and Vinokur, A. (1992). *The Soviet Household under the Old Regime*. Cambridge: Cambridge University Press.

van Ours, J., and Ridder, G. (1992). 'Vacancies and the Recruitment of New Employees', *Journal of Labor Economics*, 10 (2): 138–155.

Palacios, R., and Rocha, R. (1997). 'The Hungarian Pension System in Transition'. Mimeo, World Bank.

Pencavel, J. (1991). *Labor Markets Under Trade Unionism*. Cambridge, Mass.: Basil Blackwell.

Petkov, K., and Thirkell, J. E. M. (1991). *Labour Relations in Eastern Europe; Organisational Design and Dynamics*. London: Routledge.

Pissarides, C. (1979). 'Job Matchings with State Employment Agencies and Random Search'. *The Economic Journal*, 89, December: 818–833.

——— (1990). *Equilibrium Unemployment Theory*. Oxford: Basil Blackwell.

Pohl, G., Anderson, R. E., Claessens, S., and Djankov, S. (1997). *Privatization and Restructuring in Central and Eastern Europe*. Washington, DC: The World Bank.

Przeworski, A. (1993). 'Economic Reforms, Public Opinion and Political Institutions', in L. C. Bresser Pereira *et al.*, *Economic Reforms in New Democracies*. New York: Cambridge University Press.

Richter, A., and Schaffer, M. (1996). 'Growth, Investment, and Newly-Established Firms in Russian Manufacturing', in S. Commander *et al.* (eds.), *Enterprise Restructuring and Economic Policy in Russia*. Washington: EDI/World Bank.

Rodrik, D. (1995). 'The Dynamics of Political Support for Reforms in Economies of Transition'. London: CEPR Discussion Paper no. 1115.

Roland, G. (1994). 'The Role of Political Constraints in Transition Strategies', *Economics of Transition*, 2 (1): 27–41.

——— and Verdier, T. (1997). 'Transition and the Output Fall'. London: CEPR Discussion Paper no. 1636.

——— ——— (1999). 'Law Enforcement and Transition', mimeo. Université Libre de Bruxelles.

Rusnok, J., and Fassman, M. (1995): The True Effects of Wage Regulations in the Czech Republic'. in: D. Vaughan-Whitehead (ed.): *Reforming Wage Policy in Central and Eastern Europe*. Budapest: International Labour Organisation.

Rutkowski, J. (1996). 'Changes in the Wage Structure During Economic Transition in Poland'. *World Bank Technical Paper* no. 340. Washington, DC: The World Bank.

——— (1997). 'Low Wage Employment in Transitional Economies of Central and Eastern Europe'. *Moct–Most*, 7: 105–130.

Sachs, J. (1993). *Poland's Jump to a Market Economy*. Cambridge: MIT Press.

Sakova, S. (1996). 'Changes and Differences in Earning Structures'. Unpublished Thesis. Budapest: Economics Department, Central European University.

Saint-Paul, G. (1993). 'On the Political Economy of Labour Market Flexibility'. London: CEPR Discussion Paper no. 813.

——— (1996). *Dual Labor Markets*. Cambridge Mass.: MIT Press.

Schaffer, M. (1998). 'Do Firms in Transition Economies Have Soft Budget Constraints? A Reconsideration of Concepts and Evidence', *Journal of Comparative Economics*, 26 (1): 80–103.

Schnabel, C. (1999). 'Collective Bargaining under Stress: Decentralization and Opening Clauses in Germany'. Available at: www.rdb.unibocconi.it.

Shapiro, C., and Stiglitz, J. (1984). 'Equilibrium Unemployment as a Worker Discipline Device'. *American Economic Review*, 69: 17–25.

Shleifer, A. (1996). 'The Origins of Bad Policies: Control, Corruption and Confusion'. *Rivista di Politica Economica*, June.

Shorrock, A. (1978). 'The Measurement of Mobility'. *Econometrica*, 47: 153–162.

Socha, M., and Sztanderska, U. (1993). 'The Labour Market', in H. Kierzkowski, M. Okolski, and S. Wellisz (eds.), *Stabilisation and Structural Adjustment in Poland*. London and New York: Routledge, 131–152.

Standing, G., and Vaughan-Whitehead, D. (eds.) (1995). *Minimum Wages in Central and Eastern Europe: From Protection to Destitution*. Budapest: CEU Press.

Svejnar, J. (1999). 'Labour Markets in the Transitional Central and Eastern European Economies', *Handbook of Labour Economics*, vol. 3B, Chap. 42, Holland: Elsevier.

Terrell, K., and Munich, D. (1996). 'Evidence on the Implementation and Effectiveness of Active and Passive Labour Market Policies in the Czech Republic', in OECD, *Lessons from Labour Market Policies in the Transition Countries*. Paries: OECD.

Terrell, K., and Sorm, V. (1998). 'Labour Market Policies and Unemployment in the Czech Republic'. The William Davidson Institute Working Papers Series, no. 216. Ann Arbor: University of Michigan.

Transparency International (1998). *TI Newsletter*, December.

Uldrichova, V. (1994). 'Position of National and Ethnic Minorities in the Labour Market of the Czech Republic', mimeo. Budapest.

UNDP (1996). *Human Development Report*.

UNICEF (1997). *Regional Monitoring Report*, no. 5.

—— (1998). *Education for All!*. Florence: UNICEF.

Vaughan-Withead, D. (ed.) (1998). *Paying the Price: The Wage Crisis in Central Eastern Europe*. Geneva: ILO.

Vecernik, J. (1993). 'Czechoslovakia and the Czech Republic in 1990-93'; mimeo. Prague: Institute of Sociology, Academy of Sciences.

—— (1996). *Markets and People*. Hampshire, UK: Avebury.

WIIW (1998). Handbook of Statistics: Countries in Transition, 1998. Vienna: Vienna Institute for International Economic Studies.

World Bank (1996). 'The Financing of Pension System in Central and Eastern Europe'. World Bank Technical Paper no. 339. Washington: The World Bank.

—— (1998). 'Social Assessment of Mining Sector Restructuring in Romania', mimeo. Bucharest.

Wright, R. (1986). 'Job Search and Cyclical Unemployment'. *Journal of Political Economy*, vol. 94, no. 1, 38–55.

Index